Yale Series in Economic and Financial History

Publication co-sponsored by the International Center for Finance at the Yale School of Management

Shanghai's Bund and Beyond

British Banks, Banknote Issuance, and Monetary Policy in China, 1842–1937

Niv Horesh

Yale University Press

New Haven and London

Published with assistance from the University of New South Wales and from the Kingsley Trust Association Publication Fund established by the Scroll and Key Society of Yale College.

Printed in the United States of America

Library of Congress Control Number: 2009921877
ISBN 978-0-300-14356-0 (hardcover : alk. paper)

A catalogue record for this book is available from the British Library.

This paper meets the requirements of ANSI/NISO Z39.48-1992 (Permanence of Paper). It contains 30 percent postconsumer waste (PCW) and is certified by the Forest Stewardship Council (FSC).

10 9 8 7 6 5 4 3 2 1

For my parents,
Itzhak and Dvora

Contents

Acknowledgments

This book could not have been completed without the helping hand that was extended to me by many individuals and institutions, but most notably by my two principal supervisors at the Australian National University. Emeritus Professor Mark Elvin was one of the first academics to show interest in the topic. He subsequently helped me secure a Commonwealth scholarship and has proven an invaluable fount of wisdom since; Dr. Pierre van der Eng has taught me the difference between "asserting" and "demonstrating" and has commented at length on countless drafts. His goodwill at critical junctures of my doctoral candidacy ensured that the project would not fade into oblivion.

My work at the Guildhall Library has been greatly facilitated by the Standard Chartered Bank and Stephen Freeth of the Corporation of London. I am equally indebted to Edwin Green, Sara Kinsey, and their staff at HSBC Group Archives, without whose hospitality and profuse counsel this research would have struck a much flatter chord. Other archival materials from around the world have furthered my understanding of foreign banking in prewar China, although they do not necessarily feature in the following pages. These materials were sent to me on a pro bono basis by, among others, Maryvonne Véjux (BNP Parisbas), Marc Meuleau (CA-Indosuez), Reinhard Frost (Deutsche Bank AG), Günter Stutterich (Bundesarchiv), Sierk Plantinga (Dutch National Archives), Dr. Mark Tomasko, and Theo van Elmpt (independent numismatists).

Some chapters in this book have appeared previously as abridged journal articles, and are gratefully reproduced here with the publisher's permission (see items listed in the bibliography under the author's surname). I wish to thank a long list of scholars, authors, and editors for their support in that regard. The list includes, but is not limited to, Emeritus Professor Nishimura Shizuya and Dr. Yokouchi Masao (Hosei University), Professor William T. Rowe (Johns Hopkins University), Professor Kathryn Bernhardt (UCLA), Professor Philip Scranton (Rutgers University), Professor P. J. Drake (Melbourne University), Professor Mark Selden (Cornell), Professor Patrick O'Brien (LSE), Dr. Frans-Paul van der Putten (Nyenrode Business University), Dr. Paul van Dyke (Macau Inter-University Institute), Dr. Zhang Jianjun (University of Inner Mongolia), Dr. Noel Pugach (University of New Mexico), Dr. Julia Strauss (SOAS), Dr. Andrea Janku (University of Heidelberg), Professor Wang Shaoguang (The Chinese University of Hong Kong), Professor Louise Edwards (UTS), Professor Tim Wright (University of Sheffield), Professor Hans Hendrischke (UNSW), and Dr. Richard Rigby (Australian Office of National Assessment).

Colleagues and friends at the Division of Pacific and Asian History have been remarkably generous with their time. I would like to thank in particular Dr. Tana Li for the confidence she has shown in my teaching ability, and for her open-door policy; Dr. Robert Cribb for his wonderful insights into academe and for always striving to give a more human face to our Division; Dr. Josephine Fox for her bibliographic tips; Maxine McArthur for bearing with my soporific English prose; and Marion Weeks for her continual administrative backup. Fellow PhD students in the Division were always fun to talk to—Vanessa Ward, Julian Kusa, Tim Amos, Yeetuan Wong, Curtis Gayle, Rev. Jeremy Clarke, Jamie Greenbaum, and Leonid Petrov to name but a few.

Elsewhere on campus, I received much-appreciated feedback and assistance from Professor Russel Craig (College of Business and Economics), Dr. Zhongwei Zhao (Research School of Social Sciences), Dr. Kent Anderson (Faculty of Asian Studies), Dr. Luigi Tomba (Contemporary China Center), Renata Osborne, Darrell Dorrington, and Anne-Marie Boyd (Menzies Library).

Outside the ANU, I owe long-standing debts to Or Horesh, Leah Horesh, Avi and Gabby Horesh-West; to Emeritus Professor Raphael Israeli, Dr. Yuri Pines, and Dr. Lihi Yariv-La'or (Hebrew University); to Professor Aron Shai

(Tel-Aviv University), Professor John Fitzgerald and Amnon Varnon (La Trobe University), Wan Wong (National Library of Australia), and two anonymous reviewers for Yale University Press.

Last but not least, I would like to thank my wife, Heli, our eldest daughter, Sivaan, and our son, Dekel. All were remarkably supportive while daddy was hammering away at his research.

Any errors that remain in the text are exclusively mine.

Abbreviations

BAT	British American Tobacco Company
CBIAC	Chartered Bank of India Australia and China
CCP	Chinese Communist Party
CMBILC	Chartered Mercantile Bank of India, London and China
DAB	Deutsch-Asiatische Bank
EIC	East India Company
GBP	British Pound Sterling
GMD	Chinese Nationalist Party [*Guomindang*]
History	*History of the Hongkong and Shanghai Banking Corporation* (King, 1987)
HK$	Hong Kong dollar
HSBC	Hongkong and Shanghai Banking Corporation
IBC	Imperial Bank of China
MBI	Mercantile Bank of India
MCFC	*Municipalité de la Concession Française de Changhai*
OBC	Oriental Bank Corporation
PRC	People's Republic of China
S$	Straits Settlements dollar

SMC	Shanghai Municipal Council
Wusa	The May Thirtieth Movement, 1925 [*Wusa yundong*]
Wusi	The May Fourth Movement, 1919 [*Wusi yundong*]
YSB	Yokohama Specie Bank

Part I

Chapter 1 Introduction

Following Marco Polo's celebrated memoirs, many Western observers recognized China as the "native birthplace" of paper currency in the eleventh century.[1] Yet it was seldom noted that, eight centuries later, British banks issued paper currency in few of China's largest cities.

This dimension of British banking in China is all the more compelling because a number of new books have done much to construe the rise of China's homegrown modern banks as of the late nineteenth century. Brett Sheehan has termed this newfound interest in the history of banking in China as nothing short of a "mini explosion"—with notable contributions by Cheng Linsun, Zhaojin Ji, and Sheehan himself.[2] One of the most salient features of this new work is that it posits banknote issuance as critical to the rise of China's own modern banks.

The following chapters are aimed at supplementing the growing literature on finance in modern China from a unique perspective. They highlight the circumstances in which British banks issued paper currency on Chinese soil, and they explain what lay behind the spread of British banknotes in the late-Imperial period (1842–1911) and how British banknote issuance unfolded through the early-Republican era (1912–1926) and the Nanjing Decade (1927–1937). The coverage ends just before the Japanese invasion of China (1937), a momentous event that saw Britain's presence in East Asia decline and curtailed the preeminence of British banks in the foreign financial sector.

This introductory chapter places British banknote issuance against the backdrop of China's own experimentation with fiduciary currency from about the seventh century onward. It weaves the story line of British banking in Asia into the broader literature on China's economy before the outbreak of the Sino-Japanese War. Finally, it foreshadows the foci of discussion and explains the choice of methodology in the chapters to come.

ON THE HISTORY OF PAPER MONEY

Some of the earliest precursors of Chinese fiduciary currency date back to the heyday of the Tang dynasty (617–907 CE). A case in point is the appearance of the *guifang* 櫃坊 or "counting houses" where, for a small service charge, merchants could deposit liquid funds in order to protect them from fire or theft, and draft checks to a third party against these deposits whenever necessary.[3] By the early tenth century, however, the *guifang* had become associated with dubious speculators, who habitually debased coin deposits for quick gains or turned the establishments they owned into gambling dens.

The monetary use of paper reemerged as a result of the proliferation of base metals in interregional trade after the collapse of the Tang and the ensuing political disunion of the Five Dynasties (907–960). Because almost all of the contending overlords at the time attempted to stop copper from flowing into neighboring regions, their kingdoms (Southern Han, Min, Wu Yue, Southern Tang, Chu, Later Tang, and Later Shu) often devised lead, iron, or even claypot coins for domestic purposes. These coins were, of course, of very little intrinsic value. As such, they represented the first step toward ridding Chinese currency of its metallic anchorage.

As Song dynasty armies were asserting their authority in Sichuan at the end of the tenth century, the Later Shu's cumbersome form of iron currency could not be adequately replaced with the new dynastic copper standard. This was mainly due to an unrealistic official exchange rate proclaimed by the authorities. Consequently, locals deposited the heavy Sichuanese iron coins in return for promissory notes issued by sixteen of the wealthiest families in the region.[4]

However, once the Song had firmly asserted its authority in the Southwest, the Imperial bureaucracy took over promissory note regulation.

During the reestablishment of political unity in the tenth and eleventh centuries, a whole new gamut of credit instruments spread into other parts of China too. There was, for example, an arrangement dubbed *she* 賒 whereby buyers would present wholesale vendors with a one-month promissory note, which was made payable only after the resale of goods. The circulation of these privately issued promissory notes (known interchangeably as *tiezi* 貼子, *huizi* 會子，*jiaozi* 交子, or *guanzi* 關子) spread alongside the Sichuanese iron-denominated notes.[5]

This credit economy had been part and parcel of what scholars termed "China's medieval economic revolution" during the Northern and Southern Song dynasties (960–1127, 1127–1279).[6] Based in Kaifeng before 1127, Song bureaucrats showed keen interest in economic reform. Momentous advancements in metallurgy, weaponry, print, and maritime navigation defined much of this era. The velocity and quantity of both fiduciary and metallic money flows rose, to the extent that silver bullion was increasingly in demand as a high-denomination means of payment. For the first time in China's history, some commercial taxes were levied in silver rather than copper coins or grain.[7]

Yet, the daily use of silver was confined to merchants and moneylenders. Silver circulated in urban centers where the inflow of bullion from overseas was significant. Peasants, who contributed the bulk of the tax revenue, were largely outside the realm of this credit economy. This meant that, while the Southern Song intake of silver bullion via overland and maritime trade increased, the output of its domestic silver mines was in proportional decline.[8]

Paper money, on the other hand, turned into a common medium of payment right across China. Song notes were denominated in base metals—first iron and then copper. Copper coinage was in turn used in transactions of small denomination. The demand for copper coinage in the vast agricultural sector put severe pressures on the state-controlled mining industry. The relatively high costs of maintaining copper hearths, as opposed to the low seigniorage revenue that the government could extract from low-denomination coinage, often resulted in prolonged periods of "coin famine" (*qianhuang* 錢荒). These chronic shortfalls propelled the renowned reformer Wang Anshi (1021–1086) to work vigorously for the pooling of metallurgic know-how to the extent that Imperial mines and foundries eventually managed to double their output, extracting 9,000 tons of copper and churning out as many as 5 million bronze coin strings annually.[9]

The credibility of paper currency diminished around 1127, when the Song retreated south in the face of Xixia and Jurchen invasions. Now based in Hangzhou, the Southern Song bureaucracy was divided by the question of spiraling military expenditure. Hawkish officials were calling to recover China's territorial integrity, while doves sought to maintain the status quo with the nomadic people of the Northern steppe lands and thereby avoid a fiscal crisis. In 1135, the Song Imperial Court had tried to introduce fiat notes in frontier areas in order to strike a balance between the two camps. However, merchants and provincial administrators rejected the new notes, to the extent that by 1160 convertibility to specie had to be restored.[10] Overall, the Song experimented first with fiduciary notes (i.e., notes partly backed by metal reserve) and then with fiat notes (unbacked). Both betokened a departure from custom, whose significance in the wider context of global monetary progression cannot be overstated.

Intermittent coin famines continued in the thirteenth and fourteenth centuries as a consequence of increasing demand in other parts of East Asia and Southeast Asia, where Chinese copper coinage became popular. Silver, in contrast, was trickling into China in ever-growing quantities from both East and West along the principal trade routes. Faced with a narrowing of the metallic money base, the Mongol Yuan dynasty, which conquered China in 1279, decided to abandon coin casting altogether. It was to rely instead on nominally convertible paper notes as a means of generating state revenue.[11]

Before long, Yuan officials could not resist the temptation of surfeit issues, thereby unleashing repeated waves of inflation and consistently undermining popular trust in paper currency. The Yuan court's use of note issuance as an inexpensive means of generating fiscal revenue became a feature of Imperial policy. Inevitably, commoners had to resort to imported silver bullion as the sole reliable store of value, forcing the Imperial bureaucracy to adapt its finances along the same lines.[12] Because of these excesses, government note issuance as a policy measure was subject to deep-seated suspicion both from within the Imperial bureaucracy and in popular discourse after the fourteenth century.

Full resumption of copper coin casting by the Ming dynasty (1368–1644) occurred only in 1522. By then, the Chinese economy had been drawing an immense overflow of Japanese silver. Unlike Tokugawa Japan, the Ming bureaucracy did not attempt to expand silver mining or cast domestic silver coinage.

New World bullion supplanted Japanese silver in the seventeenth century. It was carried on board Spanish galleons and trickled into China via Manila.

The Pacific route of the galleon trade came under Spanish hegemony by virtue of a papal decree to divide oceanic exploration into a Portuguese sphere from the Cape of Good Hope to Melaka [Malacca], and a Castilian sphere from the Philippines eastward.[13] It is roughly estimated that around 5 million Pieces-of-Eight (later known as Carolus dollars)—commensurate with 120 tons of silver—found their way to Asia during the early seventeenth century.[14]

Ming taxation policy played a critical role in entrenching silver bullion in the late-Imperial economy. In particular, the *lijia* 里甲 reform, launched by Founding Emperor Hongwu, and Emperor Jiajing's "Single Whip" reform (*yi tiao bianfa* 一條鞭法) formalized over the course of Ming rule a gradual commutation of tax-in-kind and corvée labor into a silver-denominated land tax, levied by an increasingly decentralized provincial apparatus.[15]

In economic debates at the Imperial Court, the evocation of silver overshadowed that of paper currency during the early and middle Qing reign (1644–1911).[16] The monetary standard during that period was bimetallic: silver bullion was used as the most common medium of large transactions, foreign trade, and tax collection, while round copper coins continued to serve as a daily medium of exchange in retail. Moreover, because the central government preferred bullion to its own often-debased copper coins, silver weights evolved into the most important units of account in China.[17]

The net inflow of silver into China continued, albeit unevenly, until the breakdown of the Canton (Guangzhou) foreign trade system in the 1830s and subsequent British incursions into China proper. In the 1840s, imports of Bengali opium finally succeeded in eroding China's long-standing trade surplus with the West. British trading houses faced enormous difficulty in selling other manufactured products in China: opium and bullion were coveted more than anything else that the British could offer in return for tea and silk. Consequently, opium became the great equalizer of trade between India and China at a time when both had been on a silver standard.[18]

By the time British traders began selling Indian opium in South China, Britain's economy had already been unrecognizably transformed by paper money and exchange bills. In England and Wales, paper instruments totaled approximately 15 million pounds—arguably 56 percent of the money stock—as early as 1698.[19]

Monetary progress in Europe, however, was slow. The recovery of mints during the Carolingian era after a protracted post-Roman hiatus paved the way for a significant increase in continental trade. Concomitantly, the emergence of Florentine banking in the twelfth century dispelled many of the papal interdictions on interest and capital accumulation. Widening trade links then provided the impetus for a distinctly European phenomenon: the rise of joint-stock enterprise.[20] Joint-stock companies were emerging alongside guilds in Europe from the sixteenth century. Many had received a Royal Charter, which helped them monopolize the most lucrative commodities in foreign trade. At the same time, the transferability and scope of share ownership consolidated the companies' purchasing power and institutionalized their independence of the monarchy. Politically, this new balance of power was reflected in, for example, the way the British Parliament was displacing the Crown as the key agent of fiscal policy, and in the legalistic articulation of private property rights.

Papermaking, print technology, and bills of exchange had spread far and wide across the continent in the 1500s, but Europe's first government-endorsed banknotes appeared in Sweden only in 1661 (*kreditivsedlar*).[21] Tellingly, banknote issuance was gaining momentum in the British Isles through the work of one of the most eminent joint-stock companies at the time; soon after it had been set up, the Bank of England (est. 1694) aimed at expanding its note issue at the expense of private banknotes, but its monopoly of paper money in England was formalized only in 1844. Elsewhere in Continental Europe and Scotland, private banknotes proliferated well into the late nineteenth century.[22]

The popularization of notes in the West gathered momentum when improved printing technology had finally managed to keep forgeries at bay. During the early 1800s, Philadelphia inventor Jacob Perkins's steel plates and siderography began to change the world of note printing.[23] From 1817, the Bank of England made sustained efforts to further promote innovation in printing technology. These efforts resulted in a wave of new applications, such as the steam-powered press, compound color plates, electrotyping, and surface printing. By the 1860s, note printing in Britain and the United States had been mechanized and the need to manually date notes was all but eliminated. Printers such as the London-based Bradbury, Wilkinson & Co., the American Banknote Company, and the Continental Bank Note Company of New York made use of these new applications to become premium suppliers of notes to the rest of the world—China and Japan included.[24]

OVERSEAS BANKNOTE ISSUANCE

Family-owned or joint-stock banks issuing notes convertible to bullion were still fairly common in Europe at the beginning of the twentieth century; this phenomenon rapidly disappeared during the 1930s when central banks were taking charge of the money supply across much of the Western world.[25] In East Asia, the legacy of European banks entrusted with the supply of currency in colonies and dominions with varying degrees of official approbation continued in a few cases after World War II, and is still adhered to in Hong Kong today.[26] Such banknotes percolated in large numbers into the few interstitial domains that remained outside European suzerainty, quite often passing at a premium against indigenous currencies.[27] For example, around the 1900s, Hong Kong dollar banknotes were used in South China, while Straits Settlements dollar notes spread all over Peninsular Malaya.[28]

Monetary links between European colonies and self-governing regions of East Asia were not limited to the inflow of colonial currencies like the Hong Kong or Straits Settlements dollar. One of the least known properties of early European overseas banks is the fact that a considerable part of their note issue had been denominated in indigenous units of account and disseminated interstitially. This characteristic emerged as a tenet of overseas banking in the early nineteenth century, when British banks were allowed to issue notes in some of the newly emancipated colonies of Latin America. Similar issues were subsequently introduced in other parts of the world where Western European banks could enjoy comparatively free rein—East Asia, the Ottoman Empire, Ethiopia, and for a limited time even in Siberia.[29]

Since the British Treasury deprived British overseas banks of access to retail financial markets at home, these banks tended to specialize geographically through different groups of founding investors who had firsthand knowledge of specific colonial economies and the respective commodities flowing from them.[30] Although overseas banks could solicit deposits in London (and Edinburgh) in order to finance inbound bills, Treasury regulations prevented them from granting loans to clients domiciled in the United Kingdom. On the other hand, British saving, merchant, and clearing banks found sufficient outlets for growth in Britain's rapidly expanding retail and industrial sectors. They kept foreign engagements on the back burner until well into the twentieth century. Consequently, little competition arose between British domestic and overseas banks. In terms of corporate structure or managerial makeup, these two City of London banking communities were far from integrated. Youssef Cassis has, for example, estimated that landed aristocrats and politicians were twice as likely to be found on British overseas bank boards than on saving or clearing bank boards.[31]

In the 1890s, British overseas banks spread over no less than 710 branches around the world, while London's largest domestic clearing banks, such as

Lloyd's and Barclays, operated no branches outside Britain.[32] British investors were primarily attracted to secure colonies, and banking was no different. Thus, the largest British overseas banks in the mid-nineteenth century were those that were strictly associated with colonies and dominions: the Bank of Australasia (est. 1835) and the Union Bank of Australia (est. 1837). It was only when the growth potential in the Antipodes declined that other investment groups shifted their attention to the Americas, India, Africa, Continental Europe, and Greater China.

The fundamental restrictions on note issuance applicable to British banks in such disparate countries as Argentina, Greece, and Mainland China can be traced back to the same set of guidelines that had initially been devised for British colonies during the 1830s. Drawn up by the British Treasury, these guidelines were commonly referred to as Colonial Banking Regulations.[33] They restricted each bank's geographical branch deployment and ensured the subordination of business practices to colonial authorities. Adherence to these regulations was a prerequisite that competing British groups, bent on investment in far-flung corners of the Empire, had to meet before applying for a Royal Charter that would bestow on them the coveted limited-liability status.[34] Notably, the formal precepts of limited liability were introduced to the British domestic financial sector only in 1858. After limited-liability enterprise was introduced domestically, the provision of Royal Charters became a rarity.[35]

These features of early British overseas banks contrasted sharply with economic circumstances in Continental Europe. Most nineteenth-century French, Dutch, and German colonial banks had sprung up from initiatives jointly undertaken by well-established domestic banks and the state rather than by ad hoc groups of investors, thus mirroring a different pattern of economic development than in Britain. As a whole, European overseas banks like the Banque de l'Indochine or the Deutsch-Asiatische Bank worked more closely with French and German diplomatic missions around the world, and benefited from broader note issue prerogatives and less stringent reserve requirements than those set out by the British Treasury.[36]

Because of its rich natural resources and underdeveloped domestic financial sector, Latin America was one of the most attractive regions for European banking ventures in the mid-nineteenth century. British banks took the lead, claiming between a quarter and a third of all banking deposits in Argentina and Brazil during that period.[37] Consequently, the continent retained one of the largest amounts of overseas banknotes in circulation outside Asia (see Figure 1.1). But a decade later, political unrest cast a pall on financial stability in the region, as for-

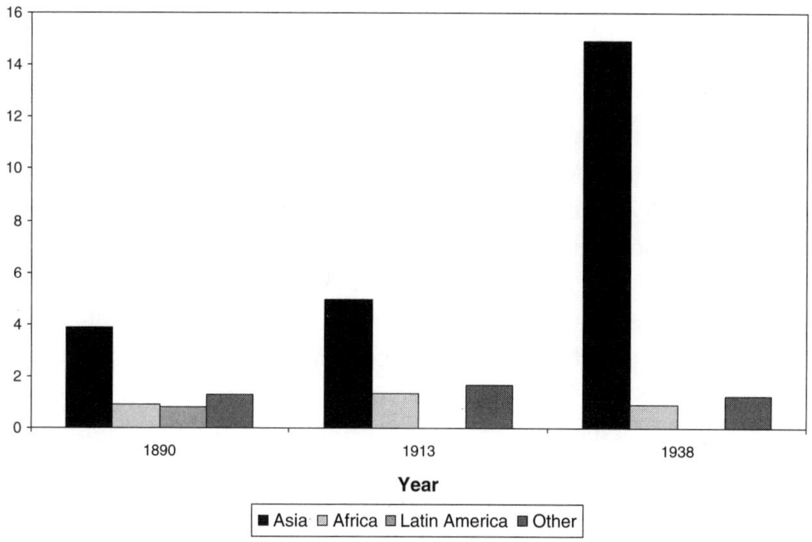

Figure 1.1. British Overseas Bank Note Circulation, 1890–1938. Unit: GBP (million). *Source*: Adapted from Jones (1993), pp. 39, 117, 215. Jones did not differentiate between overseas bank note issuance in colonial settings and foreign settings.

eign banks were progressively ejected from the monetary domain to make way for fledgling national banks. In 1904, for example, the London and River Plate Bank—then the largest British bank in Latin America—was forced to reduce its large banknote issue in Uruguay in favor of the new Banco de la Repùblica.[38]

During the early twentieth century, British overseas banks were also stripped of their prerogatives as suppliers of colonial currency in Australasia, Canada, Africa, and other parts of the British Empire, while in Asia the governments of Japan and Siam severely restricted the latitude of foreign banks operating on their soil.[39] Thus, by the 1910s overseas banknotes became a distinct Chinese treaty-port phenomenon, countenanced by European extraterritorial rights and denominated in either the traditional silver tael or local variations of Mexican dollar units.

BRITISH OVERSEAS BANKING IN CHINA

The first British banks to operate in East Asia during the 1850s had been set up in colonial India only a decade earlier. When these banks began issuing notes in East Asia, the notion of fiduciary money—let alone central banking—was still relatively novel in Europe. Like private banks of issue in the metropole, India-based banks were subject to stringent British Treasury guidelines aimed at protecting uninformed note bearers. The transition in English banking from unlimited to limited liability, which reshaped the regulatory underpinning of London as a global financial center, came into its own only in the late 1870s and was least influential in overseas banking. Therefore, the practice of banknote issuance overseas remained predicated on a nineteenth-century contingency. India-based British overseas banks were usually known as "Anglo-Indian" or "Eastern Exchange" banks. These were banks set up primarily to cash in on the breakup of the East India Company monopoly on intra-Asian trade and finance in 1833.[40] They discounted exchange bills and converted currencies, but their legal status was vague, and their ties with London's money markets and colonial policymakers remained tenuous.

In 1851, a new era began when the Oriental Bank (set up as the Bank of Western India in 1843) gained a Royal Charter, which enabled it to transfer its headquarters to London, expand its exchange business across Australasia and Africa, and issue banknotes in a large number of British colonies and dependencies. Two years later, the Chartered Bank of India Australia and China (CBIAC) gained a similar concession and swiftly established branches throughout East and Southeast Asia. In 1865, a portentous Hong Kong Colonial Ordinance gave much the same powers to a bank jointly established by few of the colony's richest merchants—the Hongkong and Shanghai Banking Corporation (HSBC).

This book will focus on the characteristics of the London-based CBIAC and the Hong Kong–based HSBC as banks of issue in China proper until 1937. Among other themes, it will propose analogies between British overseas banking in China and South America and will recount why most Anglo-Indian banks did not survive into the twentieth century. British banks, whose entry into the Chinese market occurred in the course of the late nineteenth or early twentieth century, will be only cursorily addressed because none could attain a lasting note issuance prerogative or challenge the supremacy of CBIAC and HSBC in the region.[41]

During the early twentieth century, European, American, and Japanese banks also entered the Chinese market. All these entrants—however divergent their backgrounds—cleared each other's banknotes. Foreign banks were responsible for a very large inventory of paper currency issued in China and its environs between 1865 and 1935. This is perhaps why the first observers to take keen interest in this prewar monetary phenomenon have been numismatists. The number of catalogs documenting the different specimens of foreign banknotes in China exceeds by far the number of studies on China authored by academics interested in free banking models (that is, the absence of paper legal tender and central banking).[42]

To date, Selgin's appears to be the only serious attempt to address the Chinese experience. Focusing on premodern Chinese banks, he argued that free banking in one particular locality (Fuzhou) "worked well."[43] Yet, to begin uncovering the bigger picture, Chinese modern banks, the foreign financial sector, and multiple other localities must be examined. For these reasons, Selgin himself concluded that a more comprehensive study of the Chinese banking experience "should prove a most worthwhile undertaking."[44] The following chapters make the first few steps in that direction. Although it is not concerned with free banking per se, this book seeks to correct the literature imbalance by addressing aspects of the Chinese experience that go well beyond numismatic interests, such as the circulation volumes, profitability, and regulation of overseas banknote issuance.

Foreign banknotes in China embodied influential novel design and advanced print technology, but they were certainly not the only common means of payment current in and around the treaty ports that the European Powers had carved up among themselves along the China coast during the years 1842–1914. Neither did they constitute the only form of paper money during that period. That China did not have a uniform currency during the Ming and Qing is a well-known historic fact. The most ubiquitous form of high-denomination money in the late-Imperial era was sycee—silver bullion weighing approximately 50 tael with local variations in fineness—or Spanish-American silver dollars;[45] silver bullion as well as traditional copper coinage were widespread all over China well into the 1930s. From the mid-nineteenth century, successive Chinese governments and warlord regimes had issued various types of paper currency, often imitating foreign designs, but with an uneven record of success. In addition, private moneyshop scrip, remittance drafts, military wage coupons, product certificates, and later even underground CCP paper currency were circulating in different parts of the country concurrently.[46]

Yet, owing to the extraterritorial setting in which foreign firms operated in the treaty ports, foreign banknotes acquired a contentious characteristic. Unlike Chinese currency, foreign banknote issuance was not regulated in situ by any sovereign government. While often denominated in traditional Chinese units of account, foreign banknotes were issued at will by private financial institutions operating on Chinese soil yet entirely impervious to Chinese authority.

This aspect of overseas banknote issuance was—and still is—roundly condemned by scholars in the PRC, who allege that the absence of Chinese government regulation enabled foreign banks of issue to divert much-needed capital from the domestic economy; it is the mainspring of a fairly extensive literature that, in its scope and pertinence, comes second only to that published by numismatists.[47] This book will argue that the allegations leveled by Chinese scholars, though mostly premised on questionable sources, contain on occasion valuable observations of foreign banking and its net effect on China's troubled path to industrialization.[48]

As China ventured into economic modernity in the early twentieth century, silver dollars, subsidiary coins, and banknotes gradually superseded its bimetallic standard. But for the next three decades, the leaders of the newly established Republic were unable to enforce monetary unification on breakaway provinces. A turnaround appeared in sight only in late 1935, when an invigorated Nationalist administration took China's currency off the silver standard and proclaimed its first fiat currency in the modern era, the *fabi* 法幣.

In the lead-up to the *fabi* reform, a large number of regional banks still operated outside of the central government's reach. More often than not, these banks had been amenable to warlords, who did not hesitate to milk the local civilian population through what economists call an "inflation tax." In other words, many regional banks serviced warlord debt with proceeds obtained from banknote disbursement. Still others strove to fend off the unification thrust of the GMD (a.k.a. *Guomindang*, Kuomintang, or KMT) government by maintaining a stable regional currency and securing banknote convertibility to bullion.[49]

The GMD government's intention to trim its large budget deficit helped muster support for the 1935 move off silver. A modest budget surplus, a higher degree of monetary integration, and some improvement in productivity were achieved during 1936–1937. However, in the final analysis, unchecked military spending incurred by anti-Communist campaigns and the impending war with Japan did not leave the *fabi* much chance of retaining its credibility. Considered as a milestone in Chinese monetary history, the *fabi* reform, both its background and long-term consequences, have been studied in detail and need not be recapitulated here.[50] What, however, remains understudied is how—to secure the success of monetary reform in early 1936—the GMD forced foreign banks to renounce their banknote issuance prerogatives and hand over their silver reserves.

Previous commissioned work on British overseas banking in China depict these expatriate financial institutions as generally conducive to the Nationalist cause of monetary unification.[51] This book will revisit such generalizations—particularly in the course of Chapters 4 and 5. It will argue that previous studies of British banks in prewar China (1842–1937) have been preoccupied with the portrayal of British managerial persona to the neglect of quantitative analyses. This resulted in a story line that does not accord Chinese bankers, policymakers, or antiforeign boycotts much agency. The book will seek to correct this narrative shortfall in an attempt to present what may arguably be a more balanced picture of the operation of British banks in China and their relationship with the Nationalist government.

GERMANE POLEMICS

With British overseas banking in China as its subject matter, this book will quite naturally weigh into the debates that intersect the fields of Chinese and British economic history. Two of these debates have overarching significance. A fairly recent debate concerns the performance of the Chinese economy under the late-Qing and GMD rule. Another more "ancient" debate branched off Max Weber's seminal work—published almost a century ago—on the factors that positioned Europe politically and economically ahead of China from the sixteenth century onward.[52]

The more recent debate began after Thomas Rawski and Loren Brandt published markedly positive estimates of per capita Chinese agricultural productivity growth in the century preceding the Sino-Japanese War. Rawski and Brandt revised what until then had been a dismal portrayal of living standards in the Chinese hinterland. Based on econometric analyses of land surveys and price data, they concluded that total agricultural output between 1850 and 1937 overtook population gains by approximately 1 percent annually.[53] These views have since been contested by numerous other scholars, who point to the failings in GMD agrarian reforms, and who challenge the assumptions that underlie Rawski and Brandt's findings.[54] In particular, Rawski and Brandt's assumption of efficient factor markets at work in early twentieth-century China remains at odds with a fairly large number of recent studies, including the one presented here.[55]

Interpretations of economic realities in prewar China still oscillate between the pessimistic and optimistic. "Pessimists" underscore problems in production relations that cannot be adequately covered in a study focusing on banking and the urban sector—lack of land tenure security, peasant immiserization, and overpopulation. On the other hand, "optimists" identify consistent growth in agricultural productivity fueled by what they see as the ameliorative effects of China's *integration* with world factor markets.[56]

The evidence presented in this study will contend with one of the two arguments underpinning the "optimist" view; namely, it will call into question the assumption that China's prewar economy enjoyed a higher degree of *financial integration* than previously thought. Because this study is confined to a distinctly urban segment of the economy, it cannot—and does not purport to—impact the debate over agricultural productivity or overall GDP growth rates. Instead, the study accepts Mark Elvin's suggestion that China's economy in the first half of the twentieth century should be divided into four distinct macrosystems with substantive income disparities—the poor rural hinterland, the bustling treaty ports, Japanese-managed Manchuria and Taiwan, and the separate pastureland economy of the Northwest.[57]

The variance of opinion between "optimists" and "pessimists" on the degree of market integration in late-Imperial China echoes, in a sense, a more profound debate over the root cause of European preeminence in the early modern era. Why did China's technological, monetary, and institutional head start over the West in the tenth and thirteenth centuries dissipate?

Until the mid-twentieth century, Western thinkers assumed that economic progress in China had been forestalled owing to suprastructural impediments, such as the autocratic nature of China's Confucian body politic, the self-professed "amateurism" of its officialdom, or the "passivity" of its countrymen.[58] Ironically, such sweeping cultural judgments seem to be creeping back into the academic discourse through the back door—this time not to explain underdevelopment in the prewar era but to foreshadow the rise of East Asia in the twenty-first century.[59] PRC historians, on the other hand, have consistently adhered to an inverted Marxian theory, alleging that Western imperialist incursions had maliciously trampled China's "sprouts of capitalism."[60]

Sociocultural impediments to modernization, including the low status of merchants, could certainly be found in traditional China. However, recent scholarship has substantially reshaped our views of the merchant class in the late-Qing, pointing to vertical linkages with the gentry and officialdom that were manifest, for example, in the sale of Qing Imperial degrees, or absentee land ownership.[61] Although "Confucianism" often connotes familial prejudice, cronyism, and autarkism, these are not necessarily insurmountable obstacles on the road toward economic modernization. This is perhaps why the onus of most interpretations has shifted, since the 1970s, from the sociocultural to the demographic dimension, highlighting critical factors such as the marginal rates of substitution of China's production inputs.[62]

Nonetheless, a well-rounded account of China's economic performance over the course of the prewar era cannot be produced while ignoring the critical role played by institutions. This book will touch on the broad institutional variance between China and the West, pertaining to the different vehicles of body politics, the dissimilar balance of power between government and the private sector, the composition of the bureaucracy, the evolution of central banks, and the pervasiveness of monetary regulators and financial intermediaries.

The following chapters will recount the late-Imperial relinquishment of monetary and fiscal reins. They will discuss the Qing's emaciated tax base and its minimalist central-government bureaucratic apparatus, its lack of interest in market regulation, and its miscomprehension of Western business practices.[63] Local bailiffs reported, for example, only about half of all tax revenue to their superiors in the late-Imperial era. By and large, tax revenues dwindled from about 10 percent of total agrarian production during the Ming to only about 2 percent in the late-Qing.[64] The famous *lijin* 釐金, or Likin transit duty, constituted the sole fiscal innovation throughout the Qing reign, but even this measure resulted from provincial initiative rather than central government resolve.

Peer Vries has similarly noted that China and Britain possessed qualitatively different government bureaucracies by the nineteenth century. Although China's population was thirty times larger than Britain's, the number of government officials in China was no higher than that in Britain.[65] Such global comparisons suggest that population pressures alone cannot adequately explain China's technological lag, if only because these pressures had not obstructed the economic takeoff of densely inhabited Meiji Japan.

This book will highlight market failures that help explain operative differences between expatriate and Chinese firms as a prelude to why British banknotes were sought after in Shanghai. In that sense, this work is less informed by demographics than by recognition of the significance of institutions along the lines identified by Douglass North. Heavily drawing on the European and North American experience, North and his coauthors have persuasively shown how government espousal of property rights—through the dissemination of a civil code, patent laws, insurance premia, and Royal Charters—is one of the definitive factors behind economic modernization.[66] Once the private rate of return on research and development was propped up to match the public one in the sixteenth century, Britain could embark on a course whereby imported foodstuffs gradually freed up resources imperative for the Industrial Revolution. The "institutional formula," which allowed Britain to escape many of the demographic checks that all other premodern polities had grappled with, was not unique. Much the same dynamics had first occurred in the United Provinces of the Netherlands during the fifteenth through seventeenth centuries and held out roughly until the Batavian Republic succumbed to mercantilism in the late eighteenth century. In the late nineteenth century, the same dynamics lent the American economy sufficient impetus to succeed Britain.[67]

North captured the essence of European economic "exceptionalism" for what it is worth, but the theoretical construct, which he had laid down, has since been finessed by scholars steeped in Asian and Mediterranean history.[68] Working largely within the latter category but borrowing extensively from game theory and diverse geo-generic scenarios, Avner Greif has, for example, made consistent contributions to an emerging model of institutional fluidity and optimal growth.[69] Although the empiric underpinnings of this model are still fairly raw, some of the key concepts it is advancing will be employed in a taxonomy of Shanghai's financial markets, particularly those markets relating to contract enforcement and gubernatorial coercion-constraints.

A major challenge to this institutional approach has been mounted by "California School" historians, who see much the same free market dynamism at work in the seventeenth-century East Asia without any industrial turnaround.[70] They therefore conclude that other factors better explain Europe's economic performance—for example, colonial extraction, denser coal deposits, or the competitive nation-state system.

Kenneth Pomeranz's pathbreaking book *The Great Divergence* is perhaps the most forceful iteration of "California School" views. Admirably conversant with the economic histories of both continents, Pomeranz marshaled a vast array of secondary source data to argue that England's ascendancy in the early nineteenth century should be ascribed to "shadow acres" in far-flung colonies, and to the proximity of its domestic coal deposits to arterial waterways.[71] A comprehensive riposte to Pomeranz's main thesis is yet to emerge. Nonetheless, discerning readers of his work are left with one niggling Northian question unanswered: if coal and colonial possessions, as opposed to market dynamics, were the key to England's "freak" departure from Malthusian constraints, why didn't the Iberian economy evolve in quite the same way? After all, Spain did possess colonies worldwide, was rich in mineral resources, and was not entirely bereft of coal.[72]

The abundance and accessibility of British coal deposits should not deflect scholars' attention from the large-scale exploitation of other sources of energy, which had set Britain apart from the Continental economy long before the nineteenth century: husbandry and chemicals in agriculture, and water-milling in garment manufacturing. In his influential study, David Landes cast these two factors as productivity gainers that paved the way for the Industrial Revolution; Landes then alluded to the ubiquity of financial "paper instruments" and joint-stock companies in Britain as even earlier, and equally significant, portents of rupture with the Continental mold.[73]

The Landes account ought to have been complemented with a more coherent institutional dimension. In that sense, Pomeranz's deemphasis of divergent institutions between England and China is perhaps disappointing. It is also somewhat surprising since his early work on late-Imperial Shandong had ably highlighted the degree of market imperfection plaguing much of the Chinese hinterland. That interest and currency exchange rates fluctuated wildly from one county to another, but were lower and more stable in foreign-controlled Qingdao, is one resounding symptom of this failure.[74]

Pomeranz's perception of a late eighteenth-century English departure from either European or Chinese growth patterns is supported, to some extent, by econometric analysis of secular price data presented by Shiue and Keller.[75] Theirs is a comparative research whose rigor would be truly compelling, if it were not for the devil lying in the small detail, as often is the case with Chinese sources. In contrast to Northian theory, Shiue and Keller argue that there is no strong evidence to support the existence of a unique European "institutional formula" for economic growth, because markets appear no less efficient in China than in Continental Europe right up to the nineteenth century. Yet their regressions do not seem to factor in the exchange rate fluctuations of different European currencies or regional variations in the value of the Chinese tael, and are otherwise characterized by low levels of significance.[76]

A rather different iteration of California School arguments has recently been advanced by Jack Goldstone, as if to address an aspect of the Eurasian divide that Pomeranz's analysis has "written out of the scenario," that is, science.[77] *Pace* Goldstone, readily available coal was a necessary but not sufficient factor in the makeup of Britain's Industrial Revolution. He identifies cycles of "crises" and "efflorescence"—the latter implying a per capita GDP growth rate of up to 1 percent annually—as an attribute common to many Eurasian economies before the nineteenth century, from Golden Age Netherlands in the West to Tokugawa Japan in the East.[78] He then concludes that what set the British economy apart from the Eurasian norm in the mid-nineteenth century was not merely new sources of energy, but an ardent pursuit of applicable scientific know-how to harness latent resources. Goldstone concedes, however, that the sustainability of what he terms Britain's peculiar "engine science" and its spread into popular culture was greatly facilitated by commercial law and distinct political institutions.[79]

An important tenet propounded by all California School adherents is the notion that the formation of joint-stock companies in Europe cannot be seen as unique.[80] But while Japanese scholars have, for example, traced the first Chinese joint-stock partnerships as far back as the tenth century, these have often sprung *in the face* of government policy, rather than as a result of it.[81] Furthermore, the sources that point to the occurrence of joint-stock enterprise in late-Imperial China do not come near the degree of legal detail and stakeholding transparency that characterize documents surrounding the establishment of British joint-stock firms, from their very inception in the early sixteenth century, as compiled, for example, by William Scott.[82] Scott's pioneering work is suggestive of a long continuum of institutional evolution that links publicly funded trade expeditions to the Baltic and Africa under Elizabethan patronage, with the subsequent emergence of the London stock exchange, as well as with the establishment of domestic joint-stock banks and overseas chartered banks later in the Victorian era.[83]

This is not to say that, when operating overseas, British joint-stock companies upheld transparency as a value in itself. In fact, British banks in Shanghai took advantage of the amorphous legal setting there to withhold information on banknote circulation volumes, whereas, in Hong Kong, they were obliged to disclose this type of information in the colonial government's Blue Book. Put simply, stakeholding transparency allowed British joint-stock companies to mobilize economies of scale. It was practiced in London and other places where companies raised share capital, but did not necessarily extend beyond where the British legal system obtained.

In the British context, stakeholding transparency evolved as a means of affirming the concession of property rights by the monarch. The monarch tolerated joint-stock companies because they paid for their Charters and helped raise tax revenue. Through the share capital they raised, the founders of joint-stock companies achieved a degree of investment security and economies of scale that were quite unparalleled elsewhere in the early modern world. Being the progeny of these early joint-stock companies, British overseas banks astutely utilized economies of scale acquired in London's emerging equity market to tap into China's foreign trade and into its diffuse financial services sector as of the mid-nineteenth century.

By then, Parliament had clearly displaced the Crown as the *locus* of political power in Britain. Representing a broader spectrum of commercial interest, Parliament was not only tolerating joint-stock enterprise but also actively engaged in regulating it, and laying down the legal wherewithal for its exponential growth in the twentieth century. In his important work, James Taylor has flagged the dialectical junctures that British joint-stock enterprise had to traverse before it became universally accepted in the twentieth century: the famous Bubble Act of 1720 curtailed the growth of all joint-stock companies that were not sanctioned by the state, country banks included. Later, as British public opinion grew less mistrustful of impersonal corporate entities, entrepreneurial pressure was building bottom-up for the government to permit and regulate share capital in a number of industries. Then, in 1844, the famous Peel Act formally recognized smaller joint-stock banks, but sought to eliminate private banknote issuance in return. Finally, the British corporate law reforms of 1856 meant that all joint-stock companies could apply for limited-liability status regardless of Royal Charter bestowal.[84]

On balance, the British experience seems to suggest that a stable paper currency was contingent on a mature institutional, corporate, and regulatory framework. This book will examine the inapplicability of this framework to the Chinese experience; it will foreground the immaturity of a wide range of Chinese institutions that had set out the "rules of the game" before the rise of GMD to power in 1927: central versus warlord governance, private sector versus central banks, monetary regulation, capital markets, and corporate law.

DATES AND METHODOLOGY

The period under review is 1842–1937, which scholars conventionally refer to as "prewar China." It begins with the cession of Shanghai to the British and ends with Japan's invasion of China. Strictly speaking, the first British bank to open a branch on Mainland China, OBC, did so only in 1847. Yet the book aims to address the Sino-foreign treaty-port encounter from its inception.

Choosing to focus on British banknote issuance in China has meant that the primary sources used here were mostly compiled in London. Economic historians of China have scarcely analyzed many of these materials, possibly because the large amount of archival materials made available in the PRC in the last two decades has proven a greater draw-card for scholars. With a few exceptions, however, studies weighted toward Mainland and Taiwan archives may leave our understanding of the Sino-foreign encounter incomplete.

As indicated earlier, Chinese scholars who attempted to analyze foreign banknote issuance during the 1930s often complained that the lack of disclosure by foreign bank branches in Shanghai, particularly as regards bullion reserves and note circulation volumes, compromised their findings.[85] Ever since, this topic has continued to resonate in many Chinese studies. As late as 2004, for example, the economic historian Hong Jiaguan wrote that the secretive nature of foreign bank operations in prewar China meant that extant source materials could merely yield a "guess-estimate" (*guji he cesuan* 估計和測算) of treaty-port banknote circulation volumes.[86] Now that much of the relevant data has been deposited in the public domain, we have all the more reason to revisit this topic.

The book is divided into two parts, each presenting evidence from a different perspective so as to allow readers to consider the main arguments several times over. The pith and structure of Part I (Chapters 1–3) is such that readers can, at any stage, relate British banknote issuance in China to themes of broader import, often with a global bent. This introductory chapter has explained the relevance of this book's theme to overarching academic debates in economic history. Chapter 2 will invoke anecdotal evidence to describe how financial markets in Shanghai operated, and it will try to identify where foreign and local firms intersected over the entire period between 1842 and 1937. Chapter 3 will outline the evolution of British banking in East and Southeast Asia through the annals of CBIAC. Drawing on secondary sources and on recently declassified CBIAC materials that are almost purely quantitative, Chapter 3 will also argue that previous estimates of the circulation of HK$ notes in South China were upward-biased.

The patterns emerging from this analysis are then considered in light of evidence mostly compiled in the HSBC Group Archives where Shanghai branch correspondence has been preserved but quantitative data is much more piecemeal. While Chapters 1, 2, and 3 each aim at generalizing business and monetary aspects of the prewar period (1842–1937) in its entirety, Part II (Chapters 4 and 5) plots HSBC data *chronologically* so as to foreground linkages between the changing political climate in China and the fate of British business. Particular focus will be placed on the momentous yet critically understudied period of anti-British boycotts and the rise of the GMD to power between 1925 and 1927. Where HSBC data is incomplete, we will again resort to CBIAC quantitative evidence. Chapter 6 will tie Parts I and II together in order to point out the significance of British banknote issuance in China to our understanding of Chinese history.

Previous studies have had little of substance to say about the fact that many of the British banks that operated in nominally independent parts of the developing world like China were also the main banks of issue in adjacent colonies. HSBC and CBIAC thus claimed a large segment of the money stock in both Hong Kong and the Straits Settlements during the nineteenth century. Was the colonial setting of British banknote issuance in Hong Kong any different from the one obtaining on the Mainland? The following chapters will answer this derivative question by drawing a clear, if purely notional, distinction between banknotes denominated in HK$ and banknotes denominated in Chinese units of accounts, like the tael or Shanghai dollar (hereafter quasi-foreign banknotes). The Appendix will present a long-term reconstruction of British banknote circulation volumes in Shanghai that is based on this distinction. By delinking HK$-denominated notes, whose spread in China was largely confined to the Lingnan region, from the quasi-foreign notes used in the treaty ports, economic conditions in Shanghai will be thrown into high relief.

Final conclusions will be drawn from local evidence rather than from theory, and this is by no means an arbitrary choice. As a discipline, Chinese economic history is overlaid with polar views, but at least one consensus seems to have begun forming. If scholars are to move on beyond preconceived frameworks, sweeping generalizations should make way for much-neglected provincial and county-level research, where data are substantially more reliable, and quite often more instructive, than macro-level observations.[87] Accordingly, the ideas, data, and methodology that are the basis of this study are all *localized* in essence; they highlight a neglected everyday aspect of treaty-port life by primarily consulting the records of distinct treaty-port financial institutions.

Chapter 2 The Sino-Foreign Financial Grid in Prewar Shanghai

This chapter is intended to set the scene in which quasi-foreign banknote issuance came about in prewar Shanghai; without this background one could scarcely comprehend the significance of this monetary phenomenon. Whereas the following chapters will expand on the particularities of British note issuance in Shanghai, this one will draw on a wide range of lateral and secondary sources in order to sketch out in very rough strokes how financial markets operated in the city, with particular emphasis on the confluence of foreign and local institutions.

Until recently, studies of the history of Shanghai were largely devoid of precise microeconomic data on the city's foreign sector, and those conducted in the PRC were often permeated with ideological reprobation.[1] Perhaps because of the inaccessibility of important archival sources in the city until the 1990s, other aspects of Shanghai's prewar fabric had remained for a very long time fairly enigmatic too—aspects such as divisions between and among the city's many different ethnic communities, the role of organized crime and the leverage enjoyed by foreign and Chinese financiers in municipal politics, or the formidability of Shanghai's labor movement.[2]

In the near absence of solid facts, a florid if somewhat clichéd discourse emerged to capture what had been perceived as an urban sprawl replete with opportunity and peril; Western and Chinese authors often fell prey to misconception.[3] They tended to mystify Shanghai as anything from the "Brothel of Asia" through the "Paradise for Adventurers" to nothing short of the "Pearl of the East."[4] Scholars, too, later reinforced these notions with epithets of their own, for example,. "Decadent City," "Collision Point of Cultures," or "Crucible of Modern China."[5]

Observers—Western and Chinese alike—found Shanghai a difficult place to classify because, once the Qing had ceded territory for a foreign settlement following the Nanjing Treaty of 1842, this outlying area became neither quite foreign nor quite Chinese. Whether looked at through the prism of institutions, economy, culture, or lifestyle, Shanghai tended to display mind-boggling hybridity. This hybridity could only be overturned in the postwar era, when PRC commissars cleansed the Bund (*Waitan* 外灘), Shanghai's vibrant and cosmopolitan business district on the banks of the Huangpu River, of much of its foreign heritage. That this hybridity was uncanny is perhaps best illustrated in the famous 1949 footage showing sandal-clad People's Liberation Army soldiers glaring at neon-lit skyscrapers with disbelief, as they march in from the rural Mainland to repossess the city from its equally puzzled urbanites.[6]

That said, this chapter will endeavor to avoid notions of Shanghai's "inscrutability" at least insofar as they arch into the economic sphere and insofar as the yield of newly published research permits. It will focus in particular on those institutional and financial patterns that distinguished Shanghai from the Chinese hinterland.

MONETARY FRAGMENTATION

One of the most vexing problems British businessmen faced as they penetrated deeper into the Chinese Mainland from their older strongholds in Hong Kong and Guangzhou in the late 1840s was what they saw as the Chinese Mainland's refractory currency system. At first, some tinkered with the idea of proclaiming the sterling standard in Hong Kong as an anchor of monetary stability. But by the early 1860s, most British imperial policymakers in the region had come to realize that, as complex as China's system was, it was much too entrenched to give way to a uniform currency promoted by a small number of foreigners in a colony perched on "a mere barren rock."[7] Subsequently, the Hong Kong currency was to adapt to the preferred store of value on the Mainland: the silver dollar. The Colony's subsidiary coinage, too, largely emulated China's copper cash.

While the Hong Kong currency was framed into the Chinese system, it was hoped that it would at least escape the adulteration that its generic equivalents on the Mainland suffered from and would gain wide acceptance throughout the Celestial Empire. But the limits of this conjecture soon became apparent: the Hong Kong currency remained at best one of many foreign currencies circulating in littoral China. In Shanghai, where the institutional and cadastral underpinning of British settlement was much more patchy than in Hong Kong, early attempts to introduce Hong Kong-minted silver coins denominated in the local tael failed to take root.[8] For the next century or so, the city's foreign concession areas had to rely on Chinese coinage and recast imported bullion for their metallic money supply.

Shanghai initially attracted the British because of its expedient location as a gateway to the Lower Yangzi Basin.[9] The first British bankers to descend on the region in the 1850s realized that the key to success there was mastering the vagaries of the prevailing currency, and some would later show intimate knowledge thereof. Charles Addis, a promising young Scotsman recruited by the HSBC to be sent East, observed as early as 1886:

> The only money which circulates universally throughout the length and breadth of the land is copper cash (*tung-chien*). With regard to other kinds, an intense provincialism prevails—silver lumps, silver dollars, small silver pieces, and copper cents circulating on their face value only in the province where they are minted, in other provinces at a discount. In the case of foreign [coins], there is some, which circulate throughout the treaty-ports. Some kinds of *liang* (tael) notes, dollar notes, or *chien* [copper-denominated] notes, issued by Chinese banks or exchange houses circulate only in the city where they are issued. A traveler when passing from one province to another should be careful to change the money of the former for the latter.[10]

These remarks are revealing because they were made shortly before HSBC launched its banknote issue in Shanghai. Although the passage does not bespeak anticipation of this event, it does demonstrate that British bankers had certainly come to grips with the Chinese monetary system.

What British bankers had to accommodate, though, was the fact that none of the treaties that China had signed with different European Powers in the late nineteenth century sanctioned foreign bank presence beyond the designated treaty ports, of which Shanghai became the largest. With the exception of Beijing, British banks could not set up branches in areas under effective Chinese jurisdiction. This meant that the farther one ventured out of Shanghai, the less likely one would be to come across quasi-foreign banknotes in use.[11]

But there was much more to this than jurisdiction, since notes were traditionally assessed in the Chinese marketplace based on their place of issue, while particular bank insignia were of less importance. An informed Western testimonial from 1904 described foreign bank practices as follows:

> The principal foreign banks [in China] are [HSBC], the Chartered Bank of India Australia and China, the Yokohama Specie Bank, [Banque Russo-Asiatique], [Deutsche-Asiatic Bank], and [Banque de l'Indochine]. These banks do a considerable deposit and discount business . . . [They] do their business in China without any contract with the Chinese government, and with no charter issued by that government. They are there simply on tolerance . . . with the protection of extraterritoriality . . .
>
> Several of these banks issue bank notes under the authority of their charters from home, but without any charter or other grant of privilege from the Chinese government, either central or provincial. The bank notes form a convenient medium of circulation in some of the treaty-ports and within narrow limits outside of those ports . . .
>
> A Shanghai bank note, for example, is very generally discounted if presented to the Tientsin [Tianjin] or Peking [Beijing] or Hongkong branch of the same [foreign] bank, the discount sometimes being as high as 5 per cent, although the two cities are only some three hours apart by railroad . . .
>
> The [foreign] banks are, generally speaking, known for their accuracy and carefulness in carrying out their contracts and in meeting their obligations. But they occupy a position of such advantage in many ways that it seems likely that their high profits are obtained in part at the expense of the development of trade in other directions in spite of the fact, one may add with even more emphatic truthfulness, without the facilities which they have offered, it would have been utterly impossible for trade to have developed anywhere nearly so well as has been the case.[12]

In a later note on Chinese currency, probably from the early 1910s, Addis made a similar, if less critical, remark: "Foreign coins circulated widely in all the treaty-ports and in the larger cities of China. But the [foreign] banknotes circulate only in the city where they are issued; for instance, those issued by a bank in Shanghai not being accepted by merchants of Peking [Beijing], or only at a discount."[13]

Monetary fragmentation in China intensified toward the demise of the Qing dynasty and through the Beiyang (read: early-Republican) period (1912–1927). Although both regimes promulgated countless measures to the contrary, these Beijing-based late-Imperial and early-Republican governments had made monetary fragmentation much worse by resorting to debasement in order to jack up seigniorage revenue from newly founded state mints.

Initially, Qing provincial governors purchased European minting machinery to increase the output of copper coinage, which had been in short supply throughout the late nineteenth century, as Ho Hon-wai has ably shown.[14] Once at work, the governors soon realized that modern technology extended government capacity to reduce the intrinsic value of the coins while passing them off as equivalent to time-honored units of payment. This had far-reaching, often horrendous, effects because low-denomination copper coinage was the lifeblood of retail in the Chinese premodern economy. While it expedited the recourse to private fiduciary currency in some localities, the debasement resulted in an inflationary spiral and breakdown of trust in metallic money in others.

The *Diplomatic and Consular Reports* regularly produced by British officials before World War I bear what is perhaps the most lucid testament of this transition from copper coin shortages to the debasement of copper coinage, and the ways in which it affected the demand for other means of payment in various places.

An 1898 dispatch from Fuzhou stated, for example:

> The large amount of paper in circulation helps to relieve the stringency caused by the scarcity of [copper] cash. A rough estimate of the local paper currency places the note issue of the 11 chief [Chinese] banks at 6 or 7 lacs of dollars. In addition to these there are numerous cash shops with a paper circulation of a few thousand dollars, a large portion of these notes being for small amounts. The small silver coins issued by the Foochow [Fuzhou] Mint are also much in use, but of these there are at present struck only 20c., 10 c., and 5 c. pieces.[15]

A concurrent report from the fairly peripheral treaty port of Shashi 沙市 in Hubei province seems to suggest that the interior was significantly more reliant on copper as a store of value, and therefore somewhat less receptive to new types of money:

> Copper cash and cash notes form the entire currency of the port, silver being but little used and dollars scarcely at all . . . There are said to be 130 cash shops in the town, nearly all of which issue notes. These notes are for 1,000, 5,000 and 10,000 [copper cash] . . . Those issued by the more reputable firms in Shashih [Shashi] . . . are current for some 30 miles around, but even these are useless in Ichang [Yichang]. The market is flooded with paper of 1,000 cash, mostly issued by small shops in the Manchu city of Chingchou [Jingzhou], for which it is always exceedingly difficult to get change even in Chingchou itself.[16]

The implications of Chinese central and provincial government intemperance were such that Shanghai, because it headquartered large foreign banks, soon became one of the only places in early twentieth-century China where the convertibility of paper money was standardized. To put it more precisely, it was one of the few places where banknotes—in this case primarily quasi-foreign—were readily convertible into silver dollars, or into bullion of verifiable quality, regardless of the political climate at large.

By the 1920s, J. P. Braga, scion of one the most eminent Sino-Portuguese families in Macao, could confidently state: "The banknotes of all the foreign banks, and a few of those issued by the leading Chinese banks in the treaty-ports, have the full confidence of the public and circulate freely, since they constitute (particularly those issued in dollars) one of the very few [media] of exchange on which one can rely."[17]

A handbook for Western travelers, while warning that Hong Kong and Straits dollar coins were not at all prized in Shanghai, reached much the same conclusion:

> All the leading [foreign] banks issue notes for one, five, ten dollars or upward. These notes are the most convenient method of carrying money. As the silver Mexican dollar weighs about an ounce not many can be carried with comfort . . .
>
> In dealing with money the traveler must look out for himself; nothing can save him from loss unless he does. Coinage suffers in many ways . . . There is a good deal of forged money: also occasionally, the small coinage of a particular province will come under suspicion. The rule is to have as little small money as possible, yet you must have some. Do not be offended as you might be at home, if a rickshaw coolie or shopkeeper returns a 20-cent piece saying "blass" (brass). The chances are that he is right. Pay another coin and put your dignity in the pocket.[18]

Testimonials from Chinese note bearers on what inspired their faith in foreign banknotes are harder to find, but desultory anecdotal evidence does exist. In 1879, Guo Songtao 郭嵩燾, China's outgoing minister to Britain, remarked upon his return home that he was surprised by the popularity which such notes had gained among his compatriots, while other Western innovations were still being rejected.[19]

Nearly half a century later, the *Times* correspondent in China reported that a fearsome gang of bandits in Anhui province had left the garrison town of Liuanzhou [Lu'an] 六安州 in ruins. The bandits carried off hundreds of residents for ransom, and "many others had been cruelly tortured in order to extort money." The correspondent was then bemused to report that the coveted loot had not been silver or gold. Rather, the "curious feature is that the bandits are everywhere demanding Shanghai banknotes as being easier to carry, with the view, it is conjectured, of retiring to this city when their fortunes are made."[20]

The Nanjing Decade (1927–1937), which began not long before the Liuanzhou raid, saw a much better functioning central government at work than either the Beiyang or late-Imperial periods. To be sure, debasement did not entirely disappear under the Nanjing government. However, the GMD leadership pushed fairly consistently for central banking and uniform currency along Western lines, and on balance helped improve the reliability of Chinese financial institutions.

The difference between the late-Imperial, Beiyang, and Nanjing shades of central governance did not lie in rhetoric. In fact, all three regimes employed a fairly similar reformist economic terminology, and they invited experts from overseas to help remedy monetary fragmentation.[21] All foreign advisers recommended in one way or another that China abandon the silver standard and limit private and provincial banknote issuance, but the GMD government was the only one ready to implement such measures. This was partly because the GMD did not shirk from confronting other foreign interests within China, British banks included.

The legacy of GMD resolve is, at any rate, clearly evidenced by a succession of measures that will be recapitulated in Chapter 5, but whose minutiae have been discussed at length elsewhere: the enforcement of banknote reserve policy and establishment of an embryonic central bank (1928);[22] the introduction of the Customs Gold Unit to offset China's deteriorating terms of trade (1930);[23] the withdrawal of regional tael units (1933); and the proclamation of the *fabi,* or uniform legal tender (1935).[24]

TAXONOMY OF FINANCIAL INSTITUTIONS IN PREWAR SHANGHAI

In order to understand what difference foreign financial institutions made to Shanghai's capital markets, one must first have an idea of the degree of market integration in other parts of prewar China. As explained in Chapter 1, this is an issue that is hotly debated by economic historians, and one that is permeated by regional variance. For lack of space, and owing to its succinctness, the following passage from the British *Consular Reports* has been chosen to highlight the situation in one locality, Nanning, the principal commercial hub of the then landlocked province of Guangxi through the 1910s: "There are a large number of [Chinese] banks established at Nanning, which advance money on cargo at exorbitant interest. They thrive on the discount and exchange between Nanning and Canton [Guangzhou]. Freight, insurance and interest are so high that goods sent from Canton to Nanning cost 30 to 40 percent more at the latter port."[25]

Shanghai's situation could well be described in similar terms before the establishment of the first British banks in the city during the 1850s. Since about the mid-eighteenth century, the main financial intermediary in the Lower Yangzi Basin—by far the most commercialized part of the country—were the *qianzhuang* 錢莊 known in English as "native banks" or "moneyshops." These institutions were typically small proprietorships with unlimited liability, loosely aligned along family and dialect ties.[26]

Large moneyshops lent funds and issued scrip against individual deposits called *zhuangpiao* 莊票 (shop coupon), but this could be cashed by proximate shops only after ten to fifteen days during which couriers would liaise with the issuing shop to rule out fraud.[27] The main business of *qianzhuang* was, however, advancing loans to merchants to support the junk-borne trade in agricultural commodities between the seaboard and hinterland.

As China's gateway to foreign trade began to shift during the 1850s from Guangzhou to Shanghai, and as affluent landlords and officials were seeking refuge from the upheavals of the Taiping rebellion (1851–1864) in the city's foreign concessions, the number of *qianzhuang* increased, and they branched off to invest in real estate and later in stock exchange speculation.[28]

As from the 1860s, a considerable number of *qianzhuang* began to gravitate toward a new source of capital in Shanghai: foreign banks. By 1888, sixty-two of Shanghai's largest moneyshops were borrowing capital from foreign banks to the tune of millions of taels annually. Buoyed by this new source, the moneyshops transformed themselves into an indispensable conduit for the finance of treaty-port trade. Put simply, they on-lend foreign bank funds to Chinese wholesalers of imported goods for usage of about two weeks until the latter sold their stock and paid off the debt. This form of on-call foreign bank credit came to be known as chop loans, or *chaipiao* 拆票.[29]

British, European, and Japanese banks could readily lay down funds in the treaty ports because they had cultivated exclusive relationships with established foreign trading houses, ever ready to exchange local money for sterling bills. The banks were otherwise much better capitalized than the diffuse moneyshops; the credit they advanced reinvigorated treaty-port trade, which had often lapsed into barter patterns in the early 1850s.[30] At the same time, foreign banks identified opportunities afforded by China's fragmented money markets and political instability. By 1911 they mobilized domestic resources on an order of magnitude that exceeded their initial paid-up capital several times over—largely through banknote issuance and deposit receipts.

As security for chop loans, British banks often accepted *zhuangpiao*. It is therefore plausible to assume, as Susan Mann Jones has, that the origins of the chop loan construct lie in the fact that these "shop coupons" had been so widely used when the British banks set up their first branches—that the British banks could not simply reject them, when presented for encashment by foreign purveyors. Moreover, foreign banks were also compelled to keep an account with at least one moneyshop, since only the moneyshop guild could clear the myriad forms of *zhuangpiao* through an elaborate daily mechanism dubbed *huihua* 匯劃 or "draft exchange."[31]

Chinese historians have routinely depicted the foreign bank-*qianzhuang* nexus as hugely exploitative, because the moneyshops were thought to have paved the way for foreign inroads into China's economy.[32] But in a recently published article, Professor Shizuya Nishimura has debunked much of this contention by showing that chop loans did not take up the lion's share of moneyshop liabilities and were even more marginal on foreign bank balance sheets; occasionally, the moneyshops could even lend money back to foreign banks on call.[33]

More pertinently, Nishimura's findings suggest that, quite often, British banknote circulation volumes in Shanghai were in the vicinity of total chop loan advances. Since both were a form of on-call entry on opposite sides of the banks' balance sheets, it may not be entirely implausible to assume that, at least until 1911, British banks used one to counterweigh the other. In other words, British banks may have simply reallocated *Chinese* capital on a short-term basis.

Though they had first supported foreign trade, chop loans were increasingly channeled to Chinese equity dealers by the *qianzhuang* in the early 1900s. But in 1910, Shanghai's foreign stock exchange crashed, owing largely to fluctuating world rubber prices, compounded by fraudulently induced overtrading in rubber plantation stock. The crash left scores of moneyshops insolvent and foreign banks weighed down by worthless *zhuangpiao*; the total outstanding debt of Shanghai moneyshops was estimated at 20 million taels, and their numbers dropped precipitously form 80 to 36 by 1911.[34] This, in turn, brought an abrupt end to the chop loan construct. Worse still, the stock exchange crash ramified into a nationwide crisis that crippled nascent railway ventures, and was responsible in part for the provincial discontent that toppled the Qing.

The impact of the crash meant that foreign bank prestige was rising. While scores of moneyshops became insolvent, Shanghai's foreign banks astutely weathered the storm by colluding with Cai Naihuang 蔡乃煌, the local Imperial revenue superintendent (Taotai or *daotai* 道臺) whose own funds had been heavily invested in ailing moneyshops. Cai consolidated moneyshop debts to foreign banks into a collateral loan on Chinese government security.[35]

Nonetheless, the repercussion of the 1910 crash could be felt even a few years later, as this *Consular Report* from 1913 suggests:

> Monetary stringency in the provinces, due to the timidity of capital above alluded to, is perhaps the most potent factor in the present depressed condition of the import trade. Throughout the year sycee and dollars kept piling up in the coffers of the foreign banks at Shanghai, but the system under which loans used to be freely offered by the latter to the native banks had been shattered by the disastrous experience of 1910, and the native banks were in their turn precluded from financing Chinese dealers, so that the machinery of credit, upon which the large transactions of former years were based, was almost wholly broken down.[36]

The breakdown of the chop loan construct did not affect just the standing of *zhuangpiao* in the money markets, in fact, all the other private-order arrangements that had undergirded it were badly hit. In the first instance, these arrangements related to the individual intermediaries employed by foreign firms to guarantee Chinese liabilities like *zhuangpiao*—commonly known to Westerners as "compradors" or *maiban* 買辦.[37] In the 1920s, the compradors would increasingly come under attack as "vestiges of colonialism" and as a superimposed layer of middlemen whose commission charges inevitably translated into high interest rates facing small Chinese businesses.[38]

With capital generally flowing from the hinterland in Shanghai's direction, but with foreign banks often reluctant or unable to engage the domestic sector, it was only a question of time before a new intermediary came on the horizon. The suspension of chop loans in 1911 set the scene for newly established Chinese banking institutions modeled on Western practice and run by foreign-educated executives to come out of the woodwork.[39]

If the suspension of chop loans had left a void in the Sino-foreign grid, it was in fact World War I that presented modern Chinese banks with the opportunity to gain a foothold in financial markets. The outbreak of war and its reverberations changed the overall balance of power between the foreign and domestic sectors in Shanghai in a number of ways; it retrenched foreign banks' resources, which were now mobilized to the war effort in Europe; it deterred Chinese customers from depositing money in foreign banks implicated in the war; and last but not least, the Anglo-German conflagration shattered the united stand that the foreign banks had hitherto taken vis-à-vis the Chinese government and the domestic sector.[40]

During the 1920s, Chinese banks had effectively supplanted the old chop loan construct by advancing funds to the city's moneyshops against collateral securities or goods mortgaged in the city's warehouses. The new *qianzhuang*–Chinese modern banking nexus gathered momentum and minimized the role of compradors. It could do so because, while they had a foreign flair about them, Chinese bankers were nevertheless tied to the *qianzhuang* by consanguinity and native-place bonds, and were infinitely more familiar with their intricacies than foreign bankers.[41] In 1921, the U.S.-educated economist Ma Yinchu 馬寅初 observed, for example, that homegrown banks had completely taken over two-day loans to the *qianzhuang* and that renewed interest in Chinese mutual funds and stock investment companies diverted considerable funds from the foreign banking sector.[42]

More generally, the impact of World War I on Shanghai was such that it allowed Chinese industrial entrepreneurship to thrive by producing for the local market and substituting increasingly expensive Western consumer imports. At times, these developments were offset by warlord conflicts raging in the hinterland. However, the introduction of more integrative Chinese clearing mechanisms from about 1914, as well as the surge of Chinese nationalism from 1919, helped sustain the pressure that Chinese banks exerted on the foreign banking sector.[43]

The foreign, non-British sector, on the other hand, was beset by salient bank failures through much of the same period. In 1914, the Allies forced the

Deutsch-Asiatische Bank branches in China to shut down. The branches were barely able to resume their operation in 1918, for several reasons. The Banque Russo-Asiatique (Russo-Asiatic Bank), nominally a Sino-Russian joint venture but effectively a French-owned private firm, had to be reconstituted in the wake of the Bolshevik Revolution in 1917 and ultimately failed in 1925; the Asiatic Banking Corporation, a Sino-American joint venture, was on the brink of failure in 1924 and was eventually sold off to the International Banking Corporation;[44] the Chinese-American Bank of Commerce, another U.S. joint venture, suspended business in 1928;[45] and perhaps the failure most inimical to the reputation of foreign financial institutions occurred in 1921, when the French-owned Banque Industrielle de Chine had to suspend the convertibility of its Shanghai notes until Chinese banks came to its rescue.[46]

Nonetheless, the rivalry between foreign and domestic banks during the Republican era should not be overstated. As much as Chinese banks benefited from the surge in nationalism after 1919, they seldom agitated against their foreign competitors. The two banking sectors were still interconnected and, for the most part, subscribed to a fundamental division of labor between the finance of international trade (by foreign banks) and business transacted in local currency like call loans to *qianzhuang* (by Chinese banks). Notably, archival work by Chinese scholars suggests that at least one Chinese bank and several *qianzhuang* deposited idle funds with foreign banks on a regular basis even after 1919.[47]

The compradors embodied a private-order mechanism that emerged in the mid-nineteenth century treaty ports in response to language barriers and information deficits facing foreigners who wished to penetrate Chinese markets. Compradors personally guaranteed *zhuangpiao* and other Chinese liabilities before foreign institutions, but did not have the leverage to guarantee metallic money disbursed by foreign institutions in the Chinese marketplace. In the fractured monetary conditions of the times, other highly specialized private-order institutions emerged precisely to that end: the *gonggu ju* 公估局 and *yinlu* 銀爐.

Few economic historians have paid attention to these institutions, but contemporary observers noted their vitality. This is how Charles Addis described them in 1886:

> The fineness [of "silver lumps" or sycee] is determined either by Kung-ku-chü [*gonggu ju*] (Public Assay Houses) or the Yin-lu (Silver Houses). The former are mostly private establishments, found in all large towns, where the weight and fineness of a silver lump are determined and inscribed on the face of the lump . . .

> The Yin-lu or Lu-fang, are Silver Houses, where silver bullion is melted and cast into silver lumps of certain standards and fineness. Most of the bullion is imported from abroad.[48]

The Shanghai Assay House was established in the Anglo-American International Concession by one Wang Lanting 汪蘭亭, an Anhui sojourner. At first, he faced competition from similar establishments in the adjacent Chinese-run suburb of Shanghai (*Nanshi* 南市 meaning South City and often known to foreigners as Nantao).[49] But all these soon merged to form one establishment on Ningbo Road, which enjoyed unparalleled prestige for much of the prewar period.[50] True to Addis's description, the Shanghai Assay House was at that time privately owned and had been ever since its inception in 1850. But unlike similar establishments in other parts of the country, it was not even nominally subordinate to the local Imperial bureaucracy.[51]

The Silver or Smelting Houses, which were also privately owned and usually situated in the International Concession, specialized in recasting foreign bullion into conventional Shanghainese sycee at the behest of the *qianzhuang*. Together, these two types of houses embodied a separation of powers between the production and verification of metallic money. Nonetheless, it appears that their leverage—much like the comprador-mediated arrangements—was unilateral. In other words, while compradors could *not* guarantee foreign liabilities before *Chinese* agents, the Assay and Silver Houses were *not* generally patronized by *foreign* firms.

In the absence of initiative on the part of the British-run Shanghai Municipal Council (known as SMC or *gongbu ju* 工部局 in Chinese) to create institutions dedicated to the regulation of money supply, compradors, Assay, and Silver Houses duplicated financial intermediation: assay commissions alone imposed an ex ante markup of up to 0.5 percent on business transactions in the city.[52]

By contrast, the early introduction of a uniform currency—coupled with the resolute decommissioning of Chinese coinage by Governor Francis H. May during 1912–1913—made monetary conditions in Hong Kong much more transparent.[53] There, notes issued by the same British banks soon became the most common media of payment,[54] whereas in China proper British banknote issuance never commanded a large share of the money stock; hence, it was only partly able to mitigate idiosyncratic transaction costs in the treaty ports.[55] The significance of British banknote issuance in Shanghai lies, therefore, in the provision of a convenient and reliable store of value, which eventually penetrated both the expatriate and Chinese marketplaces.

One of the most important determinants of capital mobility and market integration in most early-modern economies is the volume and fungibility of equity. In a recent study, Andrea McElderry has shown that several Chinese stock and commodity exchanges had evolved in Shanghai by the early 1880s, but remained small, diffuse, and largely dormant until the 1920s.[56]

What impinged most on equity trade was frequent Court interference in the managerial affairs of listed companies. This interference deterred potential investors and brought China's primary stock exchange, the Pingzhun 平准 brokerage (est. 1882), to a virtual standstill by mid-1880s.[57] Numerous attempts to revive equity markets were made in the 1920s, but these efforts were frustrated by the Beiyang government's inability to regulate corporate financial disclosure and by competition between various trading groups, to shore up investor confidence, or to enshrine property rights for that matter.[58]

After its establishment in 1927, the Nanjing government flooded the Chinese stock exchange in Shanghai with high-yield bonds whose proceeds were vital for the GMD's continued military buildup.[59] Between 1927 and 1935, the domestic debt that was mainly floated as bonds totaled more than 1.6 billion silver dollars, compared with a total of only $612 million in the previous fifteen years of Beiyang government tenure. Inevitably, these bonds crowded out what little trade emerged in private equity: only about 2 percent of Chinese stock exchange capitalization was attributable to private securities during the early 1930s.[60]

Chinese investors skeptical of the government's ability to honor its bonds were drawn to Shanghai's foreign-run stock exchange, formally set up as early as 1891.[61] In 1905, the foreign bourse in Shanghai was incorporated under Hong Kong law, primarily listing expatriate treaty-port firms and utilities, tobacco and rubber plantations, coal mines and cotton mills, SMC, and MCFC (Municipalité de la Concession Française de Changhai or *gongdong ju* 公董局) bonds.[62] Like its Chinese equivalents, the foreign bourse was often buffeted by speculative bubbles, but it managed to weather fleeting storms like the rubber stock crash of 1910 and grow fast in the early twentieth century.

In other words, Chinese investors' money fueled the growth of a foreign bourse that rarely listed Chinese joint-stock companies in the strict sense of the word. Similarly, Shanghai expatriates did not invest in a Chinese bourse that was little more than an instrument for floating *domestic* public debt; Chinese governments pledged substantive collateral security only against the *foreign* debt that foreign banks helped them float in the London capital market.

Why didn't the SMC push for a more integrative equity market comprising both Chinese and expatriate-run firms? For the SMC to have acted along these lines and run the risk of rankling Beijing or Nanjing's explicit fiscal incentives would have been required. However, before the mid-1920s Chinese residents of the International (and French) Concession had been willing to pay rates even without executive representation on municipal boards, if only to protect their wealth from government exactions.[63] At the same time, taxpayers in Britain—rather than expatriate SMC ratepayers—shouldered most of Shanghai's onerous maritime defense outlay.

This was laissez-faire economics in its purest treaty-port form, one in which Chinese dependence on, and preference for, foreign institutions was taken for granted too long. As Chapter 5 will show, it was precisely for that reason that the SMC came to be perceived as egregiously impervious to Chinese civic aspirations during the 1920s.

EXTRATERRITORIALITY AS COERCION-CONSTRAINT

If there ever was anything approaching a *designed* (read: preconceived) mechanism of coercion-constraint in Shanghai, this was foreign extraterritoriality (often abbreviated as "extrality" in the city's English-language press). The concept was thought to ensure the immunity of Western expatriates from prosecution by the Chinese legal system within the confines of Shanghai's International or French Concession areas, as well as a host of smaller treaty ports (then known as outports).

Westerners in prewar China were tried in Consular Courts, with each country resorting to its own code of practice. Some European Powers even maintained their own jails in Shanghai, but serious offenders were mostly sent to stand trial and serve sentences in colonial strongholds. The British relied on the legal and penitentiary system of Hong Kong, whereas the Americans relied on that of the Philippines.[64]

Although the concept had roots dating back to the fourteenth century, "extrality" in China was never spelled out in detail, so as to avoid offending Chinese Imperial sensitivities.[65] Its import was in reality *not* anchored in diplomatic agreements but rather in the projection of military might and in sufferance on the part of Chinese rulers. This also meant that the concept was fairly pliable. The first British court in China had, for example, been set up in 1833, nine years before the first Sino-British Treaty acknowledging foreign judicial privileges was signed.[66] Similarly, foreigners had established manufacturing plants in Shanghai long before the Qing formally ceded these rights in the 1895 Treaty of Shimonoseki.[67]

Owing to the lack of juridical clarity, "extrality" remained fraught with potential loopholes throughout the prewar era. The British adjudicated corporate law in Shanghai in conformity with Hong Kong Ordinances, even though the latter often overlooked treaty-port particularities. It was only in 1927, for example, that a specific Order-in-Council "for regulating the issue of [British] banknotes in China" was promulgated, even though Chinese officials in a few outports had assailed this practice as an abuse of foreign commercial privileges some fifteen years earlier.[68]

Wealthy Chinese businessmen sought to be subsumed under "extrality" by virtue of the privileges it offered. They had first looked at "extrality" as an impromptu safeguard of property rights, but they soon discovered that the concept could also imply handsome commercial gains, once they had paid their way into permanent residence in Shanghai's foreign concession areas. This was mainly because any goods transported from the treaty ports and cloaked as foreign had a better chance of eschewing the full brunt of the Likin port tax and other onerous provincial duties, which Chinese firms based in the interior had to absorb.[69]

These unique circumstances persuaded many Chinese businessmen residing in or close to the foreign concessions of Shanghai that the most sustainable course of action was (1) to invest in expatriate treaty-port enterprises, whose immunity to hinterland duties was beyond question, while relinquishing executive powers to foreign boardrooms. Others chose the opposite path: (2) to have their ventures incorporated under Chinese law, firmly hang on to executive powers, but risk government interference and lose potential tax breaks. Yet another option was (3) to avoid capital markets altogether and retain a traditional lineage-based structure to conceal taxable wealth.

By far the ideal course of action was (4) to be granted foreign citizenship by one of the Powers and to operate anywhere in China as a nominally foreign company. However, the Powers were prepared to naturalize only a tiny minority of treaty-port Chinese and were extremely suspicious of domestic firms operating under assumed foreign identity.[70] To a large extent, then, "extrality" and British corporate law were applicable to Shanghai in terms of *jus sanguinis*. While cases involving foreigners were brought before Consular Courts entirely removed from Chinese legalities, cases involving Chinese were referred to Mixed Courts.[71]

Reliable statistics are scarce, but lateral research seems to suggest that options 1 and 3 became the norm among Chinese businessmen. We can infer these patterns from the meager number of Chinese private firms, which registered with the government or were incorporated under the Chinese company of 1904, as William Kirby has shown.[72] Wang Jingyu had, in turn, first exposed the sheer scope of Chinese investment in expatriate-run companies in the prewar era.[73]

In essence, Wang proposed that Chinese entrepreneurs had been the driving force behind countless treaty-port ventures. Although these ventures targeted Chinese clientele, the entrepreneurs were prepared to entrust their ideas, know-how, and capital to Western trading houses, if only to garner a foreign halo. The picture that Wang outlined is supported by more recent archival findings: Motono Eiichi has shown, for example, that the Shanghai steam silk filatures set up in 1882 by the renowned trading house Jardine Matheson & Co. had been in fact *entirely* funded with Chinese shareholder subscription.[74]

Was the fear of Chinese investors of their own government justified? The Qing had certainly left a legacy of trampling private shareholder rights in its seminal industrial ventures, as Albert Feuerwerker has shown.[75] Predatory government interference in the private sector notoriously worsened during both the early- and late-Republican eras. The best-known examples were perhaps the two banking coups of 1916 and 1935, punctuated by Jiang Jieshi's (Chiang Kai-shek) blackmail of prominent Shanghai industrialists during his takeover of the city in 1927–1928.

In May 1916, Yuan Shikai, the first president of the Republic, tried to shore up the precarious fiscal standing of his regime by expropriating the silver reserves of the Bank of China and substituting its banknotes with inconvertible currency. What saved the bank was the fact that its branch managers in Shanghai, where much of the reserves had been stored, refused to comply. The government was unable to close in because the branch was situated within the foreign concession area, and the scheme fell through a few months later.[76]

In 1927, Jiang—the successor of Sun Yixian (Sun Yat-sen) as GMD chairman and an inveterate militarist himself—made a pact with Shanghai's underworld to rid the city of Communist sympathizers. To that end, he solicited financial assistance from Chinese factory owners and bankers equally averse to the labor movement. But, as Parks Coble has shown, as soon as he had realized his goal, Jiang ruthlessly turned on his wealthy backers with interminable demands for compensation.[77]

Perhaps the most grievous GMD disregard for property rights accompanied what was otherwise hailed as a benign move off the silver standard. The success of this move, as part of the *fabi* reform in 1935, had been predicated on bringing China's principal banks of issue under one umbrella. Yet Jiang used the brewing monetary crisis as a pretext for quietly freezing the stake of private shareholders in these banks.[78]

Chinese modern banking gathered momentum, particularly through the 1920s, when central authority was at low ebb.[79] At the end of 1925, for example, there were 132 Chinese privately owned banks with a total paid-up capital of $121 million. By contrast, the twenty-six state-run and semiofficial banks accounted for only $49 million.[80]

"IMPERIALISM," "COLONIALISM," AND "SEMICOLONIALISM"

The previous section pointed to several market imperfections in prewar Shanghai caused by a profound institutional vacuum—a vacuum derived both from the enfeeblement of Chinese central authority and from SMC inhibitions. This is, of course, not to say that China's economy as a whole would have been better off *without* the treaty-port input.

Much of the literature on the treaty-ports has been devoted to exploring their underlying racialism, or has cast them as thinly veiled manifestations of imperialism and colonialism, that is, as "semicolonialism."[81] But when the overall *economic* implications of the treaty-port mould are at stake, only *economic* yardsticks should be employed.

At any rate, historians of "world systems" question whether the treaty-port mould embodied a British strategy that was truly distinct from outright colonization, or to what extent it explains Britain's hegemony in the nineteenth century.[82] In other words, opinions vary on whether the notions of "semicolonialism" that are often associated with the treaty-port mould stand for substance or were merely colonialism in disguise.

Gallagher and Robinson initiated this debate some fifty years ago, when they described British colonial policy in the latter half of the nineteenth century as preoccupied with cost-cutting. They coined the term *informal empire* to describe British designs on late-Imperial China and postcolonial Latin America. To them, the British rationale was one of "extending control informally if possible and formally if necessary."[83] The notion that British elites had been primarily concerned with safeguarding free trade and informal hegemony where military intervention was too expensive to contemplate is supported by other scholars, most notably O'Brien and Pigman.[84]

It is in light of the onerous outlay of keeping up the colonial ramparts that we should consider the importance of entrepôts like Shanghai and the rich vein of Cobdenite liberalism that suffused British foreign policy debates from the mid-nineteenth century. British transition toward informal control and the emphasis on free trade contrasted sharply with the mercantilist mood still prevalent across the Channel.[85] In two separate articles, O'Brien and Van der Eng challenged the notion that capital exports to formal colonies could yield "supernatural" profits. Moreover, these scholars expressed serious doubts as to whether colonialism was vital to the metropolitan economies of either Great Britain or the Netherlands at all.[86]

O'Brien's conclusion, in particular, echoes the confidential pronouncements that British civil servants and politicians made in the mid-1930s. These pronouncements, which will be presented in more detail in Chapter 5, suggest that Britain's costly naval presence in far-flung corners of the world may have ultimately served a thin coterie of City rentier interests. In China, these interests were personified by "Shanghailanders" and "Old China Hands," who were regularly calling for military intervention to reassert British prestige, but retained much of their wealth in Asia, well beyond the reach of metropolitan taxation.

Christopher Platt once argued that the British government had effectively distanced itself from outspoken proponents of informal empire. Rejecting the rationale advanced by Gallagher and Robinson, Platt believed that the two Opium Wars between Britain and China (1839–1842, 1856–1860) had been fairly aberrant incidents in what was otherwise official disdain of financiers calling for British government action to enforce "informal empire" around the world.[87] The *locus classicus* of this argument is Latin America, where Platt identified only one substantive British military intervention during the nineteenth century.[88] He attributed the gap between the relatively hawkish stance taken by British officialdom on East Asia to its noninterventionist stance on Latin America to the latter's distance from *Weltpolitik* rivalries.[89]

This argument remains on the perimeters of the present book, but for lack of space cannot be treated here in full. Nonetheless, it does call for what little secondary data we can assemble to compare British banking practices in these two "semicolonial" settings, not least because quasi-foreign banknote issuance was rife in both.

The most authoritative estimates of foreign investment in prewar China remain D. K. Lieu and C. F. Remer's respective works.[90] In the late 1920s, Lieu estimated total British investments in China at GBP 149.2 million, with the great bulk attributed to Shanghai and Hong Kong. Banking accounted for only GBP 7.5 million of the total investment, insurance GBP 31.4 million, and manufacturing a whopping GBP 60 million. The remainder spread over typically invisible British exports like shipping (GBP 15.2 million), real estate (GBP 10.1 million), trade (GBP 10.9 million), construction (GBP 2.9 million), and public utilities (GBP 2.6 million). Rubber Estates and Mining—two distinct hinterland enterprises—accounted for only GBP 2.8 million in all.[91]

Remer estimated British direct investment in China proper in 1931 at GBP 197.9 million. The financial sector, broadly defined, accounted for 12 percent of the total. Trading firms led the table with 25 percent, real estate 21 percent, manufacturing 18 percent, transportation 14 percent, public utilities 5 percent, mining 2 percent, and miscellaneous 3 percent.[92] Chinese debts are still harder to estimate because of the political and economic fragmentation at the time. Remer estimated Chinese government obligations to British creditors in 1931 at GBP 46.4 million, up by GBP 18 million from 1914.[93] Lieu put the figure at only GBP 4.8 million (December 1925), but his calculus was exclusive of the British share of foreign indemnities, secured loans, and the interest they incurred—a total of GBP 92.7 million.[94]

We can now compare these figures with the data available for Latin America. Here, British investment is said to have totaled GBP 179.4 million circa 1880, with a much wider geographical spread than in China.[95] Three decades later, the total more than quintupled, with British investment estimated in 1913 at GBP 999.2 million, of which GBP 316 million were invested in various Latin American government bonds, and GBP 457 million in railways. Banking claimed a bottom-end estimate of GBP 18.5 million.[96]

Clearly, British financial stakes in Latin America were, on the whole, much higher than in Shanghai, Hong Kong, or China as a whole. The two exceptions may have been banking and manufacturing. British direct investment in Latin America alone may well have exceeded British investment in China and total Chinese foreign debt combined. This, in turn, seems to bear out Platt's thesis that *geopolitical* rather than *economic* factors explain Britain's comparative heavy-handedness in East Asia.[97]

This book argues that potentially deleterious effects of overseas banking on the host economy should be sought out in terms of capital allocation, that is, funneling local wealth to fund foreign-owned ventures. In the monetary sphere, on the other hand, quasi-foreign notes often provided the only reliable means of payment. There was no coercive dimension to this practice but, as Latin American experiments with central banking proves, one of institutional maturation.

Regrettably, the body of literature on British banking in Latin America is much less detailed than the one on British banks in Asia. Nonetheless, a cursory comparison of the literature immediately points to common ground, as well as key differences. The most salient difference between the two regions is arguably the absence of comprador-like intermediaries in Latin America, pointing to a higher degree of interpenetration between local and foreign-owned business there.[98]

Banking made up a relatively small proportion of overall British investment in both regions, but was arguably one of the most remunerative during the prewar era.[99] Crucially, observers in both places noted that British overseas banks relied, to a large extent, on local deposits to underwrite loans to foreign trading firms. Implicit in many of these observations was the allegation that the British banks depleted indigenous wealth that could have funded latecomer industrialization, and that this perpetuated the status of local economies as producers of low-value commodities.[100]

In the monetary sphere, similarities between the two regions are more evident. In both cases, British overseas banks played a reformative role, against which we can weigh up the travails of modern state formation and fiscal discipline. In both cases, powerful British banks shunned local banknotes when overprinting was suspected until, ultimately, local politicians were forced to temper their inflationary proclivities. In both cases, local banks could not effectively compete with British banks until they were infused with central government resolve to see the foreign sector of the economy minimized.[101] Equally importantly, quasi-foreign banknote issuance receded sooner in Latin America than in China, because Latin America's postcolonial polities were more cohesive and were devoid of Shanghai-style extraterritorial enclaves.

BANKING, INDUSTRIALIZATION, AND NATIONALISM IN SHANGHAI

The notion that insufficient bank credit to local entrepreneurs impeded China's industrialization has, of course, a Gerschenkronian ring to it.[102] It has been alluded to by some scholars, but vehemently rejected by others.[103] In one of the most notable contributions to Gerschenkronian theory, Daniel Verdier has recently argued that in European countries where the praxis of central banking emerged only in the late nineteenth century, commercial banks that had been granted note issue prerogatives were reluctant to invest in industrial ventures because they required a higher degree of liquidity to cover their short-term liabilities.[104] This study will draw on Verdier's proposition in a bid to determine what role, if any, overseas banks of issue played in China's industrialization.

The following section will reframe the issues involved, since historians and theorists generally disagree on the vitality of bank finance to the process of industrialization. The fundamental question posed here is simply one of resources and uses; if the treaty-port mould reproduced a *net* outflow of capital from Chinese into expatriate hands, then it was probably compromising the ability of the Chinese sector to undertake long-term projects by itself.

As mentioned earlier, no comprehensive attempt has been made to juxtapose the ethnic makeup of British bank liabilities and assets in Shanghai. Similarly, we do not know the volume of foreign bank shares subscribed by ethnic Chinese,[105] so as to compare it with Chinese boardroom representation, or their share of staff remuneration. On the other hand, comprehensive surveys of Chinese industrial ventures in prewar Shanghai clearly suggest that very few relied on credit from foreign—let alone British—sources in the early stages.

In the critical stage of formation, Chinese entrepreneurs invariably raised capital through *hegu* 合股 or the sale of a limited number of preference shares to colleagues and family-relatives. In subsequent stages, some entrepreneurs cultivated close links with Shanghai's moneyshops.[106] Extensive comprador investment in private industrial ventures would have pointed to ample sources of foreign finance. But, perhaps tellingly, compradors were the driving force behind a minority—albeit the *biggest* and most *enduring*—of Shanghai's private industrial ventures.[107]

Recent work by business historians tends to support this pattern. Sherman Cochran has shown, for example, that Rong Zongjing 榮宗敬 (1873–1938), one of China's best known and most intrepid entrepreneurs in the prewar era, began contracting loans from Japanese banks only in 1917, when his business empire had already laid down roots. We have some evidence that he contracted British bank loans in 1934, as HSBC was then *one* of the mostly Chinese bank creditors that temporarily foreclosed on his Shenxin Cotton Mills.[108]

Japanese and European banks, which were latecomers into the Chinese market, may well have been more ready to engage the domestic sector than their British competitors. In his portrayal of commerce in late-Imperial Tianjin, Kwan Man Bun has shown, for example, that the foreign banks, which helped the city's salt merchants tide over losses in the wake of the Boxer Rebellion (1899–1901), included the Yokohama Specie Bank, the Banque Russo-Chinoise, the Deutsch-Asiatische Bank and the Saigon-based Banque de l'Indochine.[109]

Tim Wright, who has written the most comprehensive account to date on coal mining in prewar China—one of largest and most capital-intensive industries at the time—cited several examples of Russian, Japanese, German, and Belgian loans to Chinese-owned mine operators or Sino-foreign joint ventures.[110] On the other hand, Wright recorded loans from British sources only in such cases where effective ownership and executive control of the mines had firmly lain in British hands.

Paradoxically, there is ample evidence to suggest that domestic financial institutions had lent profusely to expatriate-run ventures even when foreigners were not among their main shareholders. The most clear-cut example is the Imperial Bank of China [IBC] or *Zhongguo tongshang yinhang* 中國通商銀行, 73 percent of whose 1901 loan portfolio had been advanced to expatriate firms.[111]

Did British bank-lending strategy vis-à-vis the domestic sector turn potential clients away? Ishii Kanji has shown that during the 1910s the Japanese-run Yokohama Specie Bank relied heavily on deposits advanced by ethnic Chinese and Indians in Shanghai and Bombay, respectively;[112] studies of the U.S.-run International Banking Corporation similarly indicate that its Chinese client base was very large.[113] Based on an Inspector's Report from 1912, Professor Shizuya Nishimura has concluded, in turn, that ethnic Chinese advanced much of HSBC's fixed deposits in the outports, but their contribution was considerably less significant in the all-important branch of Shanghai.[114]

Pending more archival evidence, this series of findings does not easily lend itself to interpretation. Yet, it would seem safe to assume that the Chinese clientele of British banks in the nineteenth century was large. At the same time, the consistent growth of modern Chinese banks, as well as Japanese and American financial institutions, in early twentieth-century Shanghai suggests a shift in financial patterns.[115] As the following chapters will show, this shift was inextricably linked to the surge of Chinese nationalism.

The changing perceptions of, and mobilization against, foreign banks is one facet of Chinese nationalism that has not commanded the attention it deserves from historians. By and large, the few scholars who seriously tried to assess the economic impact of popular mobilization against expatriate commercial interests in early twentieth-century China have almost invariably relied on Remer's classic *Study of Chinese Boycotts*.[116] Perceptive as this work may have been, it was published in the 1930s, when there was limited access to some of the sources available to scholars today. Indeed, Remer himself was acutely aware of the provisional nature of his findings, as well as the inherent limitations of the Chinese Maritime Customs data, which he had tapped.[117] His account focused on trade flows between China and boycotted Powers to the neglect of iconic foreign-owned companies operating or manufacturing *within* China.

Interestingly, two monographs on the anti-American movement, which had broken out in Shanghai in 1905 following the Asian Immigration Exclusion Act, have been released in close proximity recently.[118] The respective authors, Wang Guanghua and Sin Kiong Wong, still dwell on Remer rather than on corporate archives when discussing the economic impact of the movement. Yet, both authors ably highlight crucial aspects of Chinese antiforeign agitation that fall beyond the purview of this book—namely, the ways in which student associations radicalized merchant guilds; the ways in which ad hoc periodicals were used to fan the sense of iniquity; and the ways in which virulent antiforeign imagery was bandied about to deter Chinese collaborators. These have been salient properties of not just the anti-American campaign of 1905; some of the same tactics and rhetoric were directed *mutatis mutandis* against the Japanese in 1919 and used with a vengeance against the British during 1925–1926.

Sin Kiong Wong, in particular, explains how demeaning caricatures of "cold-blooded" (*lengxue* 冷血) dogs and turtles were invoked to distinguish the allegedly callous Americans and their "collaborators" from the victimized or "hot-blooded" (*rexue* 熱血) Chinese.[119] That much the same imagery was later directed against British and Japanese firms is manifest in books published by Wong's Ph.D. adviser, Jeffrey Wasserstrom, and by Sherman Cochran, Donald Jordan, Harumi Goto-Shibata, Karl Gerth, and others.[120]

CONCLUSION

This chapter has drawn on a wide range of lateral sources as well as on newly published studies in a bid to present a fluid (if cursory) overview of important aspects of Shanghai's economy over the course of the prewar era. To avoid oversimplification, the chapter has consistently pointed in the direction of quantitative data uncovered by recent scholarship, wherever these had some potential of clarifying gaps in our understanding of the city's economic fabric of life. Particular emphasis was put on the function of characteristic Shanghainese institutions and on the ways in which the city's economy differed from either that of the Chinese hinterland or other global settings.

In economic terms, Shanghai's allure during the prewar era was found to be *not* so much predicated on the (selective) introduction of Western administrative and legal institutions. These institutions appear, on balance, to have played only a negligible role in generating fiscal revenue for the British Empire, and were otherwise much less coherent than, for example, in Hong Kong. Rather, Shanghai seemed to have attracted British merchants, financiers, and entrepreneurs because it provided easy and secure access to China's wealthiest provinces, while retaining a distinct laissez-faire environment.

Chinese people of means appear to have continually converged on Shanghai *not* because Mixed Courts necessarily administered Western-style justice, equity, or civil liberties, *but* because the city's extraterritorial status transformed it into a Chinese government tax-free zone of sorts; Shanghai's laissez-faire environment probably minimized the perceived risks of voracious taxation on the part of the foreign municipal administration; it enabled Chinese entrepreneurs to compete in domestic markets in preferential foreign garb, but fell short of consolidating capital markets. The same environment failed to produce uniform municipal currency or to alleviate shroffing costs. This vacuum was partly filled by a host of foreign and domestic banknotes. The following chapter will expound on one of these foreign banks: the Chartered Bank of India Australia and China.

Chapter 3 The Chartered Bank and Its Note Issue

This chapter explores the history and banknote circulation patterns of what, by the 1910s, had become one of the leading British financial institutions in East and Southeast Asia: the Chartered Bank of India Australia and China (CBIAC).[1] The bank's story and balance-sheet figures are used as the basis for a comparative discussion of the role that British and other foreign banknotes played in the Chinese economy before World War II. By assessing quantitative evidence, linkages are found between the bank's principal branch circulation volumes and monetary reform in East Asia. The argument advanced here is that Hong Kong was politically crucial to the overall growth and durability of British overseas banknote circulation.

The following sections will describe the progression of CBIAC's corporate identity and mode of operation in comparison to other British banks. They will also analyze CBIAC's overall note circulation pattern in East and Southeast. Finally, an attempt will be made to assess what CBIAC banknote circulation figures might tell us about the history of British banks in Asia.

CBIAC AND OTHER BRITISH BANKS COMPARED

CBIAC was established in the City of London in 1853 through the provision of a Royal Charter similar to the one given in 1851 to the first British overseas bank in Asia—the Oriental Bank Corporation. The original CBIAC Charter delineated the permissible scope of operations for limited-liability entities, but had to be reaffirmed by Supplemental Charters every ten years or so.[2] Although the bank's full name suggested large territorial dispersion, it chose to focus on South and East Asia and was soon to become one of the dominant overseas banks operating in British India. The bank's decision to localize in Asia followed what seemed to be an adverse political climate in Australia where, by the mid-1850s, the colonial government was less receptive toward new London-based banks.[3]

Officially, CBIAC abridged its title to become the Chartered Bank only in 1956, when regional designations had already lost much of their appeal. It then merged with the Standard Bank, one of the leading British overseas banks in South Africa, to form the Standard Chartered in 1969. Alongside HSBC, it is the only European bank with a name that still bears some testimony to the era of treaty-port finance.

The driving force behind the expansion of early British overseas banks into East Asia—known collectively at the time as the Eastern Exchange Banks—was increasing opposition in early and mid-nineteenth century England to the tight grip of the East India Company (EIC) on the finance of the lucrative opium trade.[4] The monopoly rights that EIC retained in India and China were revoked in 1813 and 1834, respectively, and it was to lose much of the exchange bill traffic between Asia and London soon afterward.

During 1829–1834, leading Calcutta agency houses with which EIC had been associated, such as Palmers, Alexanders, Colvin & Co. and Cruttenden & Co., were succumbing to competition from new, smaller trading firms that took advantage of the breakdown of monopoly rights to undercut mercantile banking business.[5] Financiers in the City of London, colonial policymakers, and local Indian mercantile groups then identified exchange banking between India and China as pristine ground for investment. Nevertheless, the absence of effective limited-liability laws overseas, as well as persistent EIC obstruction, frustrated new banking ventures.[6]

By the 1850s, small Anglo-Indian co-partnerships involved in exchange banking had set up branches in Guangzhou and Hong Kong and operated there without explicit official patronage and, initially, without a charter: the Agra Bank, the North Western Bank of India, and the Bank of Western India.[7]

This fait accomplit paralleled initiatives by well-heeled groups in London to lobby the government for a limited-liability status in the form of a Royal Charter, which was first given to the Oriental Bank in 1851 (successor of the Bank of Western India) and later to CBIAC, the Mercantile Bank of Bombay, and the HSBC. Chartered and nonchartered banks alike sought to capitalize on the thriving opium trade between British India and China by selling bills drawn on their Indian branches to China-based importers of the narcotic. The silver proceeds from the sale of opium could then be used to purchase discounted sterling bills from exporters of silk and tea, with which the Indian branches could cover their drafts on London.[8]

Yet the first generation of Eastern Exchange Banks disintegrated by the turn of the century. In 1866, there had nominally been eleven foreign banks operating in Hong Kong—the Oriental Bank, HSBC, CBIAC, the Chartered Mercantile Bank of India, London, and China (CMBILC), Comptoir d'Escompte, the Agra Bank, the Commercial Bank of India, Asiatic Bank, the Bank of Hindustan, the Bank of India, and the Central Bank of Western India. Within a year, the last six went into liquidation, leaving behind important client accounts that were quickly taken over by the CMBILC, CBIAC, and above all the newly formed Hong Kong Bank, to be known later as HSBC.[9]

This trail of bankruptcy was largely the result of the Overend Gurney crisis in the City of London. The failure of this pivotal clearing bank was one of the most notorious financial failures in Victorian Britain.[10] It set off a chain reaction right across the city, because Overend Gurney had been one of the most important clearing banks on which financial institutions—including a large number of overseas banks—depended whenever they needed to discount drafts. The clearing bank stopped payment in May only a year after it shed its old Quaker family image to register as a joint-stock firm. The circumstances invited rumors about the founders' motives in floating the bank, while precariously diversifying into long-term investments that were well beyond the core business of discounting exchange bills. Ultimately, the new shareholder acrimoniously dissolved Overend Gurney, having to settle approximately GBP 11 million in debt, owed in part by now-defunct overseas banks.[11]

In 1884, the Oriental Bank failed too. In this case, the prime factor was not a third party but the bank's overambitious distribution of agencies, which aimed to bridge numerous currency zones from Europe to Australasia but thinned out cash reserves in principal branches. One contemporary opined that the Oriental Bank had been "reckless" in its pursuit to pile up business in every corner of the world.[12] The downfall of the Oriental Bank heralded the second phase of exchange banking in East Asia, during which more regional specialization was introduced. Henceforth, the British Treasury subjected note issues by private British banks in Asia to more scrutiny because, at the height of its payment crisis, the convertibility of the Oriental Bank's notes in Ceylon, Burma, and Mauritius had to be guaranteed by the colonial governments concerned in order to stave off wider financial implications.[13]

For the Exchange Banks, mobilizing funds in Asia by issuing notes and accepting deposits was an imperative from the very outset because, as indicated above, their charters precluded similar activities in Britain. CBIAC, for example, was not permitted to undertake any retail banking activities in London until 1909 and had to refer clients to its acting agent, the City Bank, whenever withdrawals were made from Head Office current accounts.[14] Worse still was the toll that international currency fluctuations were taking on the Eastern Exchange Banks' stock, which was usually subscribed in gold-based pound sterling, but employed throughout silver-based Asia. While shareholders expected to net a proportionate amount of dividends in pounds, local branch operations and attendant profits were denominated in silver currencies that were rapidly depreciating against gold as from the 1860s.[15]

CBIAC's general manager during 1871–1892 was J. H. Gwyther. Like other staunch bimetallists at the time, Gwyther failed to preempt the decline in the gold price of silver by not reining in capital flow toward Asia. Only in 1885 did the CBIAC Head Office recall all liquid funds from its Asian branches in order to strike a balance between gold and silver assets. But despite repeated bimetallist campaigns in England, the price of silver had deteriorated by 1887 so much that Gwyther was compelled to order an adjustment of all remaining silver assets in the East to their exchange value in gold in order to avoid further capital write-offs.[16] The balance sheets of the bank's Shanghai branch reveal, however, that except during World War I when silver prices were rising, the bank's internal exchange rate continued to understate the fall in asset values. This is illustrated in Figure 3.1.

Polemics between monometallists and bimetallists were one of the salient characteristics of English economic thought in the late nineteenth century. It was only after the base of India's currency switched from silver to gold in 1898 that the bimetallist cause died out. Gwyther and several CBIAC directors were enthusiastic members of the Bimetallist League, which tried to promote

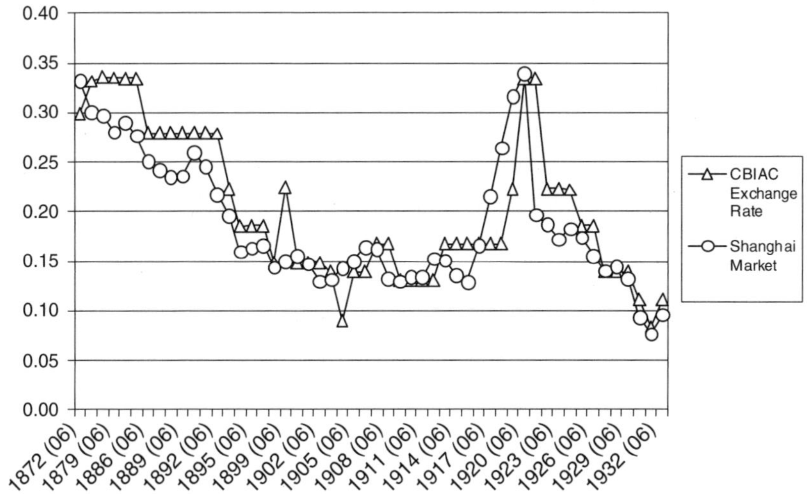

Figure 3.1. CBIAC versus Shanghai Market Silver Exchange Rate, 1872–1932. Unit: Gold-based GBP (decimalized) for 1 Haiguan Silver Tael. *Source*: The CBIAC exchange rate is calculated from its balance-sheet collection in Guildhall Library [hereafter CBIAC GL] Ms 31519. Shanghai Taels were converted to Haiguan Taels based on 0.897 parity—see Morse (1921 [Rep. 1967]), pp. 170–173; average market rates are based on Hsiao Liang-lin (1974), pp. 190–192.

an international concord whereby silver could be reinstituted as part of the money supply in the West.[17] This cause was largely championed by British exchange bankers and textile mill owners, who were convinced that an overvalued gold sterling would disrupt British exports to India. But their views did not sway the Treasury, which held that recourse to silver would blemish the stability of British currency and London's position as the hub of international finance.[18]

At the root of the depreciation in silver prices was an ongoing spate of events, which tumbled the global metallic equilibrium. Silver and gold discoveries in Nevada, California, and West Africa during the mid-nineteenth century altered bullion stock ratios, triggering off a chain reaction, which saw Germany, Scandinavia, Holland, and the Latin Union going off silver as a monetary base one after the other.[19] Attendant monetary tremors were equally felt in East Asia, prodding Japan to re-base the yen on gold at the turn of the twentieth century, in order to be on an equal footing with its Western trading partners.

More pertinently, the depreciation dealt the ultimate blow to those of the first-generation of Eastern Exchange Banks that had survived the Overend

Gurney crisis. It left a badly affected CBIAC to contend with HSBC (est. 1865) for mercantile business in East Asia. The New Oriental Bank Corporation, a short-lived venture, which had carried over from the Oriental Bank after the loss of its charter, floundered in 1892. The Chartered Mercantile Bank of India, London, and China also lost its charter but narrowly survived as a new reconstructed entity on the sidelines of treaty-port finance—the Mercantile Bank of India (MBI). Many overseas banks in other parts of Asia were affected too; even the semiofficial Imperial Bank of Persia, which had close links with HSBC, had to write off a third of its capital by 1894.[20]

HSBC was the only British bank operating in Asia that could partly bypass the depreciation of silver, thereby gaining momentum against its rivals. This was due to two crucial factors. First, HSBC was incorporated in Hong Kong with much of its stock already subscribed in silver and employed locally.[21] Second, as the primary British creditor to the Chinese Imperial Court, HSBC could indemnify itself against silver depreciation by securing gold loans on an increasing proportion of China's silver-based tax revenue.[22] Consequently, HSBC was somewhat less exposed to metal price fluctuations than its smaller competitors, which in turn were almost entirely dependent on exchange bill flows between Europe and Asia. By the same token, other banks could not partake of the close ties that HSBC nurtured with the British diplomatic establishment in order to bolster its bargaining power vis-à-vis the Chinese officialdom, and were mostly excluded from Chinese state loans before World War I.[23]

These inherent advantages were compounded by managerial prudence. To be sure, HSBC did lend token support to the bimetallist lobby, but it did not let this build up expectations of an imminent reprise in silver prices.[24] Unlike other exchange banks, HSBC was to remain at all times "on an even keel." Essentially, this managerial jargon meant that sources and uses would always be kept level in any given currency zone. Thus, HSBC sterling deposits in London were never to exceed outbound sterling bills sold by branches in Asia to importers of British goods. Similarly, when expansion of business potential in Asia called for more resources to be allocated from the Head Office, HSBC managers usually chose to retrench or raise capital locally rather than solicit more sterling deposits.[25]

By the late nineteenth century, the special connections that HSBC had nurtured with British officialdom in East Asia paid handsome dividends. They effectively kept the involvement of other British banks, most notably that of CBIAC, in Chinese government loans to a minimum.[26] CBIAC mangers had initially been averse to requests for credit from Chinese officials, but when they later showed interest in financing China's Boxer indemnity (1901) and a provincial railway line in Hubei (1905) they were promptly rebuffed by the Foreign Office. CBIAC continued to be marginalized in state loans to the chagrin of its executives in China, who thought that the country was on the eve of industrialization following the establishment of the Republic in 1911. The bank ultimately came to terms with its secondary position in the region and helped forge an international consortium of Western banks around HSBC that would negotiate new loans with the Republican government *en bloc*.[27]

CBIAC and MBI's secondary status in China was also reflected in a branch network that trailed far behind HSBC's strong presence in Hong Kong and the treaty ports. CBIAC was conceived in London and gradually gravitated toward Southeast Asia,[28] while the Mercantile Bank had evolved from a Bombay-based Anglo-Indian partnership that leveraged itself to enter exchange banking between India and China, but remained firmly anchored in South Asia. Both banks were managed from London, but HSBC kept its Head Office in Hong Kong ever since it was set up by a few of the Colony's prominent trading agency houses.

Though constricted in China, CBIAC had considerable leeway in Malaya where it too enjoyed a certain degree of Foreign Office patronage.[29] As one of the leading foreign banks in Southeast Asia, CBIAC was instrumental in funding British colonial forays into tin mining and rubber plantations and was the first to open agencies in Taiping and Kuala Lumpur (1888), followed by Klang (1909), Seremban (1910), Melaka (1910), and Ipoh (1912). Typically, such forays tapped preexisting Asian networks already engaged in mining.[30] At the same time, Europeans followed the Overseas Chinese lead in introducing rice milling, which rapidly transformed Burma, Siam, and Cochinchina from subsistence rural economies to a regional grain basket. By the turn of the century, intra-Asian rice exports soared fivefold to over 4 million tons annually, as foreign banks in Southeast Asia were funneling capital to cultivators via Chinese or Chettiar mediation.[31]

Yet CBIAC operations in Southeast Asia had to accommodate competition by an increasingly vigorous Chinese banking sector.[32] Overseas Chinese firms began to complement foreign banking hegemony in the region from the 1920s, with family-owned modern enterprises like the Ho Hong, Chinese Commercial Bank, Overseas Chinese Bank, and Sze Hai Tong setting the tone. Such banks usually expanded by partaking in the remittance business of Overseas Chinese communities to Mainland China, amounting to 421–650 million silver dollars annually.[33]

Asian and British financial institutions have always been more closely knit in Malaya than in China owing to the nature of mining and revenue farming in the Southeast Asian interior, which critically depended on an influx of migrant labor. In contrast to the Chinese treaty-port paradigm, CBIAC managers in Malaya were much more receptive to secondary moneylending and business ventures undertaken by Asians. Both CBIAC and MBI formed lasting working relationships with Chettiars in Southeast Asia that were based on the *hundi* scrip system and bore a striking resemblance to the contemporary Shanghainese *zhuangpiao*. Shanghai moneyshops, however, fell short of channeling foreign bank capital to farmers and—unlike the Chettiars in the Southeast Asian setting—did not mortgage crops. Relationships between Chettiars and British banks in Southeast Asia were also more egalitarian than in Shanghai: local confidence in CBIAC was often determined by Chettiar willingness to accept their notes during the 1920s.[34]

More generally, British overseas banking could preserve its lead over other foreign banks in Asia until the 1920s largely because of London's preeminence as the world's clearing hub and because U.S. banks had been preoccupied with Latin America until the 1910s. U.S. multinationals were latecomers into Southeast Asia and the Chinese treaty ports. Although they gradually became leading creditors elsewhere in the world, American financial institutions kept a modest regional presence outside the Philippines before World War I.[35]

THE CBIAC NOTE CIRCULATION PATTERN

Note issuance was to complement resource accumulation through local deposit acceptances in the Asian branches of overseas banks and through discounting export drafts flowing along the trade routes between Britain, India, and China. This triangular traffic entrenched Britain's economic supremacy in the latter half of the nineteenth century, whereby Chinese silk and tea exports to Britain would be essentially financed by Indian-grown surplus opium or by American-produced bullion.[36] India, in turn, absorbed British manufactured goods, particularly factory-spindled textiles, to offset British trade deficits with continental Europe and the Americas.

One of the principal attractions of overseas banking in the eyes of financiers in the City of London during the mid-nineteenth century were the comparatively high interest rates prevalent in East Asian entrepôts and the Australasian dominions.[37] Note issuance was arguably one of the most convenient ways of realizing quick gains from such market conditions, because note bearers provided the banks with commensurate interest-free bullion that could be turned into high-yield short-term loans. At the same time, banknote issuance was important as a source of working capital for newly established overseas banks because attracting fixed-term deposits in the dominions, colonies, and concession areas took years and was hampered by competition from traditional financial institutions.

In the 1830s, banks of issue across the British and French colonial Empires were often more profitable than mercantile banks. East Asia was particularly appealing to British bankers, since private banknote issuance at home was progressively phased out by the Bank of England, and since the semiofficial Presidency Banks were assuming a monopoly on paper money through much of the Indian subcontinent during the 1870s.[38] Unlike their British counterparts, French overseas banks rarely had to apply for supplemental charter renewal and normally enjoyed monopolistic legal tender benefits in colonial possessions. However, British and French banks often shared similar charter guidelines relative to their note issues: a minimum of one-third bullion reserve against notes was considered elementary in Europe during much of the nineteenth century.[39] Notably, monetary conventions in Shanghai and other Chinese treaty ports differed from colonial possessions in that many types of quasi-foreign banknotes were circulating there *concomitantly*, and no European Power could effectively enforce the paper currency of its preferred banks on local bearers as legal tender.

The British Treasury and Colonial Office were at pains to prevent chartered British banks from forming issue monopolies and made sure that private notes did not attain legal tender status in any single territory across Asia. To protect undiscerning or impecunious bearers, the Treasury often imposed double liability on private bank issues and aimed to confine note values to large denominations.[40] The Treasury's line quite often conflicted with colonial governors, who were anxious to see the money supply in their cash-starved entrepôts increasing without shouldering any of the printing and administrative costs associated therewith.[41]

CBIAC's founder, the renowned economist James Wilson, sought in 1852 a Royal Charter that would not only minimize the risks for prospective shareholders through limited liability, but would also authorize the bank to issue notes payable to bearers at any of its overseas branches outside India.[42] Nevertheless, the Colonial Banking Regulations exhorted CBIAC—like all other royally chartered banks—to keep its total note circulation volume below paid-up capital (GBP 500,000). To that end, the Treasury rendered any issue beyond paid-up capital unprofitable by requiring that the excess amount of notes in circulation be covered with a 100 percent bullion reserve.[43]

Unlike HSBC, CBIAC seldom chose to engage in excess issues even when the bullion supply was abundant. On the one hand, this strategy spared the bank printing costs and made its cash reserves less vulnerable to sudden runs. On the other hand, it meant that any diminution in the total note circulation volume (below paid-up capital level) would by definition impinge on its profits.[44]

CBIAC's Charter stipulated a common reserve requirement for the authorized (read: non-excess) issue, which obliged branches to maintain in their vaults an average monthly amount of specie equal to one-third of its local circulation volume.[45] The bank's balance sheets suggest that this requirement was largely met by maintaining total liquid reserves that were normally well above local circulation figures, albeit having to support current accounts and other liabilities at the same time.[46]

With more rigorous Treasury regulation during the 1910s, CBIAC specie reserves were progressively complemented through the purchase of interest-bearing British and colonial government securities on the order of one-third of the authorized issue. The bank simply deposited those securities *en bloc* with the Bank of England.[47] But Treasury supervision of overseas banknote issuance in Greater China was further tightened in the 1920s, and CBIAC was now required to place a one-third reserve in the custody of the Hong Kong government, and as from 1928 to entrust a proportionate share of securities at the hands of the British consul-general in Shanghai.

Meanwhile, British monetary regulation in the Straits Settlements was taking a different direction than in Hong Kong and China after colonial administrators resolved to introduce legal tender notes covered by sterling reserves in 1896 and to abandon the silver standard in 1906.[48] Re-based Straits Settlements government notes rapidly replaced older HSBC and CBIAC issues, thereby forcing the two banks to rethink their global circulation strategy. Profits accruing from overseas banknote issues in East Asia must have been considerable, since CBIAC began to actively petition the Treasury to permanently increase its authorized circulation quota in Greater China in recompense for its diminished position in the Straits Settlements.[49]

The upshot was that, from the 1910s, Hong Kong became the focal point of British overseas banknote circulation in the region, far exceeding both Mainland China and Southeast Asia, as Figure 3.2 clearly shows.

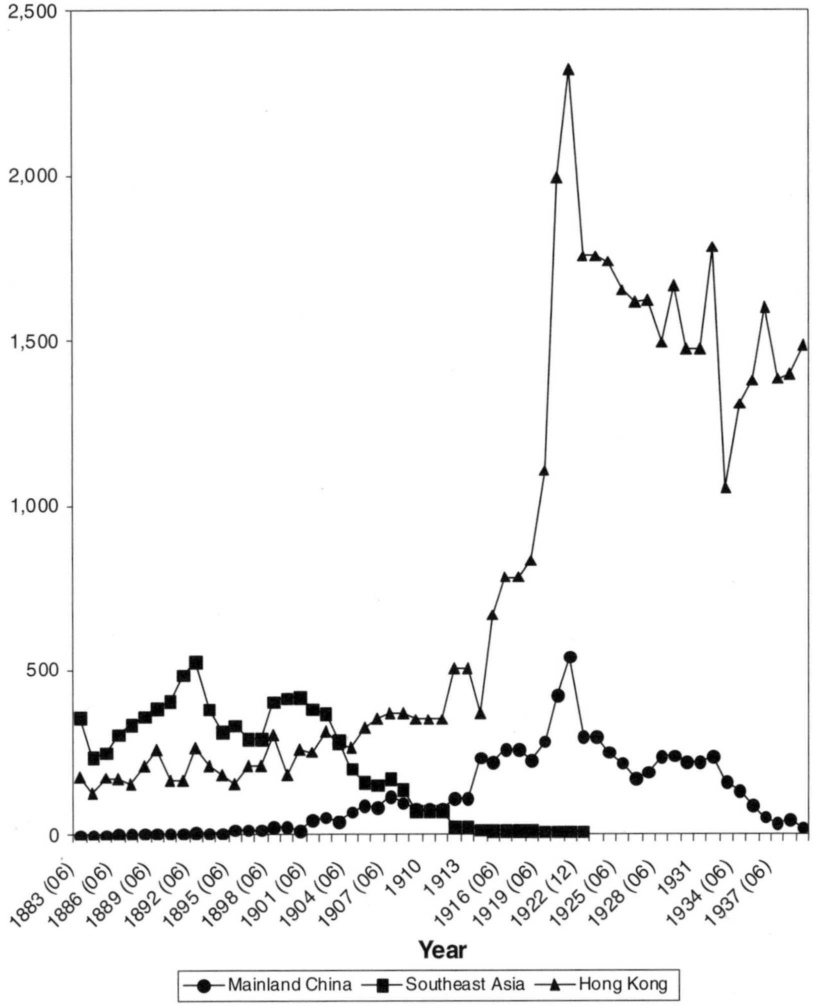

Figure 3.2. CBIAC Note Circulation: Regional Disaggregation, 1883–1939. Unit: GBP (000). *Source*: Adapted from CBIAC GL Ms 31519; missing data for 1897, 1910, 1911, 1913, 1917, 1923, and 1931 were added based on midyear figures from the previous year; the Mainland China aggregate covers tael and Mexican dollar note issues in Shanghai, Tianjin, and Hankou; the Hong Kong aggregate covers all notes issued in the Crown Colony regardless of whether they circulated locally or in South China; the Southeast Asia aggregate covers Singapore, Penang, and the bank's small issue in Siam. Conversion from local currency to GBP is based on CBIAC's own exchange rate, as used in the balance sheets.

Recognizing that economic growth would require a larger money supply, the Hong Kong government welcomed the global reallocation of British overseas banknote circulation quotas. It was wary of radical currency reforms like the one implemented by the Straits Settlements government, because Hong Kong's prosperity largely depended on direct trade with silver-based China. At the same time, because the Hong Kong dollar did not take root in Chinese treaty ports north of Guangzhou, locally denominated notes issued on the Chinese Mainland were an essential (but quantitatively minor) auxiliary to CBIAC's circulation of HK$.

The twentieth century saw a moderate decline in CBIAC's note issue as a proportion of the bank's overall activity: between 1903 and 1935 the bank's total liabilities and paid-up capital grew by approximately 360 percent, while its note circulation expanded by 245 percent.[50] Higher balance-sheet totals were nonetheless indicative of the rapid growth of intercontinental trade—as well as of intra-Asian trade.[51] During this period, CBIAC's Southeast Asian strongholds countervailed, in effect, the bank's inferior position as a creditor in China, while its diminishing role as a bank of issue in the Straits Settlements was compensated by a surge of issues in Hong Kong. This development pattern meant that the Hong Kong branch was becoming increasingly differentiated from other CBIAC branches around the world in that an unusually high proportion of its business activity was derived from note issuance, as Figure 3.3 indicates.

The expatriate mercantile community in the treaty ports and Hong Kong recognized from its inception that China's monetary fragmentation posed a hindrance to trade. Interprovincial coinage and weight variations encumbered the movement of foreign goods and services into the interior and intensified foreign reliance on financial intermediaries. Premodern institutions—like the Shanxi banks and the Shanghai moneyshops—maintained a sophisticated remittance network throughout China, which nevertheless fell short of rationalizing credit or propagating impersonal trust.

The British banks, on their part, quickly realized that this fragmentation could serve as a source of additional commission income. The difference between the foreign and traditional banking structures lay in the fact that British banks offered longer term loans to foreign firms, actively solicited deposits from foreigners and Chinese alike, and circulated notes payable on demand, whereas traditional financial institutions did not embrace reserve ratios and relied almost exclusively on remittance turnover to offer short-term credit.

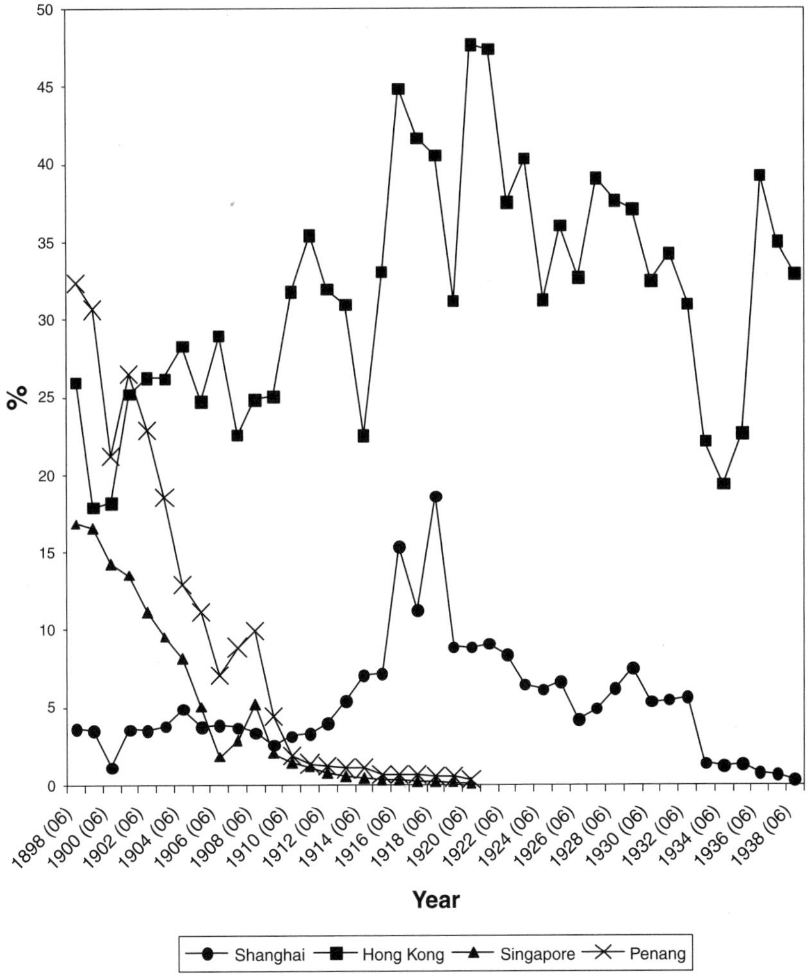

Figure 3.3. Note Circulation as Percentage of Liabilities in Principal CBIAC Branches, 1898–1939. *Source*: Adapted from CBIAC GL Ms 31519.

Like other British overseas banknotes, early CBIAC issues resuscitated—rather than revolutionized—fiduciary money markets in Asia. What British bankers indiscriminately called Bazaar Bills in the early nineteenth century had actually been a time-honored component of *local* transactions from Tehran to Osaka in many shapes, forms, and names, albeit on a limited scale.

The ingenuity of British overseas banking in Asia lay in its ability to control the flow of *international* and intra-Asian exchange bills in order to maintain an economies-of-scale advantage. The control of foreign trade finance meant in turn that British bank credit capabilities were far beyond what indigenous institutions or other foreign banks could muster. However, outside the large urban entrepôts, British paper instruments had to accommodate local realities, which necessitated unique clearing mechanisms with traditional onlenders.[52]

Reliance on compradors, Chettiars, shroffs, or *sarrafs* set prewar overseas banking in Asia distinctly apart from European financial institutions in Latin America, Africa, and the Middle East, where expatriate staff were expected to have a reasonably good command of local languages and to engage the rural sector directly.[53] Communication barriers between senior management and local clientele in Asia were further exacerbated by executive promotion policies, which underscored frequent relocation between branches and the Head Office. A managerial appointment in an overseas branch was worth twice as much as in the City of London, but there was little material or social incentive in remuneration packages to encourage the study of Asian languages and cultures prior to assuming posts abroad.[54]

At a great distance from the Head Office in London, local branch idiosyncrasy required greater autonomy, which could result in corporate inconsistency. London-based boards of British overseas banks were acutely aware of the dangers of losing control over overseas staff. Tensions between enterprising branch managers and company directors inevitably became one of the most enduring themes in overseas banking. By the end of the nineteenth century, most British overseas banks would appoint inspectors to frequently shuttle between the branches and audit local lending practices.[55]

THE CHINESE SETTING

One form of branch autonomy is manifest in inconsistent Chinese-language signage, advertisements, and banknote captions from the prewar era. CBIAC, for example, set up its branch in Shanghai as early as 1858. Chinese clients soon dubbed it the *Maijiali* 麥加利 Bank after the first expatriate manager, John Mackellar.[56] The title would remain in some way or another associated with the CBIAC right up until the 1890s, and although it was apparently never ratified by the Head Office, branch managers in Tianjin, Hankou, and Singapore subsequently adopted it as their own. Curiously, another Chinese title had taken root in Hong Kong, where the bank is still known today as *Zhada* 渣打 ("The Chartered"). Then, from the 1910s, the official title *Yindu Xinjinshan yinhang* 印度新金山銀行, or the India and New Gold Mountain Bank, became more commonly used on the Mainland but was ultimately abandoned in favor of *Zhada* in the postwar era.[57]

The inconsistency of captions on British banknotes circulating on the Mainland should also be understood in the context of China's own monetary fragmentation. As described in Chapter 1, myriad forms of paper money were still in use in littoral China during the early nineteenth century, but uniform fiduciary money per se was becoming but a fading historic memory. During the Shunzhi reign (1644–1661), there had been extensive but short-lived Imperial recourse to thirteenth-century-style copper-denominated notes, which resulted in runaway inflation and aversion to this means of payment in much of the subsequent Chinese discourse on statecraft.[58] Later-Qing governments simply lapsed into a passive acceptance of overseas silver coins as China's de facto mercantile currency.

A last-ditch attempt to issue Imperial paper notes was made during the Xianfeng reign (1851–1861). However, these notes depreciated rapidly when widespread rebellions threatened the Imperial Court. By 1859, they were worth a fraction of their nominal value and were seldom redeemed by Imperial tax inspectors.[59] Unless they had robust *local* credentials, paper notes—as any other form of nonmetallic money—were regarded with a high degree of suspicion by the Chinese, as British banks were establishing their first branches on the Mainland. This may be one possible explanation for why customary local branch names were not swiftly overruled in favor of consistent corporate identity.

CBIAC's balance sheets suggest that Chinese suspicion of quasi-foreign notes dissipated circa 1900. Only half a century after the first issues on the Mainland did British overseas banknotes make inroads in the Chinese marketplace. CBIAC's first issue in Shanghai was one of the earliest, dating back to 1863. Like other quasi-foreign note issues in the city, its notes were first rejected by Chinese clients, not least because the city's *daotai* had refused to accept them in customs payments.[60] It is also plausible to assume that the Agra Bank and the Oriental Bank failures weighed heavily on the standing of the remaining British banks in the eyes of Chinese treaty-port dwellers. CBIAC did not resume large-scale issues until 1885, but initial results were still marred by widespread suspicion.[61] In comparison, early issues in Singapore and Hong Kong were more welcomed. HK$ notes issued as early as 1862 by the CBIAC branch in the Crown Colony were in wide circulation three years later and were even used as cash reserves by local moneylenders.[62]

By the early twentieth century, contemporary observers had noted that Chinese provincial banks feverishly emulated foreign banknote designs with little regard to adequate reserve policy.[63] Though successful in attracting funds at first, most of these banks eventually fell prey to the fiscal excesses of warlords, leaving a trail of irredeemable notes. For this reason, CBIAC shunned most Chinese banknotes throughout the prewar era.[64] When repaying loans or remitting funds, specie, bullion, and quasi-foreign or colonial notes were the only media acceptable.

British banks did not aim at reshaping China's regional monetary fragmentation. Neither could they command a large portion of China's money supply from their treaty-port enclaves. In Shanghai, the Western community relied on the Chinese mercantile class just as the latter counted on foreign judicial and military protection. The period from 1895 to 1914 marked the zenith of European imperialism in China proper, but even then—with decades of local experience behind them—British overseas banks could scarcely engage the agrarian interior of the country without the mediation of local compradors and treaty-port marketing guilds.[65] The European colonial Powers could break into Chinese Imperial coffers through the imposition of war indemnities and would browbeat a motley crew of warlord-dominated governments into surrendering custom revenues and railway concessions. However, none of these factors could fulfill the hyperbole of the propaganda holding out the prospect of hundreds of millions of consumers in the hinterland eager for foreign manufactured goods.[66]

Chinese consumption habits changed little in the hinterland because the average purchasing power of most rural communities did not rise significantly in per capita terms from the 1840s.[67] Affordable imported kerosene was becoming popular, and Indian-made yarn could find buyers when market conditions allowed, but both had inferior local substitutes in the form of vegetable oil and hemp. Even Bengali opium had been partly replaced by the 1890s and could no longer fetch quick gains for expatriate trading houses.[68] Those foreign firms that ventured out of the treaty ports soon found out that success in the Chinese market was a function of either intimate acquaintance with local practices and the employ of the right go-betweens, or of unrestricted access to corruptible officials.

The volatility of the European Powers' informal *imperia* in East Asia became abundantly clear after the Russo-Japanese War (1904–1905), whose unanticipated outcome reverberated throughout the region for many years to come. Japanese expansionism was then precipitated by the ousting of Germany from its Asian concession areas during World War I and by the erosion of the Anglo-Japanese Alliance (1902–1923). In the 1920s, the three principal

British overseas banks in East Asia—HSBC, the Chartered Bank, and the Mercantile Bank of India—were still unchallenged financially, but with the rise of Chinese nationalism and the phenomenal leap in homegrown modern banking, their future prospects in the treaty ports were becoming increasingly uncertain.[69]

Faced with an unremitting popular outcry, extraterritoriality was first ceded by British garrison forces in Hankou and Jiujiang as early as January 1927,[70] paving the way for British government rapprochement with a resurgent GMD two years later and a long process of accommodation between Jiang Jieshi's (Chiang Kai-shek) proxies and the leading British bankers in Shanghai.[71] The most sensitive issue in contention between the ruling GMD and Shanghai's expatriate banking community during the Nanjing Decade (1927–1937) was the future of China's mammoth foreign debt service. The hold of foreign banks on domestic deposits and their right to issue locally denominated notes were of secondary importance, because a hostile GMD could potentially suspend debt repayments to foreign creditors, but do little to interfere with the banks' other prerogatives as long as extraterritoriality in Shanghai was in effect.[72] Nevertheless, GMD officials continued to view the free circulation of quasi-foreign banknotes in the treaty ports as an affront to Chinese national aspirations and as a major obstacle along the way to comprehensive monetary reform.

When Jiang Jieshi fatefully decided to break with his CCP allies and tighten his hold on disaffected warlords in 1927, overtures between the GMD and Britain—whose diplomats had hitherto described the GMD brand of Chinese nationalism as ominously "Bolshevized"—were already underway.[73] Jiang's drift to the right later that year facilitated a thaw in GMD-British relations. This thaw was followed by pressure from the British government on recalcitrant British bankers in Shanghai to scale down their operations in return for a Chinese commitment to honor foreign debts in abeyance.

Realignment between the Chinese and British governments was equally spurred by Japanese territorial exigencies, which threatened the interests of both countries. In November 1935, cooperation between the two governments culminated in a concerted effort to take China off the silver standard and introduce a fiduciary national currency pegged to the pound sterling (*fabi*). This new legal tender was to replace the myriad media of exchange that had been prevalent in the Chinese economy, including quasi-foreign banknotes. Compliance of the British banks in Shanghai with the *fabi* reform was formally enforced by the British consul-general, who promulgated an edict obliging all British firms in the city to hand in their silver possessions and convertible paper notes to GMD-run banks in return for legal-tender notes. Ultimately, the British government sacrificed note issue rights with surprisingly little opposition from the British banks.[74]

How many CBIAC-issued HK$ notes had actually circulated in China proper at that time? In order to answer this question, it is first necessary to reconsider previous accounts of the role played by HK$ notes in Guangdong's economy. Estimates of the proportion of HK$ notes circulating in China proper during the first half of the twentieth century vary markedly between Tamagna's 20 percent (for 1937) to Rawski's notional 66.6 percent (for the entire prewar period).[75] In the mid-1920s, HSBC executives in Hong Kong believed that 70 percent of their notes were circulating in South China, but in the early 1930s the suggestion was 60 percent.[76]

Rawski's influential book drew quite liberally on previous work done by Xian Ke.[77] Xian had grossly overstated foreign banknote inroads into China proper, and his conclusions as regards the ubiquity of HK$ in Guangdong are therefore suspect. For example, he advanced the implausible proposition that at least one-third of the Banque de l'Indochine piastre notes issued in Annam found their way to two of the poorest provinces in South China—Guangxi and Yunnan.[78] While Rawski chose to reject this particular proposition, he embraced Xian's suggestion that two-thirds of the total Eastern Exchange Banks' note issue circulated in China proper, thus ignoring their considerable share of the money supply in the Straits Settlements until the 1900s.

A comprehensive survey made by the Guangxi provincial government in 1933 indicated that piastre coins or notes were circulating in only twenty-eight of its ninety-nine counties. Within these twenty-eight counties, piastre notes in most cases made up only 5 percent of the money stock, with the notable exception of Pingxiang 凭祥, right on the border with Annam. But even in this frontier area piastre notes were reported to account for no more than 60 percent of the money stock.[79]

Frederic Lee observed in 1926 that piastre and HK$ notes were fairly common in Yunnan, but that locally issued notes had been the mainstay of financial markets.[80] Similarly, there are ample contemporary Chinese observations to suggest that the circulation of Banque de l'Indochine notes in Yunnan province was rather confined to the cities of Mengzi and Kunming, and that its value could not have exceeded 20 million silver dollars in 1919, that is, less than a third of Xian Ke's estimate for Guangxi and Yunnan that year.[81]

In an in-depth survey of provincial economic performance before World War II, David Faure has suggested that payments in kind and silver bullion typified rural Guangdong. From 1870, silver dollar coins were also becoming a common medium of exchange in Guangzhou and Shantou (Swatow). To some extent, paper notes could be found circulating in those two cities alongside silver coins, but they "did not alter the bimetallic basis."[82] Even as late as 1949 when hyperinflation in China was rampant, and most prices in Guangzhou were quoted in HK$ rather than provincial currency, contemporary observers estimated that only half of the notes issued in Hong Kong had found their way to South China.[83]

That the prevalence of HK$ notes in Guangzhou largely depended, on the demand side, on ready convertibility by local British bank has been alluded to by Frank King.[84] This is also manifest in correspondence between British and Chinese officials that was relayed to the Chinese Maritime Customs. For example, on May 6, 1936—well after the demonetization of silver currency in China—British envoy Sir Frederick Leith-Ross tried to persuade Kong Xiangxi (H. H. Kung), the Chinese finance minister, that the bullion reserve once used by HSBC and CBIAC to cash their notes in Shamian be allowed across the border into Hong Kong.[85]

On the supply side, the prevalence of HK$ notes in Guangzhou was a result of the province's trade surplus with Hong Kong. This surplus seems to be reflected in the makeup of the CBIAC Guangzhou agency balance sheet in 1920 (see Table 3.1). The balance sheet indicates that, in contrast to the Shanghai branch, the Guangzhou agency paid out loans to Chinese-owned filatures producing raw silk—a major provincial export at the time (a branch that did not issue its own locally denominated notes was termed "agency" in overseas bank jargon).[86] The balance sheet is notably devoid of exchange bill flows, which suggests transshipment of silk cargoes via Hong Kong by foreign trading firms.[87] The balance sheet is denominated in HK$ units of account throughout, and the cash reserves therein were almost entirely made up of HK$ notes rather than silver coins.[88] Short-term "silk loans" represented as much as 56 percent of agency assets and would have been quite profitable since they garnered a lending margin of up to 6.25 percent over interest payments to depositors.

Within the bank, the Guangzhou agency was clearly a net debtor. Interagency capital inflow—most probably from Hong Kong—accounted for 85 percent of total liabilities. The volume of current accounts that the agency operated was relatively minor (HK$90,446). It was nonetheless dominated by multinational firms (see Figure 3.4). Only nine out of fifty-four accounts—or merely 15 percent in terms of total account volume—were attributable to Chinese individuals and firms.

Given that 97 percent of all deposit receipts were from Chinese individuals and firms, their small ranks among current account holders may perhaps

Table 3.1 CBIAC Guangzhou Agency Select Balance-Sheet Entries, December 1920 (Unit: HK$)

Deposit Receipts (up to 1 year)	
From Chinese Individuals and Firms	14,600
From Foreign Individuals and Firms	400
Loans against Collateral (up to 1.5 years)	
To Chinese Individuals and Firms	441,400
To Foreign Individuals and Firms	0
Balance-Sheet Total	**779,000**

Source: CBIAC GL Ms 3159/53.

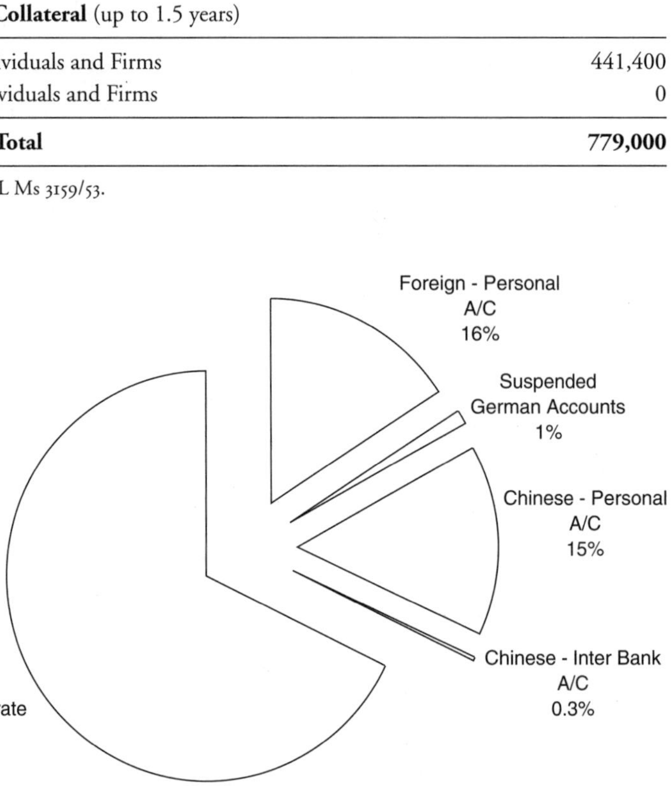

Figure 3.4. CBIAC Guangzhou Agency: Current Account Profile, December 1920. Total: ~ HK$90,446. *Source*: Adapted from CBIAC GL Ms 3159/53.

suggest that British agency managers were reluctant to engage local clientele on an open account basis.

What proportion of CBIAC HK$ notes circulated in South China then? Two alternative approaches can be used to approximate this proportion: (1) The volume of total assets in the Guangzhou agency and (2) the ratio of the value of notes in circulation to liquid reserves (notes, silver coins, and sycee) in all Greater China branches. In 1920, CBIAC had no other agencies in Guangdong, and it is therefore unlikely that its note circulation in the province far exceeded local balance-sheet totals. As elsewhere, the ubiquity of banknotes in South China depended on prompt convertibility, and this is one reason why they were not commonly used in rural areas. There were numerous border checks on movement between Hong Kong and the Mainland, which offset the premium that Hong Kong-issued notes usually had over provincial currency. CBIAC's note circulation volume in Hong Kong was HK$11.7 million in December 1920,[89] while Guangzhou balance-sheet totals during the same period were only 6 percent thereof. Even if we allow for another 6 percent to account for CBIAC HK$ notes brought into the province by moneychangers and itinerant workers, we still have a figure that is considerably lower than previous estimates for the 1920s suggested.

Turning to the second approach, we find that average CBIAC note/cash ratios during 1900–1935 differed enormously. While Hong Kong registered 10.1, Tianjin was far behind with 0.25.[90] This, in turn, points to immense variation in economic conditions and monetization levels across China. Even assuming that the ratio in Guangzhou was closer to that of Hong Kong, the result would still be far below earlier estimates of currency substitution. In other words, when we multiply the 1920 cash reserve in Guangzhou (HK$209,318) by the average CBIAC note/metallic cash-reserve ratios nominally prevalent in Hong Kong (10.1),[91] the result (HK$2.1 million) would amount to just 17 percent of CBIAC HK$ circulation volume in 1920 (HK$11.7 million). Allowing another 17 percent for private trafficking of CBIAC notes into Guangdong, produces a result (34 percent) that still falls well below Rawski's upper-end estimate of 66.6 percent.

CONCLUSION

Though rarely discussed in depth by economic or business historians, the issue of convertible banknotes was one of the defining features of nineteenth-century British overseas banking. Established in both colonies and sovereign countries, these highly specialized banks underpinned the surge in global and intraregional trade as from the 1830s, demonstrating impressive growth in some cases but damning vulnerability to currency fluctuations in others. The three principal British overseas banks in East Asia—commonly known as the Eastern Exchange Banks—came to play a decisive role in the formation of the Hong Kong and Straits Settlement currencies and for some time were the sole suppliers of paper money in these colonies. The same business rationale led these banks to disseminate locally denominated notes beyond the colonies. Such issues were initiated in the treaty ports of Siam, Japan, and China, but China proved by far their largest and most durable market.

This chapter has focused on CBIAC, the second largest of the Eastern Exchange Banks. It explained how customarily high interest rates in mid-nineteenth-century Asia made note issues a lucrative pursuit for this bank, while highlighting the ways in which regulators at the British Treasury and Colonial Office sought to restrict any excess issues. CBIAC's Hong Kong branch was found to have crucial importance to the sustainability of the bank's note circulation volume during the early twentieth century, as the Straits Settlements government introduced a re-based legal tender.

HK$ notes were fairly common in Guangdong but do not appear to have made up as large a proportion of the province's money stock as previously thought. At the same time, notes disseminated in the Chinese treaty ports, and denominated in either local tael or dollar units of account, served as an important auxiliary to the HK$ notes issued by the bank, particularly between 1911 and 1920.

CBIAC's note issue in East Asia makes for a complex story. In Siam, the Rama dynasty first welcomed and then rejected the notes. In British Malaya, they were the first form of paper money to spread into the interior but have long since become a collector's item. On Mainland China, they were never recognized by local authorities and were ultimately stamped out by the *fabi* reform of 1935. In Hong Kong, the CBIAC note issue was secondary to HSBC's (the latter issue will be further explored in the next chapter). But, ironically, 1935 was also the year in which CBIAC HK$ notes finally attained legal tender status in the Crown Colony.[92] In sum, CBIAC notes circulated across East Asia during the prewar era in the liminal space stretching between legal and illegal tender.

Part II

Chapter 4 HSBC and Its Note Issue in Shanghai, 1866–1925

> The financial mandarin Wan mao-in [Wang Maoyin 王茂蔭] took it into his head one day to lay before the Son of Heaven a proposal which had the secret purpose of transforming the assignats of the Chinese Empire into convertible banknotes. The committee on the assignats, in its report of April 1854, severely rebuked him for this. Whether he also received the traditional thrashing with bamboo-sticks is not stated.
> —Karl Marx, *Capital*

This chapter explains how banknotes first issued by the Hongkong and Shanghai Banking Cooperation (HSBC) in 1866 had helped resuscitate financial markets during the late-Imperial era, and how the demand for these banknotes shot up amid the political and economic disintegration that typified warlordism in the early-Republican period.

Drawing on local balance sheets and other primary sources, the chapter will argue that HSBC's note issue offset the deep-seated suspicion of paper money in China that even European thinkers like Karl Marx had been aware of. It will also argue that note issuance by British banks in China proper was a quantitatively modest but potent financial instrument that helped minimize branch dependence on metropolitan capital injection, on the one hand, and on China's intractable monetary system, on the other. Contrary to much of the received wisdom, the following evidence seems to suggest that note issuance was a highly remunerative constituent of British overseas banking in Asia. It helped tap regional economies with little risk, but was equally significant as a touchstone for Chinese reformists.

Not long after its inception in 1865, the British-run HSBC—then more informally known as the Hongkong Bank—had become synonymous throughout East Asia with managerial acumen, a powerful network of connections, and financial innovation.[1] Although Britain's share of the region's trade progressively declined by the turn of the twentieth century, no other European-owned bank operating in East Asia could achieve comparable growth rates or rival the Hongkong Bank's leverage over indigenous sovereigns. In various capacities, HSBC (hereafter also the Bank) came to play a significant role in the modernization of money markets and credit instruments throughout Asia before World War I. It assisted the Japanese government to turn the yen into an Asia-wide currency, and it facilitated the country's swift adoption of the gold standard in 1897.[2] It was behind the issue of the first banknotes in Siam, and it served as adviser to successive Chinese governments on economic development—to name but few salient examples.[3]

Nonetheless, the Bank's public image during the prewar era was far from immune to controversy both at home and abroad. While consistently favored by Colonial Office policymakers and British diplomatic legations, HSBC drew criticism from British jingoists and Chinese anti-imperialist activists on two separate counts.

In London and Hong Kong, HSBC often came under fire for what had been perceived as its intimate links with German firms in China, eventually forcing the Bank to accentuate its British identity and shed non-British directors.[4] But if postwar realignments have long since relegated this line of criticism to historic obscurity, Chinese invectives proved more abiding—so much so that even in post-Mao China one can still detect strains of antagonism toward HSBC among economic historians, who underscore some of the themes that have allegedly tainted the Bank's prewar legacy. These themes often include its perceived critical role in financing the opium trade;[5] in establishing a monopolistic banking Consortium to corner Chinese government loans;[6] in extracting indemnity payments from China;[7] in manipulating exchange rates in Shanghai;[8] and last but not least, in undermining the city's indigenous banking sector.[9]

At the other end of the spectrum, new work published in recent years mainly by Japanese scholars has helped us concretize the debate over the nature of foreign banking in China's treaty ports during the late-Qing and early-Republican eras. This new work helps disabuse the academic discourse of the abstractions of "high imperialism" and the European "scramble for concessions."[10] Such scholarship has carried the field forward by relying on declassified local branch balance sheets and other firsthand archival material, rather than on anecdotal sources or press reports.

The availability of this archival material owes much to Frank King, who had been commissioned to write the Bank's story in 1979 and, inter alia, supervised a complex operation to salvage branch records from a decrepit warehouse in Shanghai. First published in 1987, King's subsequent four-volume *History of the Hongkong and Shanghai Banking Corporation* (hereafter *History*) was hailed as a monumental achievement, winning praise from business historians and China specialists alike.[11]

Yet, partly due to commission requisites, the *History* is preoccupied in no small part with the dramatis personae that turned the Bank into a success story of epic proportions. In that sense, it is appreciably different from the new work on foreign banking in China, whose emergence it had made possible. The new work has since increasingly focused on capital flows between key branches of foreign banks, their liability makeup, and linkages between trade balances and local business practices. Moreover, the expansive scope of the *History* inevitably led King to adopt what one reviewer described as "digressive style."[12] As a result, those readers who are aware of the specificity of the accusations leveled at the Bank by Chinese contemporaries and Marxian economic historians may not necessarily find in the *History* a coherent rebuttal.

This chapter will revisit one specific aspect of the Bank's prewar operation where scholarly opinions are similarly polarized, but that has so far remained in the shadow of other contentious issues: HSBC's banknote circulation in the Chinese treaty ports. More precisely, the chapter will examine whether note issue prerogatives enjoyed by the Bank hindered or stimulated the modernization of China's monetary system during the late-Imperial and early-Republican eras; how exactly banknote circulation was embedded in the Bank's overall strategy, and whether or not it was a remunerative pursuit.

Chinese historians have invariably attributed great importance to quasi-foreign note issuance as a factor that retarded China's economic development and through which foreign banks scooped a shady windfall. Assertions to that effect had begun in 1958 and have scarcely relented since.[13] In a representative compilation, co-authored as recently as 2002 by a few of China's best-known economic historians, Zhang Guohui described those banknotes as "a vital means with which to plunder the peoples of colonized and semi-colonized lands."[14] Another voluminous survey of the history of banknotes, published under the auspices of the People's Bank of China in 2001, accused HSBC of having used "Schadenfreude tactics" (*cheng ren zhi wei de fangfa* 乘人之危的方法) to expand its note circulation, that is, disburse more notes over the counter whenever rival Chinese banks faced liquidity crises.[15] Notably, both compilations draw exclusively on secondary sources or press reports to substantiate their claims.

This chapter charts the middle ground between the assertions often made by Chinese scholars and King's summary dismissal of them.[16] It will plot, in a nutshell, the business rationale behind the Bank's banknote issue, how it was regulated and how it was perceived within the tapestry of Chinese late-Imperial economic discourse. Where quantitative data from HSBC branches have not been preserved, the arguments will be illustrated using comparable statistics from the second largest British bank in East Asia at the time—the Chartered Bank of India Australia and China (CBIAC).[17] Finally, the chapter will try to reassess the historic significance (or insignificance) of HSBC's banknote issue in China proper between 1865 and 1925.

CIRCULATION PATTERNS: CAUSE AND EFFECT, 1866–1911

First printed in London and launched in Shanghai circa 1866, HSBC's banknote issue in China proper was part of its distinctly East Asian arm—a business function subsumed locally and largely independent of conditions in the London capital markets.[18] In that sense, the note issue was coterminous with the secret of success of the Bank in the prewar era: with its Head Office firmly set in Hong Kong, HSBC could lay down funds that had been mobilized *within* Asia.[19] In other words, the Bank could channel silver-pegged assets to highly remunerative local outlets without having to remit gold-pegged capital from London, thereby exposing itself to unnecessary exchange rate risks. To be sure, discounting exchange bills in multiple currencies and standards—that is, the finance of Eurasian trade—continued to be the *locus gravitatis* of Bank operations. But unlike many of its London-based competitors, HSBC had a stronger local arm to fall back on.[20] Disbursing notes rather than silver coins over the counter was one auxiliary means by which the Bank could increase the working capital of Asian branches with little effort.

Overall, the popularization of notes by foreign banks in mid-nineteenth-century East Asia was linked with the growth of a more important local banking activity: the pooling of fixed deposits.[21] In China, foreign banks offered notes on demand with two objectives in mind. First and foremost, paper notes whose value was on a par with conventionally used metallic units and that were guaranteed on demand by prestigious foreign establishments attracted treaty-port dwellers bent on avoiding high assaying costs. Given the chaotic state of China's metallic currencies and the lack of reliable financial institutions, providing a readily convertible means of payment was an effective way of building up a retail client base in search of a secure depository for its wealth. In the second instance, the note issue was a source of revenue unto itself, since it was based on fiduciary principles—that is, the metallic reserve held against notes outstanding was invariably smaller than their face value. This meant that the Bank could free up more liquid capital, which it could lend on at call, and thereby net an interest rate margin.

The fiduciary principles in the HSBC Ordinance were partly inspired by nineteenth-century Scottish banking practices, whereby private banks enjoyed lucrative note issue prerogatives.[22] But in Hong Kong, HSBC's strategy turned out to be more ambitious than the Scottish model had foreshadowed. For example, Victor Kresser, a Swiss expatriate who served as the Bank's first chief manager, sought to take over the money supply in the Colony altogether by bidding for its ailing Mint in 1866. Kresser faced strident opposition from the Treasury in London, which precluded any form of monopoly.[23] Decades later, relations between the Treasury and the Bank remained strained over similar issues. Indeed, relations might have boiled over if not for the Colonial Office's resolute advocacy of the Bank's role as a stabilizing force in the economic fabric of Hong Kong, and the persistent reluctance of the Colony's government to administer money supply after the Mint had been dissolved.

While the Bank's increasingly potent position as supplier of fiduciary money across East Asia called for prudence among Treasury regulators in London, it was not lost on China's Imperial bureaucracy either. The growth of foreign banking in Shanghai had generally stimulated late-Qing reformers such as Zhang Zhidong and Zhang Jian to memorialize the Imperial Court on the acute underdevelopment of China's financial sector.[24] The reformers complained that without institutions operating on foreign bank principles and comprehensive currency overhaul, China would be unable to sustain a much-needed military and industrial buildup. They noted with chagrin that China's own financial institutions were not cut out for such a task because they were too diffuse. Traditional, privately owned moneyshops had been regularly issuing paper money in China from at least the late-Ming, but its circulation was constricted along regional lines, and it suffered from mass forgeries.[25]

By the late 1890s, the protestations of reformers paved the way for a mushrooming of government-run provincial banks across China.[26] These banks tried to lay down roots primarily by circulating paper notes modeled on novel designs and printing technology that were inspired by the foreign banknotes, rather than by China's own traditional drafts (*piaotie* 票帖). Nonetheless, modern Chinese banks often fell prey to the short-sightedness of their political patrons, who merely aimed at harnessing branch managers to expand their revenue base. Figuratively speaking, the first Chinese banks were made to "jump the queue": they had drawn on note issuance to attract metallic money long before they could claim a solid customer-deposit base, and their management was dismally interwoven into that of government ministries.

Quantitative economic data assembled from late-Qing sources are usually riddled with inconsistencies.[27] Yet, the trends in Figure 4.1 may still shed light on the inner workings of the early Chinese banks, when compared with individual foreign banks, represented here by CBIAC.[28]

Broadly speaking, Figure 4.1 shows that the *average* ratio of notes outstanding to total liabilities for Chinese banks between 1898 and 1911 was 7.8 percent, whereas it never exceeded 5.4 percent in the Shanghai branch of the Chartered Bank (this maximum value was recorded for December 1904). This dissimilarity is thrown into relief when we revise the Chartered Bank data temporally, in order to account for the fact that its second period of note issuance in Shanghai began in 1886—much earlier than was the case with the first Chinese modern banks. For the entire period between 1886 and 1911 the average Shanghai branch ratio was actually as low as 3.5 percent.[29]

In absolute terms, Chinese bank circulation volume had reached 20.7 million dollars by 1911, with an annual growth rate of 80 percent between 1897 and 1911. In 1911, the average circulation of notes outstanding per bank in this sector was $1.2 million. The Chartered Bank circulation volume in China proper only reached $700,000 the same year, although it was one of the largest foreign banks operating in the region.

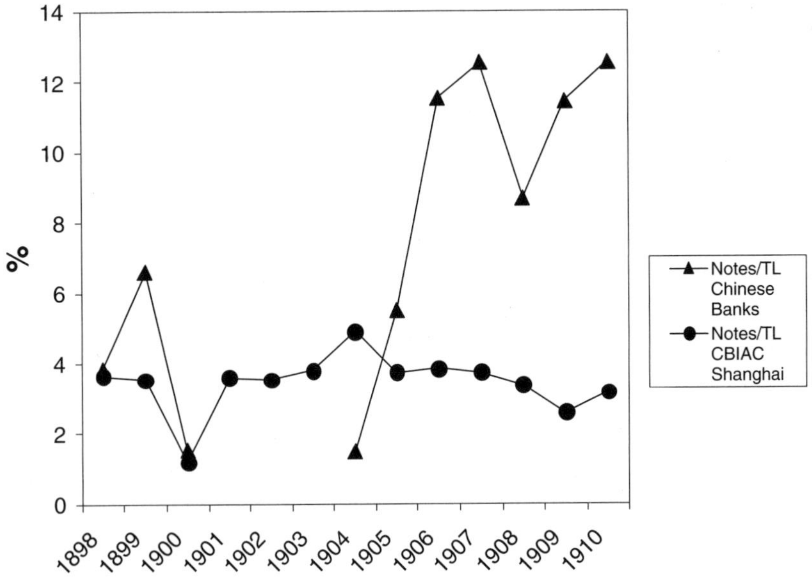

Figure 4.1. Notes Outstanding as Percentage of Total Liabilities, 1898–1911.
Source: The average ratio of notes outstanding to total liabilities for a cross section of modern Chinese banks is calculated from Cheng Linsun (2003), table 1.2, p. 34; the parallel ratio for CBIAC Shanghai branch is calculated from CBIAC GL Ms 31519.

Structural disparities between the two sectors partly derived from geographical distribution: Chinese banks had, of course, much more leeway to popularize notes in the vast hinterland that stretched beyond the confines of the treaty ports.[30] But the disparities may have also derived from the overemphasis that late-Qing reformers had placed on banknote issuance as a definitive constituent of modern banking. The reformers were quick to note how China's institutional weakness invited foreign banks to recoup profits from note issuance in the treaty ports, but failed to heed attendant reserve requirements, which set foreign banks apart from traditional financial institutions. Zheng Guanying epitomized this partiality. As a comprador for Butterfield, Swire and Co., he witnessed foreign business practices from within. Turned an official, he commented with disdain that the proliferation of quasi-foreign notes was merely a result of mercantile inertia and cronyism (*xunqing* 徇情) in China's financial sector.[31]

Zheng and others called on the Imperial Court to foster government-run banks to counter foreign economic inroads. But their frame of reference and argumentation was not wholly different from that of Qing bureaucrats—like

Wang Maoyin—who had previously tried to persuade the Manchu rulers to overprint paper money as a panacea for the dynastic decline. Nonetheless, the traditional monetary discourse did change to the extent that the early reformers had been castigated during the 1850s, whereas reformers in the 1890s could make more daring suggestions—such as the adoption of a gold standard—with impunity.[32]

The most trenchant of Zheng's commentaries on current affairs prescribed concrete measures to stem the Qing's relinquishment of macroeconomic reins. As early as 1873, Zheng suggested, for example, that Sichuan-grown opium be promoted as a substitute for imported opium from India and that Imperial consulates be opened in Singapore and San Francisco to tap Overseas Chinese wealth.[33] On monetary issues, he was unequivocal: China's monetary fragmentation could be solved only if decisive government action was taken to stamp out debasement and disallow casting by provincial officials or private businessmen.[34] Tellingly, he pinned down HSBC's success in China to its ability to raise capital from both Chinese and foreign shareholders; its strategy to entice petty cash depositors from all walks of life; and the way in which it employed interest-free proceeds from banknote issuance to on-lend.[35]

In the interim, the dilemma for the thinly endowed Qing Court remained the same: how to retain Imperial revenue without unleashing inflation that would provoke popular resistance, and without surrendering more central powers. The late-Imperial body politic was often blighted by indecision and contradictory thrusts that precluded lasting synergy between the state and private spheres in the realm of money. By the mid-nineteenth century, perhaps earlier, this shortfall had opened up a gaping loophole through which privately funded British trading houses and Anglo-Indian financial institutions could thrive on China's coastline.[36] Ultimately, it was the affluent executives of these treaty-port firms, the *taipans*, who guaranteed that the eastern thrust of Her Britannic Majesty's gunboats would remain economically sustainable.[37]

Although they benefited from China's economic malaise in the short run, British financiers and their lobbyists in the diplomatic missions had good reason to be wary of a full-blown monetary crisis that might eventually project on the prosperity of the treaty ports.[38] In 1908, for example, the British Legation in Beijing informed the Foreign Office that "[the] Shanghae [*sic*] General Chambers of Commerce has, for some months past, been concerned at the issue of dollar notes by Chinese banks without any restriction or control on the part of the government."[39] The Chambers then approached Shanghai's Taotai to clarify the restrictions under which moneyshops and banks were entitled to issue notes. The Taotai, for his part, was indignant over the foreign banks' refusal to accept Chinese banknotes of whatever provenance, other than those issued by the Imperial Bank of China. Somewhat confused, he replied that, though unenforced, government regulations restricting unbacked note issues were in effect. Consequently, the British Legation decided to join forces with the foreign banks in applying pressure on the Imperial Board of Finance (*duozhi bu* 度支部) to draw up measures for stricter control of China's banks.

In a subsequent statement, the British Legation did not mince words in an effort to rouse the Board of Finance to action. Observed from the foreign enclaves in the treaty ports, the severity of the situation in the periphery was compelling. It intensified what had already been seen as an intractable currency system:

> [It is reported that] the Provincial Bank at Hankow [Hankou], of unknown capital, has a note circulation of over 20 million dollars, that the private bank at Shanghae [*sic*] has issued notes equivalent to its paid-up capital, that another at Hangchow [Hangzhou] has notes of a face value more than three times in excess of its paid-up capital, and that two other institutions at Soochow [Suzhou] and Nanking [Nanjing], with no paid-up capital but with a guarantee from the provincial government, have placed in circulation notes of an aggregate face value of over 2 million.[40]

It should be pointed out that the good reputation that the IBC still enjoyed among foreigners at that stage was due to the fact that the bank's patron, Sheng Xuanhuai, had partly modeled it on the HSBC in 1897, despite concerns raised by Zhang Zhidong and opposition from some *Zongli yamen* 總理衙門 officials fearing excessive private ownership.[41] The IBC was China's first limited-liability bank, the first to employ foreign staff, and the first to order notes from overseas printers.[42] In conformity with early HSBC guidelines, its total banknote issue was at no time to exceed paid-up capital, and one-third thereof was to be covered by a cash reserve. However, fragmentary balance-sheet data suggest that this stipulation may not have been enforced after 1906.[43]

Imperial attempts at regulating banks and currency in China came too little, too late. When financial regulations were finally promulgated, the survival of the dynasty had already been predicated on synarchic pacts with the European Powers, so that the issue of quasi-foreign money or restrictions on foreign banking in general was hardly broached.[44] The Mackay Treaty signed between Britain and China on September 5, 1902 included, for example, an Imperial pledge to coin uniform currency "which shall be legal tender in payment of all duties taxes and other obligations throughout the Empire by British and Chinese subjects."[45] However, the Treaty made no reference to banknote issuance.

If anything, muffled protests against foreign bank prerogatives served as apologetics for the intractability of Chinese banknotes emanating from the periphery. A 1908 British *Diplomatic and Consular Report* reported, for example:

> The issue of notes has been resorted to both by provincial governments and private banks as a means of compensation for the loss of profits occasioned by the restrictions imposed by the Central Government on the output of the mints . . .
>
> The issue has been defended by the Chinese on the plea that it is not fair that the foreign banks should have a monopoly of the issue of bank notes, but this plea ignores the fact that neither the issues nor the reserves of the native banks are known with any certainty . . . [In] the case of some at least of the native banks now freely issuing notes, every principle of sound banking as recognized in Europe or America is violated, and that neither cash nor readily convertible security is held by these banks against their note issues. The foreign banks may therefore be acquitted of the absurd charge of trade jealousy, which has been brought against them for refusing to accept such notes freely.[46]

Similarly, the newspaper *Waijiao bao* quibbled in September 1909 that foreign banks could issue notes in China scot-free, only because Chinese merchants did the same without heeding sound reserve policy.[47]

A shift in attitudes might be discernible only in a July 1910 *Guofeng bao* report indicating, for the first time, that the Board of Finance was genuinely concerned about the spread of Russian banknotes in Mongolia and planned to set up branches of the Ta-Ching Government Bank (*Daqing yinhang*) there in order to disseminate Chinese banknotes.[48]

By then, however, Chinese and foreigners alike had realized that there was little substance behind the reformist rhetoric of the Qing government. In February 1910, William D. Little, chairman of the Shanghai Chamber of Commerce, concluded—based on advice received from the foreign banks—that Qing monetary measures were simply inadequate.[49]

The last reformist salvo was heard in June 1910, when the American Legation in Beijing translated yet another Board of Finance memorial urging the Imperial Court to ban all banknotes except those issued by the IBC.[50] But the directives emanating from Beijing were hopelessly contradictory, as an edict from the previous year permitted privately owned moneyshops to continue issuing notes to clients, provided that they were backed by five mercantile guarantors.[51] Good intentions notwithstanding, neither edict could have been implemented on the ground by a rapidly atrophying central authority.

THE EVOLUTION OF NOTE RESERVE REQUIREMENTS, 1866–1911

In the mid-nineteenth century, the Colonial Banking Regulations imposed fairly lenient reserve requirements against note issues by British overseas banks. In the grand scheme of things, the Lords Commissioners of the Treasury in Whitehall personified regulatory experience accumulated on the British Isles. Experience in Europe taught that private banks must be forced to keep coin reserve in proportion to the amount of banknotes they issued, and this rule was to be applied to the colonies too. However, quite often, monetary deviations from European norms had to be accommodated. The case for regulatory adjustment was made, in the first instance, by those who were more in tune with local realities—that is, colonial and dominion governments. The Secretary of State for the Colonies was their effective channel of communication with Treasury regulators. Since the East Asian treaty ports were not strictly under the secretary's jurisdiction, the Foreign Office and diplomatic corps had to be consulted too, when it came to the issue of quasi-foreign notes in China proper.

British overseas banks were generally expected to keep a specie reserve on the order of one-third of their notes outstanding in the treaty ports. However, in the absence of widespread telegraph facilities or robust metropolitan inspection, local branches were lightly regulated until the late 1890s, and the one-third reserve guideline was seldom enforced there.[52] The Hong Kong Ordinances, under which HSBC was incorporated, allowed the Bank to keep a single note reserve in its Hong Kong Head Office. In theory, therefore, banks headquartered in London were at a disadvantage because they were expected to maintain overlapping reserves to meet contingencies both in Hong Kong and in their other Asian branches.[53]

The Treasury was often preoccupied with issues other than specie reserve ratios. For example, the Treasury doggedly opposed the dissemination of small-denomination notes (valued under 5 silver dollars) in the colonies. In the main, this was predicated on domestic rather than colonial experience: acceptance of counterfeit, small-denomination notes by the illiterate or undiscerning poor was thought to have engendered the instability of country banking in mid-eighteenth-century England. The impecunious did not deal with large amounts of money (over 1 GBP in value) and did not seek to exchange bullion for anything but lower-denomination notes. Lower-denomination notes were therefore associated with forgery attempts directed at the poor.[54] The validity of this association is open to question, however. Lawrence White has argued, for example, that the instability of English country banks during that period did not stem from forgery but from restrictions on the number of shareholders, resulting in chronic undercapitalization.[55]

The British experience, which seemingly called for restriction on note denomination, was relatively easy to apply in Hong Kong and the Straits Settlements. Yet, the Treasury was uninformed about what was happening in China's treaty ports. There, British banks willfully violated the restriction by disseminating 1-tael and 1-Mexican dollar notes en masse.

The Treasury also subjected note issuance to the principle of double and, in HSBC's case, even unlimited liability. Double liability meant that note bearers were to receive preferential treatment, compared with other liability holders. If the equity of a failed note-issuing bank was depleted, note bearers could in theory foreclose on a corresponding amount from the shareholders' private property. In HSBC's case, such foreclosure could be unlimited in scope.

The failure of the Oriental Bank Corporation (OBC) in 1884—the oldest and hitherto largest British bank in Asia—was an important catalyst for intensifying Treasury regulation of overseas banks during the late nineteenth century.[56] As indicated in the previous chapter, OBC left hundreds of clients around the world clamoring for compensation. In Ceylon, where it had a particularly large note circulation, the crisis threatened to destabilize much of the colonial economy. Ceylon's governor therefore decided to underwrite the issue, setting a precedent for official protection of private note issues at which the Treasury fretted.[57]

The Treasury was now compelled to step up its scrutiny of far-flung territories to avoid a repetition of the Ceylon crisis. One upshot was that local coin or bullion reserves to support note issuance overseas were no longer deemed sufficient. When, in 1889, HSBC appealed to the Treasury for ex post recognition of its branches and note issuance outside Hong Kong, the Treasury presented a new condition: from now on the Bank was to deposit with trustees "securities specially appropriated to cover its note issue."[58] In practice, the Treasury's new guidelines entailed an additional note reserve to the metallic one, to be made up of tradable assets under lien to the colonial government. Furthermore, the reserves would now total two-thirds of the circulation volume—almost halving potential profits accruing from the fiduciary (read: unbacked) portion of the issue.[59]

Differences soon emerged between HSBC and the Treasury as to what assets could be designated as security. The Bank was naturally inclined to present idle resources: it offered over $1.1 million of the $2.5 million required in title deeds and private company bonds, which it had received against loans or purchase of branch premises. The remaining $1.5 million were to be covered by Chinese Imperial government bonds, which paid relatively high dividends, but hinged on the shifting political fortune of the Manchu Court. Unimpressed, the Treasury threatened to have the Colonial Office suspend the Bank's incorporation ordinance unless a different portfolio of securities was presented.[60] Faced with a near ultimatum and potential ramifications in the future, the Bank had to give in. In August 1890, it presented a new portfolio, which the Treasury could sanction: title deeds were to be replaced by colonial-government rupee bonds.[61]

Until the twentieth century, the Treasury did not specifically address the China issue because it was still insignificant as a share of the Bank's total issue. This was because of two very different reasons. Primarily, Chinese suspicion of paper notes had roots dating as far back as the fourteenth century, which meant that treaty-port demand for this medium of payment trailed far behind the vigorous monetization that typified Hong Kong and the Straits Settlements.[62] Apart from that, the British banks operating in East Asia were strategically concerned with the entrepôt trade flowing through the colonies. The banks, therefore, allocated a smaller portion of their global issue quotas, set by the Treasury, to the treaty ports.

The China issue became a strategic factor in British Exchange Bank thinking only in the early twentieth century, when it served as a counterweight to receding circulation volumes in Southeast Asia. As noted earlier, in 1902, moves by the Straits Settlements to replace the three private banks of issue—HSBC, CBIAC, and the Mercantile Bank of India (MBI)—with a sterling-pegged governmental currency came to fruition. A gold standard for the Straits had been on the drawing board in conjunction with a government issue a decade before, but was stonewalled by the three Eastern Exchange Banks until then.[63] Similar moves to introduce a governmental currency did not materialize in Hong Kong because its economy had been much more intimately linked with the silver-based Chinese economy. But perhaps more crucially, HSBC executives enjoyed an unusual rapport with many of the Colony's governors—a fact that may have clinched the survival of private banknote issuance there.[64]

To what extent was the loss of the Straits banknote issue a blow to the British banks? A proper answer would require an analysis of the profits accruing from local note issuance. Fortunately, some editions of the *Straits Settlement Government Gazette* recorded the reserves that the banks assigned for their local issue by virtue of an Order-in-Council, whereas reserves against the China issue were never specified in *Hong Kong Blue Book* aggregates. In August 1898, for example, HSBC assigned "unspecified specie and securities" totaling S$1.6 million against S$4 million of note circulation in Penang and Singapore.[65] This amounted to a 40 percent cover—26 percent less than the statutory reserve imposed on the Bank's issue in Hong Kong. It is therefore safe to assume that the reserve ratio was much lower in principal branches than in the Bank's Hong Kong headquarters and that local profit margins were similarly wider there.

The point can be further illustrated by using in-house data available for CBIAC. In 1898, this bank had a total reserve of S$1.3 assigned against just under S$4 million in circulation.[66] This amounted to just 33.3 percent cover for the local issue, of which only S$830,000 was metallic. With two-thirds of the issue unbacked, and allowing for a moderate interest rate of 2.5 percent, the bank was in a position to garner a gross profit of S$80,000 annually, if it channeled the fiduciary portion of the proceeds to its borrowing clients. When converted to sterling, profits accruing from the Straits issue alone may have constituted as much as 5 percent of CBIAC's total profits that year.[67]

Developments in the Straits Settlements at the turn of the century were compounded by the loss of smaller markets for banknotes in Japan and Siam, as governments there decided to revoke foreign bank privileges. HSBC's note circulation in the Japanese treaty ports of Kobe and Yokohama never attained much importance, but Bangkok had held out for some time the potential for large circulation volume. HSBC was the principal European bank entrusted with the paper money supply in Siam—the Chartered Bank and the Saigon-based Banque de l'Indochine played a much more modest role. In July 1902 all three banks were asked to withdraw their issue, which by then had amounted to about Tical 2.5 million in total.[68]

The issue quota set by the British banks for China rose immediately after they realized that they were about to lose Southeast Asian note markets. As early as 1899, the HSBC Head Office in Hong Kong informed the Shanghai branch that it had revised the cap placed on the circulation of locally denominated notes on the Mainland from $1 million to $1.5 million, two-thirds of which was allocated for Shanghai.[69] But despite the increase in HSBC circulation volumes on the Mainland, metallic and bond reserves that were meant to cover the issue remained in Hong Kong. In the absence of specific Treasury guidelines for China, the Bank had simply taken a calculated risk that it would be able to withstand possible redemption waves with minimal reserves.

Toward the end of the nineteenth century there was another important turning point in Treasury policy, which would counterweigh the gradual withdrawal of notes in the Straits. In 1898, the Treasury allowed HSBC's note circulation to exceed the Bank's paid-up capital for the first time, if the Bank was prepared to put up 100 percent metallic cover. The concession was made because the Bank and its proponents in the Hong Kong government argued that sudden demand spurts for notes in the Colony shortly before the Lunar New Year could only be met with a special "excess issue."[70] From then on, the Bank's total circulation quota grew according to a set pattern, whereby the "New Year" argument would be used repeatedly to incorporate previous ad hoc excess issues into the authorized one, while setting new excess caps for the future. This resulted, as from the end of the Imperial era in China, in total circulation levels that were far greater than paid-up capital, but backed by a larger metallic reserve.[71]

The evolution of reserve requirements imposed by the Treasury on the Bank during the late-Qing is summarized in Table 4.1.

Table 4.1 shows a steady rise in the global circulation quota that the Treasury sanctioned. However, this rise was accompanied by a narrowing down of the fiduciary (or unbacked) portion of the total issue. In other words, the potential for profit accruing from note issuance wore down over the course of time. Until 1888, the fiduciary ratio stood at 66.6 percent. In other words, as much as two-thirds of the silver bullion or coins that Bank clients paid in over the counter in return for notes could be on-lent without cover. Between 1889 and 1897 the fiduciary ratio dropped to one-third. In 1898 it stood at 22 percent, and it continued to diminish steadily thereafter. The overview suggests that profits accruing from note issuance during the Bank's formative years may have played a significant role in its meteoric rise.

How did the changes in the global issue quota project outside Hong Kong? By 1904, there were definite signs that popular suspicion of notes in China had subsided. In addition, the fact that HSBC's Shanghai branch was not required to hold metallic reserves against treaty-port circulation also made local managers keen to issue notes there. These factors were, however, tempered by a Head Office concerned primarily with the money supply in Hong Kong. In November 1904 the Head Office informed Shanghai: "We quite appreciate the difficulties you experience in having so limited a circulation, but you know the trouble we have each China New Year now in providing cover for

Table 4.1 HSBC Note Issue: Reserve Requirements, 1865–1906 (Unit: HK$ million)

	Metallic	Bonds	Fiduciary	Excess Issue	Max Total Issue
1865–1888	2.5	0	5	0	7.5
1889–1891	2.5	2.5	2.5	0	7.5
1892–1897	3.33	3.33	3.33	0	10
1898–1906	3.33	3.33	3.33	5	15

Source: Adapted from King (1987), vol. 1, pp. 119–122, 381–393, 446–447, 484–485; vol. 2, pp. 53–68.

the bank's large banknote circulation [in Hong Kong] at the time . . . After the] China New Year you may increase your limit to 20 lacs."[72]

In other words, the last tentative China quota set internally in 1899 (1.5 million silver dollars) was to increase by 0.5 million. The circulation grew apace from then on until about 1924. Extant branch records suggest that by 1908 Shanghai notes denominated in Mexican dollars reached a circulation of $1.5 million (about Tls. 1 million), and tael-denominated notes—a circulation of Tls. 115,000.[73] At the same time, demand in Tianjin and smaller treaty ports perked up. Overall, circulation of HSBC notes in Mainland China rose to a peak of $4.3 million circa 1923, by which time tael notes had largely been phased out.

On the eve of the Xinhai revolution (1911), which led to the overthrow of the Qing dynasty and the establishment of a Republic, the China issue had already supplanted Southeast Asia as the second most important market for notes in the Bank's strategy. The way in which the Head Office had come to view the issue of quasi-foreign notes on the Mainland was tersely stated in a memorandum it relayed to the Shanghai branch in December: "Your note issue in Shanghai does not embarrass us beyond our having to put up [Hong Kong] dollar for [Mexican] dollar here. So long as you do not object to incurring dollar liabilities at current price of Mexicans, and there should not be much risk in that, you may go on issuing notes moderately, say up to $30 lacs."[74]

The wording inevitably retains some of the Eastern Exchange Bank jargon. Put simply, the Head Office gave the branch permission to increase its circulation up to 3 million silver dollars (the value of the Hong Kong dollar and Mexican dollar current in Shanghai being similar). Yet, globally, the Bank had a considerable "excess issue" by 1911. Since its first priority was Hong Kong's money supply, and since no note reserves had been kept in China proper at that time, the Bank effectively designated its China issue as part of the "excess issue." Thus, the China issue required full metallic backing: one silver dollar in the Hong Kong central reserve for every dollar note disbursed in Shanghai. More importantly, the memorandum indicates that, even with 100 percent reserve set against it, the Shanghai issue was seen as a generally remunerative pursuit from a Head Office perspective.

Net profitability of the China issue may have stemmed from a combination of higher market interest rates in Shanghai, coupled with a cross-rate premium on the Mexican dollar against the Hong Kong dollar. Either way, there was another much more prosaic factor that made the China issue attractive: note issuance was exempt from both Chinese and foreign government tax in the treaty ports, whereas it incurred a 1 percent surcharge in Hong Kong.[75]

Other evidence to support the argument that the China note issue was, on balance, profitable is still circumstantial: HSBC archives contain a number of files documenting attempts by conmen to make the Bank disburse silver over the counter on presentation of fake notes, and the Bank's unstinting investment in improving printing plates and in other preventive measures. The first serious forgery could well have been the one which Charles Addis, then Beijing branch manager, entered into his private diary in 1903: "There has been a forgery of H&S Bank $5 notes, and there is alarm among the Chinese principally. The Bank has been kept open all day."[76]

This short entry also seems to suggest that most note bearers were Chinese rather than European expatriates. It is therefore plausible to assume that the first forgers were Chinese, and so were their victims. However, the quality of the forged notes was *not* such that the Bank considered forfeiting issuance altogether. At the same time, the Bank seemed to have spared no effort in trying to minimize the risk: in 1901, for example, the Shanghai branch accountant burned unsigned idle notes to the face value of over 1 million SH$.[77]

THE SHANGHAI BRANCH, 1866–1911

How important, then, was note issuance as compared with other business ends in Shanghai? Answers should naturally be drawn from local business records. The Bund was home to a large number of foreign banks of issue before the Communist takeover. Yet, not many of the prewar balance sheets pertaining to the HSBC branch survived. This section will therefore aim at describing circulation patterns from whatever little quantitative data is available.

The first generality that emerges from the records is that the Bank had assigned a very important role for local banknote issuance right from its inception, however disappointing initial circulation returns were. As early as 1866, the Bank ordered from London printers notes to the face value of SH Tls. 1 million.[78] This required foresight because quasi-foreign banknotes use in Shanghai had until then faltered; CBIAC, for example, withdrew its first issue just three years later. The earliest entry for HSBC shows a circulation of Tls. 24,000 in Shanghai in December 1866, but by January 1867 the figure dipped as low as Tls. 10,000. Year-end results show the circulation rebounding back again to Tls. 57,000, and redemption velocity much lower. HSBC could claim a circulation volume of Tls. 140,950 as early as 1873, while CBIAC resumed its issue in the city as late as 1886. In 1875, HSBC Shanghai note circulation was substantially down again at Tls. 76,563.[79]

What does this tell us? In sum, HSBC could not make good on its vision of introducing up to Tls. 1 million into circulation within a short period of time. Initial circulation volumes were erratic, reflecting the unwillingness of treaty-port clients to receive notes instead of silver over the counter. This retells much the same pattern implicit in the CBIAC ledgers, although early HSBC issues fared somewhat better. These figures might ring hollow in the ears of nonspecialists unless juxtaposed with the overall size of HSBC's Shanghai branch activities. Tables 4.2 and 4.3 illustrate the role early note issuance played in branch activity, based on two local balance sheets that have been preserved in their entirety.

Table 4.2 shows that effective midyear circulation in 1876 reached just under 1.5 percent of the local balance-sheet total—much less than the overall global Bank ratio of notes to liabilities, which stood at 4.1 percent at the same time.[80] Bullion holdings in Shanghai were about four times larger than notes outstanding, but no portion thereof is specifically set against note issuance. At 12.4 percent, the Shanghai cash to liabilities ratio is likewise lower than the global Bank ratio of 13 percent.[81] Clearly, the demand for fiduciary money in Shanghai during that period trailed far behind the vigorous demand for notes in Hong Kong and the Straits that published Bank aggregates reflect.

More importantly, the distribution of balance-sheet entries indicates that locally derived business made up a much more significant share of Shanghai branch operations than previously thought. In particular, Baster's influential work construed the first British banks operating in East Asia as institutions uniquely concerned with the provision of short-term credit for trading firms by discounting bills and foreign currency exchange.[82] Nonetheless, Table 4.2 demonstrates that the volume of entries strictly associated with the finance of Eurasian and Intra-Asian trade (interagency flows, Head Office accounts, and

Table 4.2 HSBC Shanghai Branch Balance Sheet, June 30, 1876
(Unit: Shanghai Taels [000])

Assets		Liabilities	
Cash	329.4	Branch Capital	1,092
Metallic Bullion	334.7	Note Circulation	78.5
Advances and Loans	2,383.6	Current Accounts	1,291.7
Interagency Account	1,958.3	Interagency Account	1,060.8
Bills for Collection	32.3	Deposits	720.2
Head Office Account	8.8	Head Office Account	212.8
Sundry Accounts	125.1	Suspended Accounts	695.2
Profit and Loss	163.2	Sundry Accounts	40.2
		Bills in Hand	32.3
		Bills Payable	7.5
		Profit and Loss	104.1
Total	**5,335**	**Total**	**5,335**

Source: HSBC Group Archives (hereafter HSBC GA), SHG LEDG 46. The Profit and Loss entry on the asset side refers to interest paid by the branch to depositors and general operation costs, while, on the liability side, the same entry refers to commission and interest revenue.

bill of exchange balances) made up only 37 percent of local assets or 48 percent of liabilities. The lion's share of branch activity was, in turn, devoted to business contracted locally—loans, fixed deposits, and current accounts.

It is therefore plausible to assume that from very early on the Mainland branches of the Bank engaged in the provision of retail banking services as part of their strategy. Their note issue should then be understood as a prop for locally contracted business launched against the backdrop of volatile monetary and political conditions outside the treaty ports, that is, providing a means to attract depositors, safeguard credit to indigenous borrowers, and reduce shroffing costs.

That attracting Chinese clients was at the heart of incipient branch activity is perhaps best illustrated by a letter Addis sent in 1866 to A. Leith of the Bank's Tianjin agency, in which he promised to be more cautious in the future when cashing "Drafts to Natives."[83] The letter further suggests that much of the Beijing branch meager cash balance (Tls. 1,699) had been kept in anticipation of bill redemption by clients holding HSBC drafts issued in Tianjin, and that this flow made up an important part of the Bank's business in North China.

Capital flows between Shanghai and other branches of the Bank, as captured in the 1876 balance sheet, are also revealing. Under the left-hand interagency aggregate, branches in India emerge as the single largest creditor to Shanghai (Tls. 0.85 million or 80 percent of the entire entry), suggestive of exports consigned from Bombay, with comparatively miniscule backflow of Chinese exports bound for Calcutta. London was by far the largest net debtor of the branch (Tls. 1.9 million or 97 percent of the entire entry), while traffic between the branch and Head Office in Hong Kong was surprisingly small (Tls. 8,400 in debit).[84] Globally, the Shanghai branch was net creditor (Tls. 0.9 million). Contrary to conventional wisdom, then, these figures suggest that, less than a decade after it was opened, the Shanghai branch could already draw on local resources to support a surplus of Chinese exports to the British Empire, that is, reverse capital flow from the periphery to the metropole. This sweeping conclusion should be qualified, however, by two critical variables: we do not know the exact percentage of branch capital (Tls. 1.09 million) that had been subscribed locally by ethnic Chinese.[85] Similarly, we do not have data on the proportion of loans funneled to importers of Indian or British goods.

Another rare balance sheet, dated April 9, 1881, demonstrates the pattern in which the branch expanded in its formative period (see Table 4.3). The balance-sheet total is now at Tls. 6,514,861—a vigorous growth rate of 22 percent over five years echoing the Bank's overall growth rate.[86] Note that circulation is at Tls. 126,000, up by 47,000 on 1876, but still under 2 percent of total liabilities. Fixed deposits almost doubled from Tls. 720,200 to 1.4 million, making them the fastest growing entry alongside current accounts. These changes are translated, on the asset side, into a rise of Tls. 0.8 million in loans and advances. Globally, the branch is now a much bigger global net creditor (Tls. 1.6 million), although total intrabank capital flows as a whole are down by 20 percent. The growth pattern is generalized in Table 4.3.

Table 4.3 demonstrates that between 1876 and 1881 locally derived business was by far the fastest growing arm of the branch, offsetting a downturn in trade flows with Great Britain in the late 1870s.[87] This lends credence to an insightful observation the Chinese economic historian Wang Jingyu made in 1983. Wang claimed that the founding of HSBC revolutionized the modus operandi of British banks in East Asia in that, following its lead, foreign banks began to eagerly pursue resources from treaty-port dwellers (ethnic Chinese included)—mainly by attracting fixed deposits.[88] In that sense, HSBC was very different from the OBC, which had dominated the treaty-port economy until the 1870s, because the OBC branch in Shanghai had been almost exclusively pitched at discounting bills of exchange and lending to Chinese officialdom.

Table 4.3 Changes in Main Balance-Sheet Entries of the HSBC Shanghai Branch, June 1876 through April 1881

Entry	Percentage Change
Note Circulation	+60%
Fixed Deposits	+96%
Current Accounts	+104%
Advances and Loans	+33%
Cash and Bullion	+70%
Total Interagency and Head Office Turnover	–20%
Credit Balance with Overseas Branches	+78%
Total Liabilities = Total Assets	**+22%**

Source: Calculated from HSBC GA, SHG LEDG 46.

HSBC deposit agglomeration trends in Shanghai dovetail with longer-term figures available for CBIAC, from which it appears that fixed deposits did become a more crucial constituent of British banking in Shanghai during the 1870s and 1880s (see Figure 4.2).

But while Wang was generally right in his interpretation of foreign banking trends, concrete local circulation figures explicitly disprove assertions made by other Chinese scholars. Based on contemporaneous press reports, Zhang Guohui has argued, for example, that the aggregate face value of British banknote circulation in Shanghai in 1874 was $3.5 million and that HSBC accounted for more than 51 percent thereof.[89] Notably, the HSBC Shanghai balance sheet of 1876 put local circulation at Tls. 78,563 (or $109,878), a substantially lower figure than the $1.75 million imputed to Zhang's English-language press source.

Much of the literature on quasi-foreign banknotes in prewar China has been similarly premised on amorphous circulation estimates or, in the second instance, on emotive descriptions of how foreign banks flouted Chinese monetary sovereignty. But these estimates and descriptions merely serve to deflect scholars' attention, both in China and in the West, from the fact that note issuance mainly served as the lubricant of an infinitely more significant turnaround, which saw foreign banks employing treaty-port deposits to finance international and intra-Asian trade, as well as loans contracted locally.

How deposits were employed locally is a question of particular interest to economic historians because it has a direct bearing on our understanding of access to capital in prewar Shanghai, and therefore on its unique path to industrialization. Although there can be little doubt that foreign banks mobilized

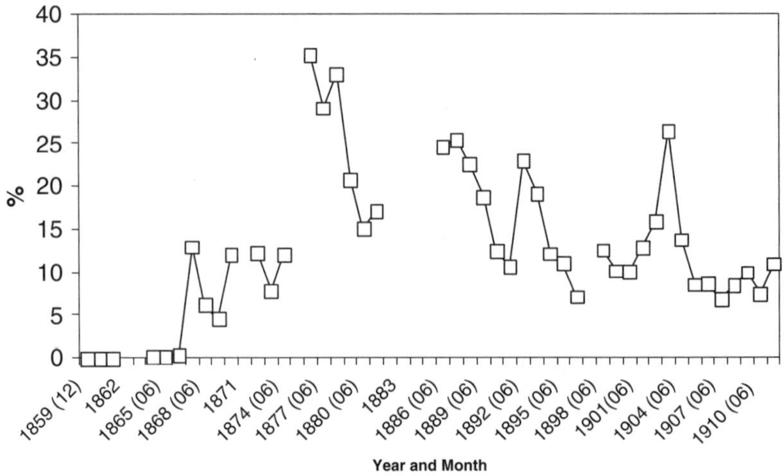

Figure 4.2 CBIAC Shanghai Branch: Fixed Deposits as Percentage of Total Liabilities, 1859–1911. *Source*: CBIAC GL Ms 31519/1–25.

vast amounts of silver capital from Chinese government agencies like the Imperial Maritime Customs, as well as from individual Chinese depositors, opinions vary as to *how* and *to whom* this capital was allocated.[90]

Any locally mobilized funds that foreign banks might have ploughed back into the indigenous sector of Shanghai's economy would have had to be mediated through the city's famous factor agents—the compradors. In a well-known monograph, Hao Yen-p'ing has concluded that the compradors were indispensable for China's seminal industrialization both as intermediaries between foreign banks and the domestic sector, and as entrepreneurs in their own right.[91] But the data presented by Hao on the import of comprador investment in Imperial and privately owned modern ventures in Shanghai conflict with other analyses, which strongly suggest that Chinese privately owned industrial firms were chronically undercapitalized right until 1930s and all but shunned by British bank decision makers throughout the prewar era.[92]

Geoffrey Jones, who has devoted many years of research to the history of British banks in Asia as a whole, offered an apt interpretation of their lending practices: "Within the context that the banks regarded their legitimate business to be trade finance and exchange operations, decisions on lending were based on risk rather than ethnicity. However, the risk assessment most definitely did take into account ethnicity, to the detriment of Asians for the most part."[93]

Hao and Jones have ably drawn two different sketches of the Sino-foreign encounter. Yet more robust data may be needed before Shanghai's prewar economy becomes fully understood. Case study analyses may fill some of the gaps in the bigger picture; the analysis presented here was conceived precisely to that end.

Was HSBC's note issue harmful in any way to the Chinese sector of the treaty-ports economy during the late-Imperial era? In the absence of coercion on note bearers or of reliable Chinese alternatives, the question may seem almost unwarranted. As shown earlier, the circulation volumes of quasi-foreign notes were much lower than previously thought, and Chinese critics largely ignored their contribution to China's reformist discourse. Having said that, it is important to remember that the note issue helped attract a large number of Chinese depositors, who unconditionally entrusted their fortunes to a Bank that was otherwise alienated from the domestic economy. In that sense, it may well be argued that the Bank's note issue in the treaty ports helped entrench a skewed capital allocation.

WARLORDISM DURING THE BEIYANG PERIOD (1912–1925)

Historians of Republican China have long grappled with the complexities of warlordism. Theorizing this phenomenon, or couching it in social-science models, is an inordinately difficult task because the term itself—*warlord* (*junfa* 軍閥)—not only carries with it onerous premodern baggage, but is also shorthand for a motley crew of militarists, myriad satrapies, and, in some cases, barely traceable alliances.[94]

The initial scholarly thrust in the West was therefore centered on an analysis of individual warlords—their characteristic shade of governance, their religious beliefs, doctrines, client-patronage systems, and so on.[95] Most scholars have since concluded, in one way or another, that the disintegration of civilian authority in China had inevitably sprung from the complete collapse of the Confucian system of values and dynastic world-order in 1911. But, recently, more and more new studies have taken a longer-term view, tracing the paralysis of central authority further back in time to the emaciation of state revenue in the face of rapid population growth, which had characterized the Ming-Qing eras.[96] Although early-Republican budget figures may not be entirely reliable, few scholars now question the fact that by honoring foreign debts incurred by the ancien régime, and borrowing yet more, the new Republican government compromised its executive powers and popular support base.[97]

For most ordinary Chinese the breakdown of central authority in the 1910s often spelled unspeakable depredation. However, for the foreign banks and for the indigenous mercantile elite operating within the safety of the treaty ports, this was a veritable golden age. Chinese bankers, for example, took advantage of the new circumstances to extricate themselves from the claws of an ever demanding, yet incapacitated, Treasury in Beijing to establish independent financial institutions that, in time, would co-opt and often outpace their foreign counterparts.[98] Foreign banks, in turn, could thrive on loans to the Chinese government, which the latter could secure only by pledging an increasingly large proportion of future customs revenue.

As long as Beijing's grip on the periphery was contested by secessionist elements, the prospect of a Chinese government opening up a second front against foreign privileges like extraterritoriality or banknote issuance was minimal. Conversely, no individual warlord had enough moral authority or firepower to mount an attack on the treaty-port paradigm: most solicited foreign military assistance in one way or another themselves.

But, ironically, it was the reckless inflationary policies (*lanfa wujie* 濫發無節) of the warlord era that made banknotes familiar to dwellers of all but the most remote counties in the hinterland.[99] Because satrapies tampered with the once more reliable copper coinage by driving their own mints to use inferior raw materials, they spread general distrust in money and blurred the traditional boundary between the fiduciary and metallic. The pervasive political uncertainty and inflationary fiscal policies of the times generally compounded a flight from means of payment identified with the central government, as well as with the warlords, toward money that was endorsed in the treaty ports by either Chinese private banks or foreign banks.

The surging popularity of quasi-foreign notes in China coincided with the phaseout of HSBC's Southeast Asian issue in the 1910s. The Bank immediately sensed that, in addition to vigorous monetization in Hong Kong, a secondary market was opening up for its notes on the Chinese Mainland. Thus, it began to lobby the British Treasury to modify its global allocation quotas in a way that would allow disbursement of more notes in China. During the early 1910s, there was a flurry of correspondence between HSBC, CBIAC, and the undersecretary of state at the Colonial Office in an attempt to seal a deal with the Treasury, whereby the large issues of the two banks in Singapore and Penang would be supplanted by bigger quotas for Greater China.[100]

The Banks' argumentation had to be adapted to suit the tastes of Treasury regulators, whose main concern, during that period, was the money supply in colonial Hong Kong, but who took much less interest in the growing demand for notes in the Chinese treaty ports. Therefore, in their representations,

CBIAC and HSBC focused solely on Hong Kong as the raison d'être of their reallocation bid.

This strategy was not lost on a reincarnation of the Chartered Mercantile Bank. CMBILC had lost its note issue prerogatives when it was reconstituted as MBI in 1893, and it was now trying to recover its position in Greater China by underscoring conditions in Hong Kong. MBI complained in letters to the Treasury that the HSBC and CBIAC duopoly on note issuance in the Colony created a premium on HK$ notes over silver coinage of about 3.5 percent. This, it claimed, was indicative of money supply shortfalls, which made the entry of another bank of issue desirable.[101] The Treasury was persuaded by the argument, but it chose to impose much stricter reserve requirements on MBI than on the bigger two banks, reflecting concerns about the Chartered Mercantile Bank's past performance. Although its profit potential was significantly cut, MBI renewed its note issuance in Hong Kong in 1911 and, as if by default, in Shanghai circa 1920.[102]

Internally, HSBC executives had been ambivalent about the long-term prospects of the China issue because successive Chinese governments were toying with the idea of unifying all forms of currency management under their wings as a form of indirect taxation. Although the central government was far too hamstrung at that stage to implement such reforms on the ground, HSBC executives were mindful of the implications such a move might one day have for the Bank's modus operandi on the Mainland. As early as 1917, Sir Newton Stabb, the Hong Kong–based chief manager, wrote to A. G. Stephen, then manager of the Shanghai branch:

> With regard to the question of abolishing sycee and making the currency of China a universal dollar, my opinion is that whether the change would suit us or not, we must support it. A universal dollar for China has been the cry for years past and I think such a currency (always provided the mints are under control and can be depended upon to maintain the standard of the coin) would be of such benefit to trade generally that you would gain much more by the change [than] you would lose over the loss of interport exchange and tael-dollar business.[103]

At the same time, the Bank's staff in China proper thought that the prevalent monetary conditions there afforded unique business opportunities. In a letter dated October 1919, A. G. Stephen wrote to Charles Addis who, at the end of his long tenure in Asia, had returned home to eventually preside over the Bank's London office: "Very possibly the fact that outside the Shanghai Banks' Notes and a small local issue of Notes by Foreign Banks at the treaty-ports, there is not now a single reliable Note available in China (of course leaving out of account Hongkong Notes), has created an unusual demand for Silver dollars all over the country."[104]

The letter also indicated that 40 million ounces of dollar coinage that the then dysfunctional Republican government had minted from imported silver in Nanjing, Tianjin, and Wuchang was already gobbled up by the Chinese interior. The comparative reliability and ubiquity of those central government dollar coins—commonly known as *Yuan da tou* 袁大頭—rendered the use of traditional silver bars ("sycee shoes") outmoded because the sycee could not be used in business transactions without a costly nod of approval from third-party assayers.[105]

Since the Bank did not itself mint coins, it was prepared to welcome universal metallic Chinese currency, provided that it was overseen by foreign advisers rather than launched independently. Chinese or British government oversight of paper money circulation in the treaty ports was a thornier issue that bank correspondence usually skirted; here the Bank was a player, not just an observer. On the whole, the Bank's guarded policy in the Republican period reflected decades of anticipation of monetary reforms that never materialized in the late-Qing.[106]

Though equally circumspect, the British diplomatic corps in China was less ambivalent than the Bank toward an imminent Chinese monetary reform, arguably because it represented wider group interests. British trading firms were one such group. They bore the brunt of the foreign banks' interport exchange commission, and they were clamoring for uniform currency. In late 1919, J. N. Jordan, the British minister in Beijing, urged the Chinese foreign ministry (*waijiao bu* 外交部) to heed the pleas of British merchants for the abolition of sycee and the standardization of dollar and subsidiary copper coinage, after previous pledges by the Imperial regime had come to naught. More importantly, Jordan warned of the grave consequences of currency debasement by provincial mints, which was tarnishing the credibility of the central government.[107]

Although they benefited from interport exchange commission, the fragmented monetary situation in China required foreign banks to closely monitor interport market trends. One such important bellwether in Shanghai was the *yangli* 洋釐—that is, the exchange rate between the silver dollar as a medium of payment and *kungkued* or shroffed sycee. A seasonal influx of commodities or sycee from the hinterland to Shanghai made the dollar comparatively dearer and vice versa. These two means of payment were far from perfect substitutes, not least because dollar coins—especially Mexican—were considered more reliable when paying for raw silk, soybeans, or tea. Movement in the balance of dollar–sycee stock immediately affected private indebtedness in Shanghai because, until 1933, current accounts were run on the basis of an abstract unit of account (Shanghai Tael), derived from "sycee shoes," but were mostly payable in hard Mexican dollar coins.

Chinese observers often noted that, as the largest single depository of silver in the city, HSBC was in a position to manipulate the *yangli* and foreign currency exchange rate to maximize commission revenue.[108] This was thought to be an unscrupulous stratagem designed to exploit China's monetary fragmentation. The allegation against the Bank has not yet been persuasively corroborated or refuted. Neither is there direct evidence in the Bank's archives to support either argument. If *yangli* exchange profits in Shanghai had been substantial, it stands to reason that the Bank would have been more opposed to single currency than extant in-house records suggest.

There is, on the other hand, sufficient evidence to bear out the Bank's primacy in Shanghai's financial markets, at least circa 1900s. Figure 4.3 illustrates the HSBC's share of the total amount of sycee in the city, based on the findings of a Head Office inspector who had been dispatched to the branch in October 1915.

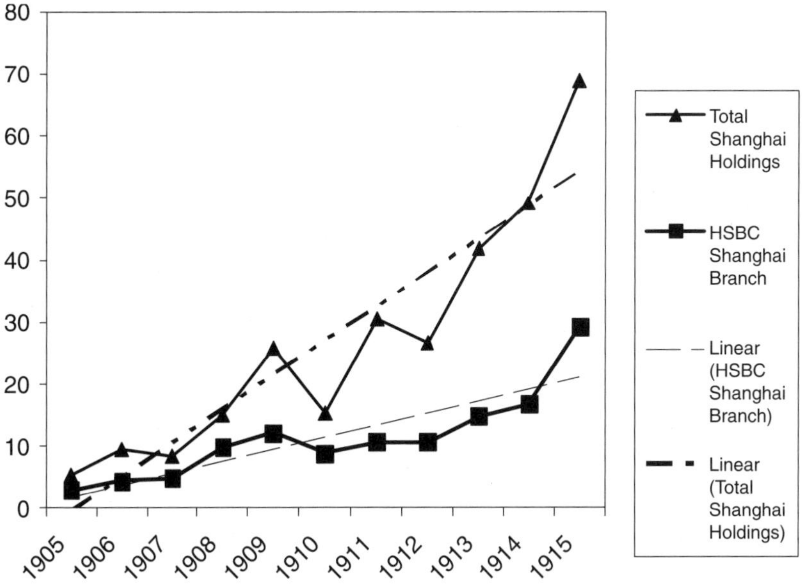

Figure 4.3. HSBC and Total Sycee Holdings in Shanghai, Year-End 1905–1915. Unit: SH Tls (million). *Source*: HSBC GA London II, Box 8, Item 123 (Inspector's Report on Shanghai, October 22, 1915).

Table 4.4 The HSBC Shanghai Branch Cash Balance Makeup, October 22, 1915 (Unit: Shanghai Dollars)

Banknote Specification		Balance Makeup	
HSBC	195	Banknotes	12,000
CBIAC	2,420	Mexican Dollar Coins	1,607,654
Banque Russo-Asiatique	1,950	Chinese Dollar Coins	3,854
International Banking Corp.	510	Hong Kong Subsidiary Coins	60
Banque Belge pour l'Etranger	490	Local Subsidiary Coins	0.55
Netherlands Trading Society	565	Chinese Copper Coins	0.02
Deutsch-Asiatische Bank	160		
Imperial Bank of China	1,440		
Bank of Communications	2,815		
Bank of China	1,455		
Total	**12,000**	**Total**	**1,623,568.57**

Source: HSBC GA London II, Box 8, Item 123 (Inspector's Report on Shanghai, dated October 22, 1915).

However fast banknote circulation volumes were growing in the late 1910s, the Bank's large silver holdings were used primarily to support other liabilities rather than serve strictly as note reserves. In mid-1915, notes outstanding in Shanghai totaled just under \$3.5 million, while the stock of sycee was estimated at Tls. 9.85 million or about \$13.7 million. In other words, sycee holdings were 3.9 times bigger than the face value of all notes outstanding. Those figures compare somewhat favorably with mid-1916 data for the CBIAC branch in Shanghai, where sycee and bullion reserves were only twice as large as note circulation.[109] In all, however, respective branch ratios were not all that far apart: the Shanghai total reserve to note ratio was 3.9 for CBIAC and only slightly higher at 4.3 for HSBC.

Fortunately, the same Inspector's Report of 1915 provides details on the makeup of the liquid cash reserve. Table 4.4 offers a glimpse at the types of currency circulating (other than sycee) in Shanghai at the time that the Bank was prepared to accept.

Table 4.4 shows that by 1915, HSBC was prepared to accept three types of Chinese state banknotes despite prevailing uncertainties about the salubrity of the domestic banking sector, whereas in the late-Imperial era the Bank accepted Imperial Bank of China notes only. The novelty may well have been related to the fact that the Shanghai branches of the Bank of Communications and the Bank of China were less yielding to Beiyang government pressure than the branches in Beijing, which were beyond the pale of foreign extraterritoriality.[110]

One other feature of the 1915 cash balance is the liminal share of dollar and subsidiary coins issued by China's Provincial Mints—merely 0.2 percent of the total. Clearly, Chinese currency, in either note or coin form—was not highly regarded.

When juxtaposed, other Inspector Reports from 1915 represent an important quantitative source on the volatile business climate in early-Republican China as they feature fairly synchronic information from several commercial hubs.[111] Several historians have identified a widening gap between economic growth rates and living standards in the hinterland and China's littoral provinces during the 1910s.[112] The Reports suggest that, at least from a monetary standpoint, bifurcation was to be found not only between center and periphery, or between various macro-regions, but also among the treaty ports themselves.

Table 4.5 shows that the ratios of paper notes to silver coinage are completely different in each of the treaty-port branches, suggesting widely different dynamics of monetization at work.[113] Surprisingly, in Shanghai notes made up only 7.4 percent of the balance (excluding sycee holding), while in Qingdao and Hankou they made up 5 percent. In less commercialized Beijing, however, notes made up as much as 21.3 percent of the balance.

One probable reason why monetization patterns were so different was the fact that principal banks of issue, be they foreign or domestic, varied spatially. Deutsch-Asiatische Bank (DAB) and Yokohama Specie Bank (YSB), for example, seem to have had a minor standing as note issuers in Shanghai. But 1,200 km further up the coast, in German-administered Qingdao, DAB and yen-denominated YSB notes made up the entire balance.[114] In inland Harbin, HSBC ledgers were denominated in gold-based Roubles, while in Dalian [Dairen] HSBC ledgers were denominated in Silver and Gold Yen.[115]

In Hankou, DAB notes are completely absent from the note balance totaling $21,409, but so are other British, European, and American banknotes, which prefigured in the Shanghai cash balance—with the sole exception of the Russo-Asiatic Bank ($2,000). Conversely, Hubei provincial government notes made up the majority ($10,929) of the branch's note balance.[116]

The degree of receptivity toward Chinese banks is similarly variegated. In Shanghai quasi-foreign notes constituted only 47 percent of all notes in the balance, while in Qingdao no Chinese bank note was accepted over the counter. In Hankou and Beijing, quasi-foreign notes made up 25 percent and 67 percent of the total note balance, respectively.

This large HSBC stock of Hubei Provincial Bank note holdings in Hankou contrasts sharply with all other branches and illustrates the difficulty of

Table 4.5 Liquid Cash Balances in HSBC China Branches, 1915 (Unit: Silver Dollars)

	Quasi-/Foreign	Chinese	Total
Shanghai			
Banknotes	5,710	6,290	12,000
Silver Coins	1,607,714	3,854	1,611,568
Sycee	N/A	40,465,864	40,465,864
Total			**42,089,432**
	Quasi-/Foreign	Chinese	Total
Qingdao			
Banknotes	7,424	0	7,424
Silver Coins	131,613	21,450	153,063
Sycee	N/A	73,400	73,400
Total			**233,887**
	Quasi-/Foreign	Chinese	Total
Hankou			
Banknotes	5,470	15,939	21,409
Silver Coins	27,574	381,411	408,985
Sycee	N/A	1,077,559	1,077,559
Total			**1,507,953**
	Quasi-/Foreign	Chinese	Total
Beijing			
Banknotes	33,525	15,802	49,327
Silver Coins	74,000	157,543	231,543
Sycee	N/A	1,197,273	1,197,273
Total			**1,478,143**

Source: Inspector's Report in HSBC GA L II 8.123; sycee figures for Qingdao, Beijing, and Shanghai were originally given as Jiaozhou Tls. 49,417.6, Gongfa Tls. 823,125.27, and Shanghai Tls. 28,933,092.87, respectively. These were converted to silver dollar units based on Morse (1921 [1967]), pp. 174–175, 178–180; *Zhongguo jindai zhibi shi* (2001), p. 23.

applying uniform guidelines from the Head Office to a vast and fragmented country. In the Beijing branch, for example, the Inspector remarked that attitudes were circumspect even as regards much more reputable Chinese banks—that is, the Bank of Communications and Bank of China—than was the case in Hubei:

> It will be seen that the notes of two Chinese banks appear in the Cash Balance. The amounts are not large and I am informed that particular care is taken not to allow the holding of such notes to exceed say $20,000 . . . There does not appear to be any special reserve of cash against the note issue [of the Bank of Communications and the Bank of China].[117]

Through the late 1910s, as debasement and overprinting in warlord-dominated areas grew completely out of control, small strides toward internalizing the specifics of Western reserve requirements and the implications of their sheer lack of enforcement in China became noticeable in the popular press.[118] For foreign banks, however, overprinting was a living proof of the incorrigibility of China's finances; for China's need to continue maintaining the presence of foreign advisers, and for the indispensability of foreign financial institutions. Foreign banks decried the lack of central banking, but at the same time were secretive with respect to the larger volumes of notes they had printed to satisfy demand for secure means of payment in the Republican era. In a joint statement they published in early 1920, the foreign banks stated:

> In foreign countries the issue of paper money is generally an exclusive prerogative of the central government, and is entrusted to the government banks. Lately, mercantile establishments have multiplied and the note issue has increased daily. Officials have regarded this as a way to accumulate funds, and the merchants as a way to make profit. If a method is not devised to control this, there will soon be no ready money for the official receipts and disbursements, and in the market there will be nothing but worthless paper. Prices will rise, and the people will suffer poverty. The danger is hard to appreciate . . . [Chinese dollar coins] are now circulating all over the Northern Provinces and are penetrating into Manchuria and Mongolia, displacing the discredited Chinese bank notes.[119]

A second round of inspection of HSBC's Mainland branches was conducted in 1922, by the outspoken Thomas S. Baker, whose long and versatile career with the Bank had comprised the roles of Yokohama branch accountant and Singapore and San Francisco branch manager.[120] In the introduction to his internal report, he gave a sobering appraisal of China's predicament, which was less diplomatic in tenor than the joint statement published by the foreign banks in 1920:

> The form of government at the present time in China is ostensibly a Republic, but actually the principal Provinces are more or less in the hands of Military Dictators who are ravaging and ruining the country by plundering revenues of Railways,

> imposing levies on towns and villages and in some cases seizing the revenues of the Salt Gabelle, whilst as a rash expedient of raising funds for military purposes a fiduciary note issue of $30 million in copper value is seriously contemplated by the Tuchuns [Dujuns] of Chili [Zhili].[121]

Baker's impressions are valuable because they provide a financial expert's perspective on the degree of destruction that warlordism wreaked upon China's hinterland economy. This is supported by more recent work. In a comprehensive study of warlordism in central China, Edward McCord has shown, for example, that pernicious inflationary policies, extortion of merchants, arbitrary taxation, and pillaging of property rights may have been much more ruinous than shrapnel.[122]

Baker wrote at the time that he had "little doubt" that economic conditions in China deteriorated since Republicanism had been introduced, with sycee gradually disappearing from the interior in favor of locally minted dollars of uneven quality, and with worthless paper money inundating Hunan, Hubei, and Guangdong.[123]

A Maritime Customs report from the early-Republican period resonates with much the same judgment, as it exemplified the consequences of warlordism in the southeastern reaches of Sichuan province:

> Heavy military taxation . . . and an abnormal high price for rice—nearly 100 percent higher than in ordinary times—counteracted in part the favorable conditions under which the port was trading. The high price of rice was due, it is said, partly to lack of proper attention being paid to the preceding year's crop, owing to the conscription of many agricultural laborers on the part of the military, and partly because many of the farmers are substituting poppy cultivation, as being more profitable, for rice. Whatever advantages the Chungking [Chongqing] trade may have gained during the first quarter of the year were lost during the following quarters, on account of . . . the increased military taxation, already very high, and, finally, the outbreak of hostilities between rival [warlord] factions.[124]

Clearly, it was the troubled interior that was pulling China away from the traditional tael system—a world apart from the relative security of the treaty ports, where sycee holdings amassed; possessing sufficient quantities of metallic money, British banks in the treaty ports were nevertheless not inclined to meet the voracious demand for reliable money that followed the debasement of traditional coinage. Disbursing more notes in the treaty ports than they already had would have contravened their global issue quotas. The disparities between the foreign and domestic banks of issue were now more pronounced compared with the late-Qing era. Chinese paper money increased by leaps and bounds, becoming a more dominant feature of the money supply.[125]

Thomas Baker's visit to the relatively new Chefoo (Yantai) branch in September 1922 coincided with preparations for the first HSBC issue in this outport. It thus provides an intimate account of the underlying rationale behind the China issue. The inspector noted that common currencies in Yantai had hitherto included Tael-denominated bars, silver dollars, and HSBC notes transported from Shanghai. Baker warned of a precedent whereby small outport branches like Yantai disbursed inordinate amounts of HSBC Shanghai notes, since the silver reserve held against them was not held locally, and sudden inability to redeem them could harm the Bank's reputation. Instead, Baker recommended that HSBC China notes be strictly prescribed per locality with on-site backing.[126]

Nonetheless, Baker was not entirely sure if a *local* issue in Yantai was feasible, owing to its ambiguous legal status: "I understand it is intended that this Agency [Yantai] shall have a small note issue of its own, but I am not sure that the Taoyin [Daoyin] of [Shandong] or the Peking Government would allow our bank to issue notes of its own in [Yantai] where no Foreign Settlement exists."[127]

Short of providing data to compare with other local cash balances in 1915, Baker's tour of 1922 did contain background information that might help us better understand the dynamics of quasi-foreign banknotes.

On Shanghai, Baker commented that quasi-foreign notes "circulate at par with one another," but that YSB and the Bank of Taiwan had to curtail their issue due to their "unpopularity." This was undoubtedly an allusion to the swingeing anti-Japanese boycott during the May Fourth or *Wusi* Movement (1919).[128] In Qingdao, on the other hand, Baker observed that YSB Silver Yen notes had become "the actual currency of this port," thus supplanting DAB notes, which had been predominant until the outbreak of World War I.[129]

Regrettably, Baker did not seem to have produced reports on South China branches and agencies, which had probably fallen under Head Office purview. Nonetheless, the monetary fragmentation in South China was described in other correspondence between the Banks' nodes in Hong Kong, London, and politically sensitive Beijing. This correspondence also demonstrates the extent to which HSBC played a role in the politics of South China.[130]

In September 1922, A. H. Barlow, then deputy chief manager at the Head Office, wrote to Sir Newton Stabb, the London office manager and a former chief manager himself, that Guangdong was "flooded" with paper money issued by the once GMD-backed provincial bank and, consequently, "trade is very much hampered." In the same breath, Barlow was pleased to communicate the news that the warlord Chen King Ming (Chen Jiongming 陳炯明) had just deposed the Nationalist caretaker government in the province and would put currency matters "on better footing."[131] The Head Office was to extend a helping hand to Chen by temporarily accepting in its Guangzhou-Shameen branch a deposit of $10 million from the provincial bank paid in provincial notes on twelve months' maturity and generous 8 percent interest made payable in metallic silver, with the hope of tiding Chen's regime over.

Public pronouncements aside, the Bank continued to display ambivalence about China's political and economic fragmentation. Yet, this ambivalence can only come to light if banking praxis is disentangled from executive views, as expressed in quotidian correspondence between the Head Office and Mainland branches. The first disbursement of HSBC banknotes in Yantai in 1922 is a case in point, because it came about at a time when the Bank's management projected indifference to its China issue as a whole.

A letter from A. H. Barlow to E. G. Hillier, HSBC's representative in Beijing, is probably one of the best documentations of the Bank's ambivalence.[132] Barlow indicated therein that vigorous demand for notes in Hong Kong meant that the Bank was forced to retire its small circulation in Amoy (Xiamen) and Foochow (Fuzhou) in order to free up reserves, and that "we have restricted the circulation in Shanghai and the Northern Ports for the same reason."[133]

Barlow's letter was sent in January 1922. A few months later a substantial amount of notes would be disbursed in Yantai, and circulation figures in China proper would steadily grow until 1925, in contrast to the Bank's policy, as described by Barlow in 1922. Moreover, in another section of the letter, Barlow expressed adamant opposition to any concession to nationalists, which might result in the Chinese banning HSBC notes and disrupting "the convenience of the public, Chinese and Foreign [alike]."

Barlow's inconsistent stand on the Mainland issue may have partly derived from fledgling Chinese antagonism—both at the grass-roots and official levels—which he himself observed:

> There have never been any objections raised by the Chinese to our note issue, until the Shanghai Chinese Banks raised the point a few months ago; on the contrary, the difficulty has always been to keep it within bounds, and the Chinese would be the first to object to any measure tending towards depriving them of this safe and convenient form of currency.
>
> If the Chinese had a really powerful State Bank of undoubted solvency, to which we could go for currency, the note issue of foreign banks would automatically

disappear in China, except in Hongkong. That is a long way off yet, however, so I hope matters will be left as they are for the present.[134]

But whether the Bank's management was genuinely ready to welcome a "powerful" Chinese central bank in the 1920s is questionable; maintaining the status quo was the overriding goal. The Bank's top echelons identified the rise of Chinese modern banking with hothead antiforeignism too easily. Seven months later, Barlow addressed the China issue again in a letter to Hillier. He complained bitterly of the manager of the Bank of China in Shanghai—in a probable allusion to Song Hanzhang 宋漢章, one of the least politically minded figures in Chinese financial circles—who was allegedly fomenting antiforeign sentiments: "He is now mentally deranged at times I am sorry to say."[135]

Barlow's attitude toward the rising tide of Chinese nationalism should also be understood in the context of the long-standing extraterritorial privileges in Shanghai, which by the early 1920s had begotten a complacent British expatriate community amenable to almost no one but itself. The apogee of expatriate complacency came to be symbolized, in a sense, by the inauguration of a new lavish HSBC headquarters on the Bund in 1923. The *North-China Herald* explained that this occasion had taken on political dimensions since "the Hongkong & Shanghai Bank is a cause of special pride to the British community [in Shanghai] . . . [I]t was here that it was born, here that it was nurtured, here that its policy was shaped and executed. It owes nothing to London and exists as a monument of spontaneous British financial genius continually adapting itself to the needs of a peculiar environment."[136]

The sentiments that Barlow had expressed led the Bank, as a whole, to critically underestimate the magnitude of the changes that were transpiring in China and the degree of adaptability it would have to show in the future in order to preserve its status in postcolonial East Asia. Like most "Old China Hands" at the time, or the *North-China Herald* for that matter, Barlow misunderstood the polychromatic nature of the Chinese nationalist movement as well as the profundity of popular grievances on which it had fed. In February 1924—just two months before he embarked on his three-year tenure as chief manager—Barlow typically confounded the GMD's objectives with those of their more radical ally, the Chinese Communist Party: "I cannot think that Bolshevism will ever take great hold in China . . . Sun [Yat-sen] himself dare not put his Bolshevist theories into practice."[137]

CONCLUSION

Based on unpublished in-house archival data, this chapter has aimed at explaining the evolution of HSBC's note issue in China between its inception in 1866 to the eve of Nationalist reawakening in 1925. It sought, *en passant*, to examine claims made by Chinese scholars that the note issue was part and parcel of an imperialist grand design that brought China to its knees.

Analysis of Treasury policy and local branch balance sheets indicates that the regulation of British banknote issuance was progressively tightened. In East Asia as a whole, note issuance was in all likelihood remunerative, thereby contributing to HSBC's ascendency during the 1880s. Initial circulation volumes in China were, however, negligible compared to Hong Kong and the Straits Settlements, most probably because of deep-seated suspicion of fiduciary money.

As note issuance became a more important constituent of foreign banking in the region during the early twentieth century, the British Treasury strove to narrow down its remunerative elements and risk potential. In spite of the fact that China-specific stipulations and special reserves continued to be conspicuously absent from the Treasury's agenda, HSBC circulation volumes during that period suggest that the Bank succeeded in instilling confidence in its note bearers.

Note issuance was used indirectly to facilitate the ponderous transition of British overseas banks in China from institutions solely catering for foreign trading firms to institutions that efficiently tap domestic resources. The contours of this transition have been discussed here, but in order to determine its long-term consequences, future research will have to better explain *how* and *to whom* foreign banks allocated capital in Shanghai.

The last section described how internecine warlordism and the erosion of central authority during the early-Republican or Beiyang period (1912–1925) unleashed bouts of paper-money overprinting in the hinterland, thereby increasing the demand for secure means of payment within the treaty ports. Note circulation volumes in Shanghai, and to a lesser extent in the outports, shot up considerably through the Beiyang government tenure. But, in hindsight, the spread of quasi-foreign money in the treaty ports during the early 1910s was a significant turning point neither because of its absolute volume nor because of its implications for Chinese sovereignty.[138] Rather, quasi-foreign note issuance was historically significant because it was one of the first features of modern banking that engaged reform-minded officials, as they deliberated on what was wrong with China's finances.

The late-Qing and early-Republican governments paid obeisance to this reformist rhetoric, but their grip on power was too precarious to effectively combat the spread of quasi-foreign notes in China proper. Whether the Nationalist government proved more adept at regulating foreign banks afterward will be the focus of our next chapter.

Chapter 5 HSBC and Its China Note Issue in the Late-Republican Era, 1925–1937

Foreign banks constitute another kind of economic oppression. They print banknotes in order to bag our stock of hard currency and goods in return for worthless paper. They also fleece us with their exchange commissions. But those among us, the Chinese, who have money prefer to deposit it in foreign banks of all places. These deposits total hundreds of millions of dollars. Even when they deign to on-lend this money to our modest businessmen, foreign banks charge a hefty interest rate. Each year they cream a hundred million dollars in profits off us.
—*Sanminzhuyi qianzike* (a 1928 GMD primary school textbook)

In British India, the Exchange banks began to be criticized for not lending sufficiently to Indians, and for not employing Indians at a senior level. British banks were attacked and boycotted alongside British political institutions, with these sentiments peaking in the 1930s . . . In China there was *less of an explicit attack* on British banks, but their roles were changed as a modern and unified nation state emerged.
—Geoffrey Jones, *British Multinational Banking, 1830–1990* (emphasis added)

This chapter aims to explain how the GMD's rise to power projected on HSBC's China banknote issue. Examining a period that stretches from the May Thirtieth Incident (1925) to the outbreak of the Sino-Japanese War (1937), the chapter will challenge the notion of little resistance that British banks are thought to have faced in China, as demonstrated by Jones's passage above. Quite to the contrary, it will show that antiforeign agitation, mounting competition by Chinese-owned modern banks, and GMD government reform heavily impinged on the operations of British banks in China and contained by implication the spread of quasi-foreign banknotes.

This chapter roughly follows the chronology of the late-Republican era. It shows that the May Thirtieth Incident (*Wusa can'an* 五卅惨案) marked a veritable watershed in Sino-foreign relations, after which HSBC's unchallenged position on Mainland China rapidly eroded.

In order to draw out the significance of 1925 to the history of British banks in China, HSBC data will be juxtaposed with comparable CBIAC figures. It is subsequently argued that GMD state-building efforts during the Nanjing Decade (1927–1937) forced HSBC and other foreign banks to downsize and, ultimately, renounce their note issue privileges.

The penultimate section will revisit the role played by Sir Frederick Leith-Ross, the special British envoy to East Asia, in delivering the GMD's *fabi* reform (November 1935). The *fabi* reform saw China briskly parting with the silver standard and introducing sole fiat currency for the first time since the fourteenth century. Public and confidential pronouncements that Leith-Ross made during his sensitive mission to China provide insights into the GMD's economic performance and into its relations with British banks, not just in 1935 but throughout the period under review. Finally, a brief assessment will be offered of the significance of HSBC's note circulation figures for our understanding of Republican China.

This chain of events outlined above is by no means self-explanatory. It should be noted that most Western accounts of foreign banking in prewar China either gloss over the implications of the May Thirtieth Movement (1925–1926) or depict foreign bank attitudes toward Chinese monetary reform in the mid-1930s as cooperative.[1] It is therefore critical for China scholars to consider whether the overall picture of Sino-British relations during the Republican period might not require some readjustment.

THE BIG BANG OF MAY 1925: SHANGHAI

The May Thirtieth Incident broke out in Shanghai in 1925, when a labor dispute in a Japanese textile factory situated in a British-policed concession area rapidly escalated into bloody demonstrations and a year-long nationalist boycott against British goods, sweeping across other treaty ports and Hong Kong.[2] The protest movement sparked by the Incident proved a definitive turning point in Sino-foreign relations. Not only did it force the Powers to enter negotiations with the Chinese government over treaty revision and the eventual abolition of extraterritoriality, but it also changed long-standing Western perception of the Chinese people as servile.

The violent demonstrations rocked British diplomatic legations, and militated an increasingly assertive group of Chinese modern banks to fold back cooperation with their British counterparts.[3] In early June 1925, Shanghai moneyshops and Chinese-owned banks had struck in solidarity with the victims of the May Thirtieth Incident, and an all-out ban on British note clearing had been formally declared.[4] Even British firms operating deep in the interior were not spared: the Peking Syndicate mines at Jiaozuo (Henan Province), for example, had been forced to shut down and did not recover until 1933.[5]

Despite the relative insulation of British banks from the hinterland economy and the transient nature of the boycott, by then their banknotes had become one of the most tangible aspects of the British presence in the treaty ports and were therefore particularly vulnerable to popular rejection.[6] However, the boycott of British banknotes in Shanghai during 1925 has not attracted much scholarly attention, mainly because it had been transpiring backstage and was played down in expatriate press reports. In other words, while the relentless campaign against British consumer goods produced immediate repercussions in bilateral trade statistics and was constantly decried by the British expatriate community in China, accurate information on the extent of British banknote redemption and deposit withdrawals was largely confined to confidential branch correspondence.

The *North-China Herald*, the most influential English-language newspaper in Shanghai, had been traditionally dismissive of the ability of student movements and popular discontent to bring about change in Chinese political consciousness.[7] Initially, the general tone taken vis-à-vis the Incident was low-key: the *Herald* rarely mentioned the run on British banks. When it became clear that the disturbances, strike, and boycott would not end soon, as the newspaper's coverage had first implied, editors shifted their attention to physical attacks on British nationals in China.

Most of the reports on British banknote redemption were made by the lower rung of Chinese newspapers in Shanghai. During 1925–1926, these newspapers took a more militant line than well-established newspapers like *Shen bao* and were therefore less reliable.[8] They reported quite extensively on student activists who demanded that Shanghai's merchant and banking guilds declare an all-out currency war against quasi-foreign notes; that wayward moneychangers who accepted quasi-foreign notes be punished; and that all Chinese residents of the city withdraw their deposits from foreign banks. But in the lack of substantive information on the outcome of such calls, Chinese newspapers eventually turned to cover the boycott of British-made products, which had readily available—and fairly reliable—local substitutes: cigarettes, sweets, kerosene, drugs, toiletries, and luxury items.[9]

Advertisements in the Chinese press denigrating rival British consumer goods—particularly cigarettes—were very common through 1925. Chinese bank agitation was usually not as extensive and less pronounced than the one carried out by students, but notable exceptions can be found. On August 4, 1925, for example, the *Yinhang zhoubao*, whose readerships was made up of Chinese businessmen and banking professionals, carried this Shanghai Commercial and Savings Bank advertisement:

> The tragic events following the May Thirtieth iniquity startled the entire nation. What has since been uppermost on everyone's mind—apart from protesting foreign aggression and bullying—is finding a way to save lives and property. The pursuit of industrial development and the setting up of factories are important collective means of helping the nation cope. Nonetheless, if we are to do that, we must first pool our capital into solid savings. If only each and every one of our four hundred million compatriots opened a savings account—many a little would make a mickle [*jiye chengqiu* 集腋成裘]. We will then mutually benefit from enormous resources with which to promote industrial development. Nothing will be beyond our reach, and no trade will remain unprofitable.
>
> This bank prides itself on reliability and the ample reserves backing all its business activities. Our service is at its very best when it comes to opening savings accounts, and we offer generous interest rates to clients. We would be honoured to answer expressions of interest from patriotic sires, and are able to send printed brochures by mail.[10]

The unprecedented vehemence with which British businesses were attacked sounded alarm bells in Britain and stirred Whitehall to quiz the Eastern Exchange Banks on the viability and safety of their bullion reserves.[11] At the height of the conflict, both HSBC and CBIAC were buffeted by a collective walkout of their Chinese staff in Shanghai.[12] More importantly, the Chinese boycott of British goods in 1925 began to tilt the overall performance of the Eastern

Exchange Banks, since a large segment of their revenue hinged on the finance of trade between the two countries. While CBIAC's total real profits in 1925 fell by 15.5 percent compared with the previous year, HSBC at first suffered an overall drop of only 2 percent.[13] The Mercantile Bank of India was even less dependent on the Chinese market. Its returns in South Asia smoothed over poor results in China, with an overall profit hike of 5.8 percent in 1925. However, local statistics available for the Mercantile Bank reveal that its Shanghai branch was incurring heavy losses during 1920–1926 and that the bank's note circulation there plummeted from the equivalent of GBP 56,000 to just GBP 19,343 during the same period.[14]

In the mid-1920s, challenges to British economic hegemony in China were palpable in a wide range of sectors. Domestic firms took advantage of the political climate to lure away clients from British multinationals in a wide range of sectors; Nanyang Bros. produced cigarettes in Shanghai that snatched a significant market share from the British American Tobacco Company (BAT); Chinese shippers stung British steam navigation hegemony on the Yangzi, and most Shanghai department stores catering for the masses were dominated by Overseas Chinese.[15] In his study of Sino-foreign corporate rivalry in the treaty ports, Sherman Cochran found that the 1925 boycott had considerably boosted Nanyang's profit margins, but could not ascertain BAT's performance in China presumably because he had been denied access to the relevant company archives in London.[16] He therefore concluded that the economic effects of the May Thirtieth Incident were "not fully understood, and deserve further research."[17]

Based on British consular sources, Richard Rigby suggested, in turn, that BAT sales in China dropped by as much as 40 percent in mid-July 1925. The psychological impact of this downturn was so dramatic that by the end of the month, the China Association—a body aligning the biggest British firms operating in the region—had petitioned the Foreign Office to refrain from using military force in Shanghai and to try mollifying student anger with promises of ending extraterritoriality in the distant future.[18]

Hong Jiaguan argued that, perhaps more than any other event in the twentieth century, the May Thirtieth events helped modern Chinese banking flourish and pointed to a 71.4 percent rise in the volume of funds deposited therein through 1925.[19] While such dramatic advances cannot be ruled out of hand, available CBIAC data do not indicate a commensurate drop in foreign bank deposits. CBIAC fixed deposits in Shanghai merely dropped from Tls. 7.9 million in December 1924 to Tls. 6.3 million in December 1925, while current accounts actually climbed from Tls.7.7 million to Tls. 8.5.[20] Considering the fact that the CBIAC note circulation volume in the city was almost halved during the same period (see Figure 5.2), deposit levels clearly show that Chinese response to the antiforeign agitation was by no means uniform. It is plausible that Chinese bearers were keen to redeem quasi-foreign banknotes, which were of highly visible nature, but less inclined to entrust funds long deposited in foreign banks to Chinese equivalents.

What available data there are in HSBC's branch ledgers, Inspector's Reports, and correspondence with Whitehall ministries clearly point to a similar dramatic drop in Mainland banknote circulation volumes in 1925.

For Shanghai, data assembled in Figure 5.1 show that the level of notes outstanding, which had reached $3.6 million midyear, was more than halved toward the end of the year.

That the mid-1925 shrinkage in note circulation volumes could not have been on the Bank's own initiative is evidenced by a wad of five Bills of Lading

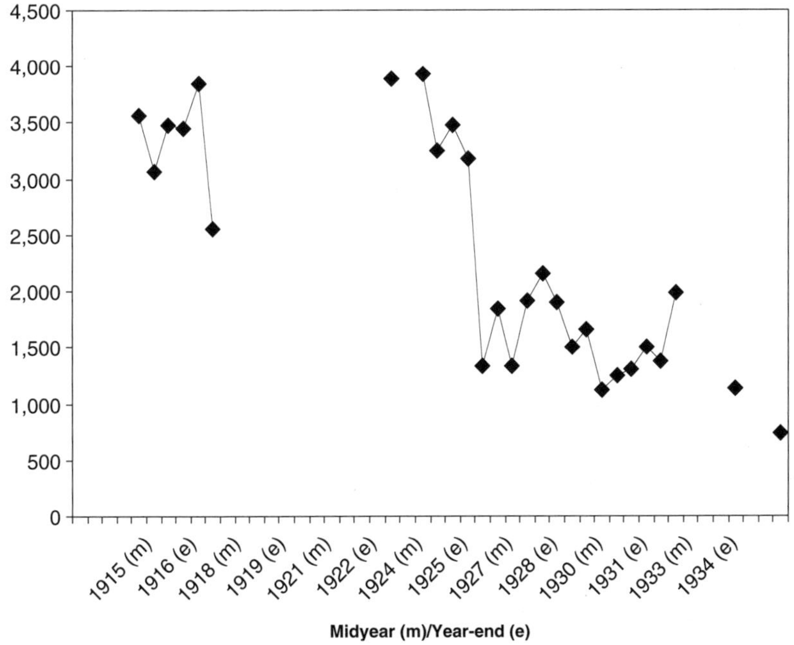

Figure 5.1. HSBC Circulation Volumes in Shanghai, 1914–1935. Unit: Shanghai Dollars (000). *Sources*: In HSBC GA: SHG II, 1023; SHG 343.1-5; SHG II 1044; London II, Box 8, Item 127 (Inspector's Report on Shanghai); GHO 96.2; GHO 13.2; SHG LEDG 294; In PRO: FO 371/13193; FO 371/18130; year-end 1935 based on King (1987), vol. 3, p. 247.

Table 5.1 Note Printing, Shipment, and Miscellaneous Costs (B/Ls Aggregate), August 1924–February 1925

Total Face Value of Notes Ordered	SH$2 million
Shipping and Packaging Cost	GBP 87
Total Printing Costs	GBP 2,550
Design and Security Cost	GBP 1,065
Total Cost	**GBP 3,702 or SH$33,142**

Source: HSBC GA SHG LEDG 294; total cost does not include insurance for the five consignments involved other than that provided by the shipping agency; pound sterling is converted into (Shanghai) silver dollar values based on an implicit exchange rate for 1925 (1 SH$ = GBP 0.1117) calculated from Hsiao Liang-lin (1974), p. 192.

in the Bank's records. The bills were issued by a banknote printing company in London between October 8, 1924 and February 11, 1925. Their inventory shows that only three and a half months before the sudden outbreak of the anti-British disturbances, the Bank had actually been preparing to *increase* its Shanghai issue.[21] The armored note consignments were ordered from London in separate batches within a short space of time, most probably due to security reasons—the leading Western banks in Shanghai never employed local printers.

The bills also provide insights into the production costs of quasi-foreign notes, to the extent that one may better determine their profit potential. The breakdown of printing and delivery costs is compiled in Table 5.1.

Merely allowing for a lower-bound call-loan interest rate (3 percent per year), considering the fact that the notes often carried a premium over metallic money, and assuming a moderate shelf life of 20 years, it appears that at least during its pre-1925 halcyon days, the Bank's branch in Shanghai could reap a return on banknote issuance, even if a worst-case scenario required the immobilization of one-third metallic reserve. In other words, the branch could earn approximately SH$760,000 in profits over a period of nineteen years on a circulation volume of SH$2 million, if it efficiently channeled silver proceeds to on-call borrowers. This proposition calls into question previous accounts of quasi-foreign banknotes in China, which tended to overstate the deadweight of production costs, while deprecating the notes' remunerative aspect and presenting foreign banks as essentially concerned with rendering "public service" to Shanghai's denizens.[22]

It would be implausible to assume that the Bank was prepared to commit considerable resources to combating forgeries regardless of the contribution of note issuance to corporate revenue. Numerous records do in fact suggest that the Bank instilled counterforgery alertness in its staff and invested heavily in advanced note designs.[23] When necessary, branch managers did not hesitate to complain to the Head Office about the poor quality of notes received from the London printers. In 1922, for example, the manager of the Shanghai branch accused Bradbury, Wilkinson & Co. of producing easily falsifiable notes, and suggested that a new batch for Shanghai be ordered from Waterlow & Co., a firm that had previously been commissioned to print the Bank's Beijing notes.[24]

Whatever ambivalence the Head Office had expressed about the China issue before 1925, it did *not* arise as a result of disappointing returns or the amorphous legal framework of extraterritoriality. Rather, it arose because global Treasury quotas meant that bigger circulation volumes on the Mainland offset the Bank's ability to issue in Hong Kong, where demand for notes, the premium they carried, and circulation velocity were much higher.[25] Until 1925, therefore, the dynamics between the Head Office and China branches allowed the China branches to expand their issue in order to capitalize on the growing demand for reliable media of payments, but only within a range that did not imperil the Bank's status as arbiter of the money supply in Hong Kong.

In the latter half of 1925, the *Wusa* disturbances were not just affecting banknote circulation in Shanghai; they were rapidly translating into turmoil in stock exchanges too. Just prior to the May Thirtieth Incident, HSBC shares traded in Shanghai at SH$1,300, while fetching GBP 143 in London per unit. By August 29, the share price had fallen by 15 percent and 11 percent in Shanghai and London, respectively.[26] HSBC shares were most adversely affected in the Hong Kong stock exchange. In early June 1925, the share traded at HK$1,290. By early March 1926, it had dipped as low as 1,065, a drop of 17.5 percent.[27]

THE BIG BANG OF 1925: HONG KONG

Was 1925 equally dismal for British bank performance in Hong Kong? In view of these stock exchange indices, we might expect a similar drop in circulation figures there. In some respects, Sino-foreign friction was even more pronounced in South China than in Shanghai, because the GMD had by then set up a provisional government in Guangzhou, which vowed to outlaw HK$ notes and coins on the Mainland, and to which the Hong Kong colonial government was openly hostile.[28] Moreover, opposition to quasi-foreign note issuance was one of the most vehement facets of Sun Yixian's (Sun Yat-sen) otherwise ambivalent stance vis-à-vis the Powers.[29]

On June 23, 1925, a mass demonstration in solidarity with the Shanghai strikers escalated into a bloody confrontation that rocked the Shamian 沙面 [Shameen] foreign concession area of Guangzhou. It resulted in a death toll considerably higher than in the disturbances farther north. The June 23 events in Guangzhou were to be named the Shaji 沙基 [Shakee] Incident, after the creek separating the Chinese city from the concession area, from which French and British soldiers had shot demonstrators.[30] Much as had happened in Shanghai, a comprehensive strike and boycott of British goods immediately followed in Guangzhou. But rather than students, it was the GMD that *directly* coordinated—and was reinvigorated by—the protest movement in South China.[31]

Unfortunately, the HSBC Head Office balance sheets for 1925–1926 have not been preserved. However, comparable data available for the local CBIAC branch do not show any significant drop in banknote circulation volumes (or fixed deposits) during the mid-1920s.[32] It is therefore likely that the balance-sheet totals of British banks in Hong Kong were only negligibly affected by antiforeign agitation in 1925. But this was not because antiforeign sentiments in South China were any less pronounced than those in Shanghai. Rather, it is likely that swift action taken by Hong Kong authorities to restrict silver withdrawals managed to defuse an imminent run on British banknotes there.

In anticipation of the May Thirtieth disturbances spreading south, the Hong Kong government imposed martial law and introduced a series of other draconian measures.[33] It enforced strict censorship of the Chinese press, it mobilized the Colony's Volunteer Defense Corps to patrol the streets, it banned silver and foodstuff exports, and it prohibited Chinese residents from leaving the Colony with jewelry valued more than HK$5.[34] Similarly, reports emerged of an extensive Hong Kong police crackdown on valuables concealed in departing ships and outbound terminals, resulting in confiscation of goods and jewelry worth HK$1.6 million.[35]

In the meantime, GMD propagandists were calling to encash HK$ notes, or exchange them for Chinese banknotes.[36] As in Shanghai, a run on British banks was in the offing. But there was one principal difference in subsequent developments. Whereas there was no legal precedent for the Municipal Council in Shanghai to come to the rescue of private banks, Hong Kong's governor general, Sir Edward Stubbs, intervened personally with sweeping emergency powers designed to shield the British banks from a wave of withdrawals.[37]

The Shaji Incident, which broke out on July 23, confirmed British premonitions. It precipitated a massive walkout of Chinese temporary workers from Hong Kong in protest against British use of force in the foreign concession areas of Shanghai and Guangzhou. British banks in the Colony remained open, but were propped up by fresh emergency regulations restricting maximum individual withdrawals of silver from the banks to HK$100 per day.[38]

Those hit hardest in the Colony were therefore Chinese-owned banks, which relied on the remittances and deposits of migrant laborers. By July, thousands of these workers had already deserted the Colony, and some apparently managed to carry their deposits across the border.[39] Chinese-owned banks and moneyshops in Hong Kong were effectively depleted of silver reserves following two serious runs in June and September.

Yet, in Guangzhou, Chinese industrialists thrived by producing substitutes for foreign-made goods, and HK$ notes were for the first time trading on a par with—and sometimes even below—GMD-issued banknotes.[40] Chinese sources claimed that, at the GMD's instigation, Guangzhou merchants had been able to withdraw no less than HK$5 million from local foreign bank branches during 1925–1926.[41] CBIAC Guangzhou balance-sheet data seem to lend qualified support to this description: the bank's deposit receipts there were minor compared to the ones in other China branches. They dropped from a total of HK$140,635 in June 1925 to HK$89,525 in December 1926.[42]

Despite Hong Kong's dire economic condition, the British press in Shanghai singled out the Colony as one place where the nationwide disturbances had been adequately dealt with. On August 15, 1925, an editorial in the *North-China Herald* praïsed Stubbs for his firm action in the crisis. In the face of bleak trade statistics that were emanating from the Colony, the newspaper suggested that the Hong Kong government "should congratulate itself on the successful handling of the boycott."[43]

The standoff between Guangzhou and Hong Kong ended formally in October 1926, when the GMD-led strike committee reached a comprehensive settlement with the colonial authorities. By then it had become apparent that the *North-China Herald* praise was premature and that Sino-British relations were on the cusp of a new era. Predictably enough, the view from Britain—which would have had to shoulder the cost of military intervention if Hong Kong had been attacked—was much more somber than the British expatriate press could portray.

On May 22, 1926, the London-based *Economist* captured the impending turnaround in British foreign policy:

> The natural impatience and disgust of the European towards the excesses of the [Chinese] student agitation of last year has practically disappeared, and has given way to a more sympathetic spirit, which it may be hoped, will eventually secure a willing response from young China. Galling as it has been for the British merchant to suffer from the unjustified ban on his right to trade, [his] demand for military intervention has died away, and there is now a general feeling that the Home Government's policy of patience and conciliation will ultimately prove to be the better course. It is fully realized that while the Chinese have shown little gratitude for the benefits of living in peace under British rule, they have had to put up with good many minor disabilities, which have developed a sense of soreness and resentment. There is a generally awakened desire to remove all cause for irritation.[44]

THE BIG BANG OF 1925: THE OUTPORTS

Another set of HSBC data juxtaposing Shanghai with China's smaller treaty ports further highlights mid-1925 as a watershed in the vicissitudes of the Bank's China issue. This set of data leaves very little doubt as to the linkage between the May Thirtieth or *Wusa* Incident and the subsequent winding-down of Bank's Mainland issue (see Table 5.2).

HSBC circulation volumes on the Mainland can be much better understood if they are compared again with the more comprehensive data that are available for CBIAC. When combined, HSBC and CBIAC records shed light not just on the Shanghai banknote boycott, but also on how this boycott played out across different outports. Moreover, such a comparison helps construe the vicissitudes of British banknote issuance in China throughout the period under review.

Figure 5.2 lends support to the argument made in previous chapters, namely, that the demand for quasi-foreign money had dramatically shot up as a result of the breakdown of the Imperial order (1912). The minor drop in CBIAC's circulation volumes beginning in mid-1915 and the subsequent four-year trough may have primarily stemmed from the effects of World War I on the leverage of British banks in the city, as discussed in Chapter 2.[45]

The ultimate drop in CBIAC's Shanghai circulation volumes after June 1933 may well be attributable to concurrent legislation in the United States, which allowed President Roosevelt to tackle the Depression by drumming up the price of silver. (This U.S. legislation, the Silver Purchase Act, will be discussed at greater length in the next two sections.) The most pronounced drop

Table 5.2 HSBC Note Circulation in China through 1925 (Dollar-Denominated Notes Only)

	January	February	May	June	July	August	October	November
Shanghai	3,604,060	3,426,060	3,645,060	3,169,286	2,133,060	1,877,060	?	?
Beijing	498,525	491,060	?	?	?	142,050	?	?
Tianjin	324,405	328,405	?	?	186,177	130,577	104,805	101,402
Yantai	118,536	101,555	?	?	?	97,230	?	?
Hankou	63,980	59,980	?	?	?	38,280	?	?
Xiamen	963	963	?	?	?	756	?	?
Fuzhou	?	660	?	?	?	660	?	?
China Total	**?**	**4,408,683**	**?**	**?**	**?**	**2,286,613**	**?**	**?**

Sources: HSBC GA. For Shanghai, see SHG LEDG 294; GHO 96.2; GHO 13.2; for Tianjin, see SHG II–28.2 and GHO 96.2; for Fuzhou [Foochow], see SHG LEDG 1177 and GHO 96.2; for Yantai [Chefoo], Beijing, Hankou [Hankow] and Xiamen [Amoy], see HSBC GA GHO 96.2. Very few Tael-denominated notes had been circulating in the treaty ports by 1925; the majority of Tael notes outstanding were thought to have been hoarded or lost.

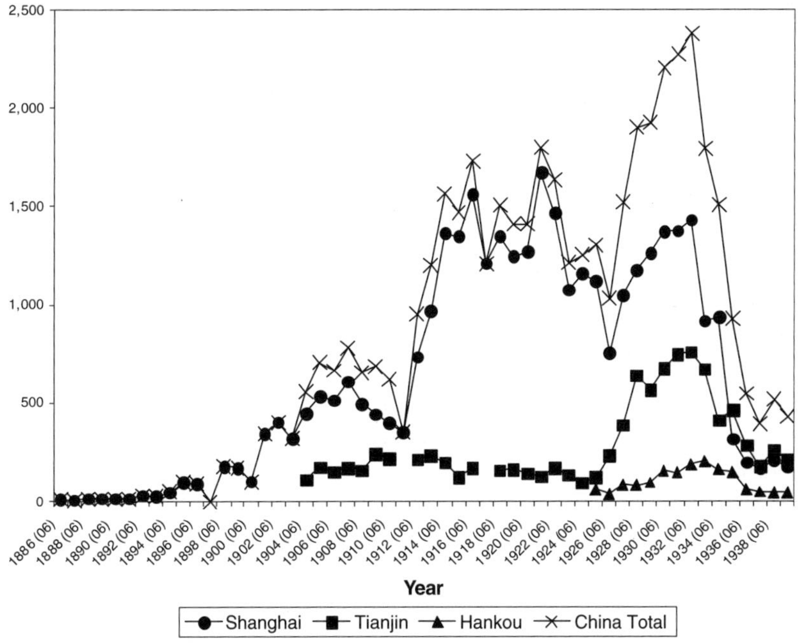

Figure 5.2. CBIAC Note Circulation: Mainland China Denominations, 1886–1939. Unit: Shanghai Taels (000). *Source:* CBIAC GL Ms 31519; the value of banknotes denominated in Mexican dollars and Tianjin Taels were converted to Shanghai Taels based on the bank's implicit exchange rate.

in CBIAC's circulation volumes occurred between June 1925 and June 1926. This, in turn, points again to a strong circumstantial linkage with *Wusa*.

CBIAC started issuing local dollar notes in Hankou during the latter part of 1924 and achieved some headway in the following months. But there, too, circulation decreased markedly between June 1925 ($89,950) and June 1926 ($57,150) without a commensurate effect on deposit receipts or current accounts.[46]

In Tianjin, a substantially different pattern emerged—a factor that may point to the varying monetary and political pulses that set North China apart from the Yangzi basin. Notably, the spasmodic wave of anti-British demonstrations that had convulsed Shanghai in June 1925 generally spread southward but was much less pronounced in the North.[47] However, as the following paragraphs show, HSBC eventually capped its entire outport issue in anticipation of further antiforeign agitation during the Nanjing Decade (1927–1937).

The fact that HSBC introduced a cap on its circulation in Tianjin and that the city was distant from the Nationalists' power base in the South meant that the demand for substitute CBIAC notes in the city actually shot up in 1925. Demand for CBIAC notes in Tianjin was high enough in the following years to offset the fall in the bank's Shanghai banknote circulation volume. In fact, thanks to its Tianjin issue, CBIAC's aggregate China circulation volume had increased by June 1927 compared with its level on the eve of *Wusa*.

The linkage between the *Wusa* anti-British boycott and the dramatic drop in British bank circulation figures is not only manifest in quantitative data; it is also mentioned in in-house HSBC correspondence. For example, in a telegram exchange between Barlow and the new Shanghai branch manager, G. H. Stitt, dated June 19, 1925, Stitt warned Barlow that reserves at the branch were "running low" and asked him to intervene with the British consul-general so that the latter would agree to immediately unfreeze the Bank's $4 million reserve under his custody. Barlow, for his part, advised Stitt to conserve his cash tightly because of the long anti-British strike that he now anticipated.[48]

That the Shanghai consul-general was a custodian of a reserve roughly tantamount to the circulation volume in China did not imply that the Mainland issue per se had to be fully backed at that point in time.[49] Attention should be paid to the fact that the Bank's Head Office in Hong Kong had to be called upon to contact the Hong Kong authorities, so that they in turn would approve the release of the reserve by the consul-general in Shanghai. This suggests that the China issue was simply conceived of as part of the Bank's global excess issue, which *by definition* required 100 percent backing in Hong Kong.

The Bank managed to have part of the excess reserve placed outside the central note reserve in Hong Kong no sooner than 1921. This is attested to in an upbeat telegram that Charles Addis sent from London to Stephen in Shanghai:

> Arrangement [is] now concluded with the Colonial Office regarding security of the Banks' note issue. a) HM Government had no objection to the increase of the Bank's authorized capital to $50 million. b) An ordinary note issue equal to issued capital of $20 million shall be one-third fiduciary and the balance of two thirds covered by coin or approved securities at the Bank's option, while any excess issue over $20 million shall be fully covered in coin. c) It remained to be agreed what portions of the security should be held in places other than Hong Kong.[50]

The conceptual tie-up of the China issue with the excess issue is attested to again in a memorandum sent, on Secretary Winston Churchill's instruction, by the Undersecretary of State for the Colonies to the deputy of George Curzon, then the British foreign secretary. The memorandum indicated that HSBC had asked the secretary to allow part of the note reserves to be kept outside Hong Kong, in Mainland localities where circulation was increasing.[51] Churchill, the memorandum went on to report, consulted the Lords Commissioners of the Treasury, who approved Shanghai and Tianjin as sites accessible enough to house a secondary reserve. It was, then, HSBC that had suggested that British consuls in China be appointed as trustees of the said reserve and that they report from time to time to the Hong Kong government on the amount of securities entrusted to them.

Addis's telegram and the undersecretary's memorandum imply that any Mainland note reserves that the Bank would have kept before 1921 was at the Bank's discretion. Until then, any treaty-port note reserves could *not* be deducted from the central reserve held against the total global issue in Hong Kong and were certainly not required of the Bank by the Treasury or the Foreign Office. Moreover, it was the Bank rather than the Treasury that sought to buttress the China reserves by having the Mainland issue linked with the global excess issue. This was a measure designed not only to protect the Bank from local runs, but also to abrogate an onerous overlap between informal local reserves and the formal central reserve.

The regulatory framework underlying HSBC's banknote issuance *after* 1921 is summarized in Figure 5.3. In essence, it shows the Bank of England as the ultimate arbiter of British monetary policy and as a trustee of HSBC's nonmetallic reserves. Charter guidelines and banknote reserve ratios applicable to

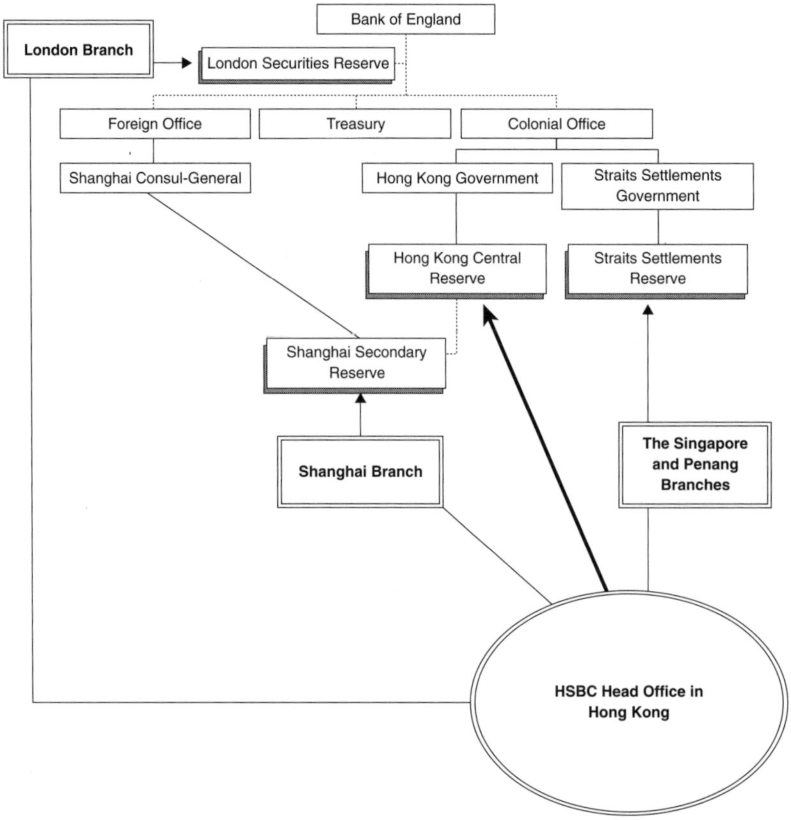

Figure 5.3. Regulation of HSBC Banknote Issuance in East Asia, circa 1925. *Source*: Adapted from the Archival Material cited in Chapters 4 and 5. Caveat: By 1925, the metallic reserve in Singapore was purely notional, since the Straits government had taken over banknote issuance. The January 22, 1926 edition of the *Straits Settlements Government Gazette* (p. 103) indicates that the value of securities (mostly colonial consols) still deposited by HSBC with London Crown Agents against its pre-1907 note issue in the Straits exceeded by far residual circulation figures in Singapore and Penang.

all Eastern Exchange Banks, as well as the day-to-day monitoring of financial conditions overseas, were carried out by the Treasury in consultation with the Foreign and Colonial Offices. Colonial governments were then answerable to the Colonial Office insofar as reserve ratio enforcement was concerned. HSBC's bullion and coin reserves were locked up in vaults under colonial government jurisdiction. But since Shanghai was nominally a part of the Republic of China, enforcement of HSBC reserve ratios there became the responsibility of the local British consul-general, a Foreign Office employee.

The measure to formalize and buttress the status of the Shanghai reserves in 1921 may have saved the Bank's reputation on the Mainland from a more severe thrashing during the tumultuous days of mid-1925. Even so, HSBC was hard-pressed to meet the redemption wave. The problem was that the Shanghai note reserves held under the consul's trusteeship had been largely made up of precious Mexican dollars. These dollars carried a premium over debased Chinese dollar coinage, and the Bank was loath to disburse them. Hence, the Bank persuaded Hong Kong's treasurer to allow it to transfer the Mexican dollars to the central reserve in the Colony, while replenishing the Shanghai reserves with Chinese dollar coins.[52]

By early July, the enormity of the situation in Shanghai had finally registered with Barlow, who telegrammed Stitt: "It looks to me as if this British Boycott is the most dangerous thing we have been up against for many a long day and will, if it is maintained for any length of time, strain our resources severely."[53]

On July 18, 1925 the *Beijing ribao* reported on a massive run that had occurred on the HSBC Shanghai branch:

> Since a popular boycott was declared on the British-owned HSBC, Shanghainese depositors of this bank have flocked there to withdraw funds, especially clients elbowing their way to cash paper notes. At the time [of the present run], the Bank had already been squeezed between a rock and a hard place. It scraped through by the skin of its teeth with crucial assistance from a [Chinese] bank related to Yu Xiaqing [虞洽卿] and from some other avaricious banks, to the extent that it could breathe alive again.[54]

The fact that the mainstream Chinese press in Shanghai did not report any dramatic anti-British bank stampede and that only a Beijing-based daily raised the allegations against "collaborating" Chinese banks diminish the credibility of such reports. It seems more likely that the pressure on British banks was applied incrementally, as student agitation was gaining ground. A rare local reference to the dynamics of boycott may be detected in a report carried by the Shanghai students' mouthpiece *Rexue ribao* [Hot-Blooded Daily] on June 7, 1925: "Ever since calls for the boycott of quasi-foreign banknotes spread across Shanghai, there has been unusually heavy traffic of clients wishing to withdraw funds from foreign banks or encash quasi-foreign banknotes. The HSBC was worst affected, [with clients streaming to withdraw funds] . . . from morning to noon without respite. This Bank's predicament is now extremely precarious."[55]

Either way, Barlow was so alarmed at the anti-British wave that he recommended the immediate withdrawal of treaty-port issues except in Shanghai. This was because, unlike Shanghai, outport issues had always been covered by the central Hong Kong reserve and because no other local reserve in China was recognized by the Treasury. The outport issue was therefore "weapons in the hands of agitators." Then, Barlow went on to compare the volatility of the Bank's issues in China with the monetary setting in Hong Kong: "In Hong Kong conditions are not the same, as we can always rely on the Hong Kong Government to enact protective legislation in the event of a concerted attack being made on our note issue here."[56]

Barlow knew, of course, what he was talking about. As indicated above, shortly before the *Wusa* disturbances had spread to the Pearl River Delta, the Hong Kong government had imposed severe caps on note redemption, silver withdrawals, and capital movement between the Colony and the Mainland. This emergency legislation was a precondition set by the Bank and CBIAC for the grant of a loan on the order of HK$6 million designed to bail out "native banks" in the Colony. The new restrictions unleashed a frantic wave of silver smuggling across the border into Guangdong province, but may well have saved HSBC and CBIAC from a run on their banknotes within the Colony.[57]

Meanwhile, the situation was rapidly deteriorating in Shanghai. On July 2, Stitt telegrammed Barlow that local note circulation was already down by $0.5 million since the disturbances started and that Chinese clients were also withdrawing funds from current accounts "rather freely."[58] A week later the circulation volume sank to a record low of $2.7 million in Shanghai and $0.66 million in the outports, whereas total liquid cash reserve (excluding the Mexican dollars entrusted to the Consul) stood at only $1.8 million.[59]

The permanent shift in the Bank's strategy with regard to its China issue occurred in the course of the following two months. On July 13, Stitt reported that the cash position of the branch was improving, and that he might not have to draw on the $4 million consular reserve.[60] Three days later Stitt even thought he detected signs that the vehemence of the boycott against HSBC notes on the Mainland was subsiding, with the Shanghai circulation now at $2.4 million—only $ 0.3 million less than the week before.[61]

Barlow, however, who would have witnessed the spillover of disturbances into South China in late June, remained unconvinced. On August 5, he instructed Stitt to stop reissuing redeemed notes in all Mainland branches in anticipation of more runs.[62] And on August 17, he imposed a cap of $2 million on the Shanghai circulation volume.[63] Apart from helping to stave off future runs in Shanghai, Barlow also hoped that the decreased circulation volume in China would free up the reserves held against it in Hong Kong to use as cash in claims on the Bank in the Colony or, alternatively, underpin an increase of note issuance there.[64]

Ironically, while the *Wusa* disturbances put a downward pressure on the Bank's circulation volumes in China, they buoyed up demand for HSBC notes in Hong Kong, because the new colonial government restrictions there meant that individuals could not withdraw silver from the banks freely. Receipt of a limited amount of notes was the only way to draw deposits from either Chinese or foreign banks in the Colony.[65]

The other factor that stoked the demand for HK$-denominated HSBC notes was the fact that trade between the Colony and the wider Delta was effectively cut off. This meant that Cantonese silk producers whose goods had been exported via Hong Kong's deep-water port could not use the sales proceeds to purchase imported products for transportation upriver because border passages were blocked. Many, therefore, chose to smuggle the proceeds over the border—and notes were harder to detect than goods.[66]

By mid-1926 the impetus of the disturbances had clearly begun to wane across the Mainland. The Maritime Customs report published in 1926, though lamenting the impact of the anti-British boycott, could point to a silver lining:

> The Shanghai incidents of the 30th May, with their counterblast in the South, bade fair to paralyze trade; but the strike and boycott movements were soon restricted to certain centers only, and what could not be shipped or imported through Shanghai or Canton [Guangzhou] found its way in many cases through neighboring ports or through other large seaports such as Tientsin [Tianjin]. Exception being made for the southern and, principally, the West River ports, the Shanghai incidents were but a temporary set-back to trade in general.[67]

The subsequent period saw intermittent conflicts between locals and expatriates in some of the outports that never degenerated into a countrywide backlash. Nonetheless, the enormity of the events during the past year resonated as far as Whitehall, as Western attitudes toward China gradually began to shift. On June 4, 1926, Barlow informed his new branch manager in Shanghai, A. B. Lowson, that the British government was sounding out prominent figures among its nationals in the treaty ports on the future course that its China policy should take.[68]

In the years to come, Whitehall would come to question the views of its hard-line expatriates in China—wealthy *taipans* and plebeian Shanghailanders alike. The sheer import of the shift in Britain's China policy is beyond the scope of the present book, however. Suffice it to say that, among other things, the shift ramified into tighter administrative supervision of British banknote issuance in the treaty ports during the late 1920s.

The first harbinger of a shift in Whitehall policy toward British expatriates in Shanghai surfaced in August 1926, when the Head Office informed Lowson that, henceforth, the British authorities would require all British banks of issue in China to apply for a license if they wished to continue disbursing notes.[69] But the new Nationalist government would pose far more stringent demands.

THE NANJING DECADE (1927–1937)

Recognizing the linkage between *Wusa* and the fate of British banks in China is crucial not only because of the drop in HSBC's circulation volumes or share prices, but because the pertinent literature seldom mentions the 1925 events by name.[70] Yet GMD rule over China, which "had gained in feasibility" as a direct result of the turnaround in Chinese public opinion during the 1925–1926 disturbances, put an end to one of HSBC's main sources of revenue: loans to successive Chinese governments.[71]

Fragmentary data notwithstanding, recent work by business historian Yasutomi Ayumu indicates a drastic diminution in Mainland China's share of the Bank's global business following the GMD rise to power. In 1913, for example, HSBC's Shanghai branch accounted for 22 percent of total balance-sheet assets. By 1941, Shanghai's share had dropped to just 9.5 percent.[72] HSBC's global profit in 1935, eight years into GMD rule, was only half that which had been posted in 1924, on the eve of *Wusa*.[73]

The shift in Britain's policy toward China was taking shape, while the GMD's Northern Expedition (*beifa* 北伐) was underway. The Expedition saw the Nationalists pushing from their stronghold in South China toward Shanghai against regional warlords between 1926 and 1927, and finally proclaiming their capital in Nanjing in 1928. Short of eliminating warlordism, the Expedition was an attempt by Jiang Jieshi to claim the center stage of Chinese politics.

The notorious bloodbath in Shanghai on April 12, 1927, during which Jiang joined forces with the city's underworld and mercantile elite to crush the Communist Party and its local sympathizers, was the cue Whitehall needed to endorse its new agenda in the region.[74] A unified China under Jiang now seemed less of a threat, as long as the generalissimo was prepared to reach a compromise over the future of extraterritoriality without taking unilateral steps.

For HSBC and the other British banks this meant trouble, because their strength and prestige in China hinged on the privileges that extraterritoriality had afforded since 1842. The British bankers in Shanghai dreaded challenges to the status quo that a new Nationalist government might pose. When its sway was confined to Guangdong, the GMD introduced tough measures to discourage people from using British HK$ notes or dealing with foreign banks in general.[75] If the Nationalist thrust were to assert itself over a larger swathe of the country, then the British banks' domination of the Chinese foreign exchange market, as well as their ability to mobilize resources locally, would be jeopardized.

But the degree of unification that GMD territorial expansion ushered in proved much less of a threat to foreign banks than was first thought; the first few years of nationalist rule were marred by residual warlordism and an irresolute stand on the foreign presence. Monetary fragmentation prevailed, while the enthusiasm that had fed the *Wusa* Movement had been consumed by the killing of hundreds of labor activists in the 1927 raid on the Communist Party. With fresh doubts emerging as to the new government's power, demand for HSBC banknotes in Shanghai soon reached the SH$2 million cap, which Barlow had imposed in August 1925. By August 1927, therefore, the upper limit on the China issue had to be revised to $2.5 million.[76]

The Bank was still wary of new runs on its notes, but it did not contemplate voluntarily renouncing the China issue. Furthermore, in late September 1927, Lowson pressed the Head Office to reconsider its positions and allow him to issue notes beyond the $2.5 million cap, but he was promptly rebuffed. This was because the Head Office feared that, under the prevailing political circumstances, any increase in the Shanghai issue would immediately be hoarded, impinging on the Bank's ability to balance off circulation volumes between the Mainland and Hong Kong when demand in either place spiked.[77]

As from early 1928, changes in Foreign Office attitudes toward China translated into pressure exerted by the British Legation in Beijing and the Shanghai Consulate on the HSBC Head Office to provide accurate monthly reports on the volumes of its notes in circulation on the Mainland and on the size of reserves set against them. The fact that such a request specifically addressed the Mainland rather than Hong Kong for the very first time suggests that foreign banknote issue prerogatives were becoming a diplomatic hot potato soon after the inauguration of the Nanjing government.[78]

While the Shanghai Consulate asked for the "total amount of [HSBC] banknotes circulating in China," the Bank could only provide accurate figures on

Table 5.3 HSBC Mainland Branch Circulation, 1925–1933 (Unit: Silver Dollars)

	January–February 1925	September–November 1926	December 1927	December 1933
Shanghai	3,604,060	1,428,060	2,158,460	1,142,254
Beijing	498,525	108,050	32,050	9,160
Tianjin	325,577	71,393	41,563	17,033
Yantai [Chefoo]	118,536	11,200	2,050	1,200
Hankou	63,980	8,270	5,577	3,382
Xiamen [Amoy]	963	701	698	615
Fuzhou	660	660	660	667
China Total	**4,612,301**	**1,628,334**	**2,241,058**	**1,174,311**

Sources: HSBC GA GHO 96.2; PRO FO 371/13193, FO 371/18130; PRO Figures are in HK$ units.

quasi-foreign notes issued from the treaty-port branches; it possessed no data on the amount of its HK$ notes in use across the border: "It is obvious of course that we cannot have the slightest idea of the amount of Hongkong notes in circulation in Canton or China."[79]

To what extent did the rise of GMD power in the late 1920s play a role in highlighting the Mainland issue? Determining the answer is of consequence, not least because the previous account of the Bank's policy toward its Mainland issue suggested that the Head Office had steadily phased out notes in the treaty ports since 1921, essentially due to lack of profitability, thereby denying any agency to Chinese policymakers.[80] But a detailed set of data for 1927 and 1933 (see Table 5.3) demonstrates that the China total clearly rebounded from the post-*Wusa* ebb by December 1927, and one cannot completely rule out the possibility that it continued to climb higher for some time afterward despite a downtrend in the outports.

That HSBC circulation volumes in Shanghai, and by implication in China, rebounded circa 1927 would be meaningless, unless we bear in mind the CBIAC circulation pattern, as shown in Figure 5.2. That figure showed a marked surge in the China total as from mid-1927 right until mid-1932, even beyond the pre-*Wusa* level. If British banknote issuance in China were becoming both politically fraught *and* unremunerative, it would probably not have rebounded in quite the same way as it had circa 1927.

A more plausible explanation is that, despite proclamations to the contrary, HSBC and CBIAC were not prepared to give up the note issue in the face of nationalist backlash precisely because the issue was, on balance, profitable.

The two banks were eventually *made* to renounce the issue by *Wusa* and its longer-term ramifications—namely, GMD monetary reform measures and the backlash against extraterritorial privileges.

The political climate in 1927 was manifest in a rare article that was published in the otherwise moderate organ of the Chinese bankers' association, the *Yinhang zhoubao*. Aptly titled "The Problem of Clamping Down on Quasi-Foreign Notes" (*Qudi waichao wenti* 取締外鈔問題), the article offered one of the first analyses of how GMD government resolve, predicated on the experience it had acquired in combating HSBC HK$ notes in Guangzhou through 1926, promised to deliver where previous Chinese governments had failed.[81]

Yet, this newfound determination to root out foreign bank prerogatives did not immediately translate into tangible achievements. HSBC data on circulation figures in the outports between 1927 and 1932 are lacking, but Table 5.3 suggests that a moderate rise may have occurred even after 1927, particularly in light of a similar pattern in the CBIAC Shanghai branch. Similarly, a letter from the Head Office to A. B. Lowson in Shanghai, dated January 4, 1930, suggests that the Bank's local note reserve entrusted to the consul-general totaled $6 million at that time, $2 million more than in 1925.[82] Apart from the heightened probity with regard to sudden runs, the figure may also suggest rising circulation volumes on the Mainland some time after 1927.

The difference in the status of the Mainland note reserve was equally significant. The same letter implies that by the early 1930s, Hong Kong's government had been prepared to recognize part of the Shanghai reserve as appropriate cover for larger circulation volumes in the Colony toward the Lunar New Year. Hitherto only the central Hong Kong reserve had been formally recognized for this purpose. This would have allowed the Bank to manage its global note circulation more flexibly, reducing overlap between formal and informal reserves.

At the same time, the large number of pertinent press clippings in the Bank's records suggests that it was closely monitoring popular sentiments against its note issue in China. In February 1930, the Head Office wrote to Lowson that reports in the Chinese press on a dramatic increase in quasi-foreign banknote circulation were "pure invention" and that the quantity of such banknotes was probably "infinitesimal" compared with Chinese banknotes.[83] Curiously, the letter did not address specific HSBC or other foreign bank circulation numbers, focusing instead on the growth of domestic banks of issue and on the fact that "[t]here has been much talk about stopping the foreign banks from issuing vast numbers of notes in China." Lowson, at any rate, was instructed to deny the reports because "as you know, we do not wish our issue to go up in Shanghai."

To what extent, then, were Chinese banknotes taking center stage in the early 1930s? In a confidential letter from G. E. Hubbard, the Bank's Shanghai-based political adviser, to V. N. Grayburn, who had been appointed chief manager in 1930, Hubbard reported that notes issued by Chinese banks in the city now formed the "chief" medium of currency in "Central China, the Yangtsze [Yangzi] Valley up to Ichang [Yichang]."[84]

Hubbard estimated that in 1930 the total circulation volume of Chinese banknotes—of which five government-backed banks were the principal stakeholders—was $290 million, while quasi-foreign money amounted to only $5 million.[85] The progress Chinese banking made was impressive inasmuch as it dwarfed the foreign treaty-port issue, but Hubbard's wording leaves some doubt as to whether Shanghai banknotes were widely used in all parts of China even at this late stage; new research by Brett Sheehan suggests in fact that China's modern banking sector remained fairly diffuse in the hinterland as late as 1936.[86]

The tightening of foreign bank supervision roughly coincided with Japan's annexation of Manchuria (1931).[87] The annexation set the stage for a closer Anglo-Chinese diplomatic rapprochement and a currency war between anti and pro-Japanese banks of issue in Northeast China. On January 1932, Hubbard envisioned a settlement whereby Japan could be persuaded to recognize Chinese sovereignty in Manchuria in return for GMD moves to curb anti-Japanese demonstrations in Shanghai and to repay the controversial Nishihara loans.[88]

Either way, Hubbard was pleased to report that, in view of its unraveling conflict with Japan, the GMD government "has indefinitely postponed the unilateral abolition of extraterritoriality fixed for January 1st." He thought that the Japanese threat might actually be a boon to foreign business, and he reported that the British Chamber of Commerce believed it averted the need for Britain to launch a costly war against China to preserve extraterritoriality.

Hubbard's dalliance with *Weltpolitik* was by no means atypical of a bank with such longstanding presence in the region. Yet, in a sense, it betrays ignorance of the changing balance of power in Shanghai's financial markets. A second glance at Figure 4.3 reminds us that as late as 1915 HSBC branch holdings, according to its own in-house data, accounted for 42 percent of Shanghai's silver stock. Yet, seventeen years later, fairly reliable Bank of China data put the figure at just 18 percent. The full data set is charted in Figure 5.4.

The diminishing share of the Bank in Shanghai finance could not have been unrelated to developments in the wider arena. Despite Japanese en-

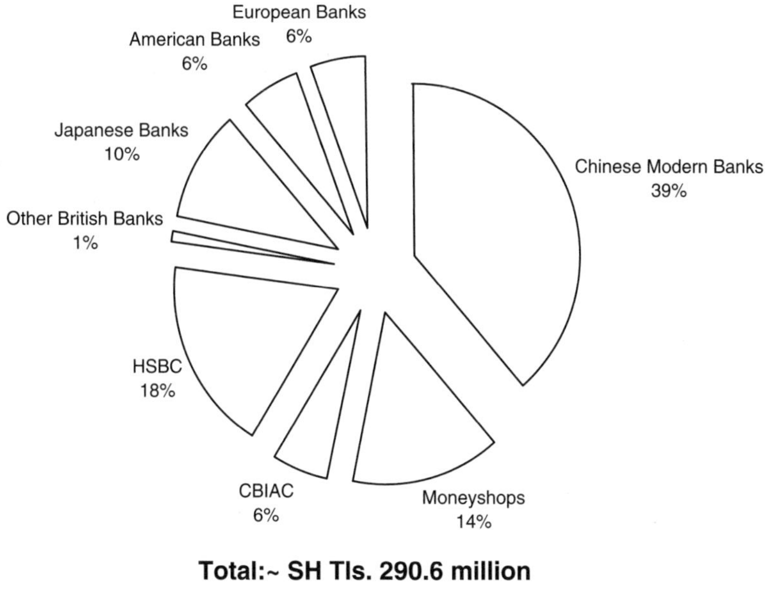

Figure 5.4. Bank Silver Stocks in Shanghai, 1932 Year-End. *Source*: *Zhongyang yinhang yuebao* [Central Bank Monthly] 1.5 (December 1932): 894–895. As from 1932, Chinese government data on the foreign financial sector seem increasingly detailed. This was arguably because prominent foreign bankers had been persuaded to join national advisory bodies like Shanghai's Joint Reserve Committee. See, e.g., *Quanguo yinhang nianjian* [The All-China Banking Yearbook], vol. 2, 1934–1935, section D, p. 32. However, foreign banks continued to withhold information on local banknote circulation volumes or China branch balance-sheet totals until the abolition of extraterritoriality in 1942.

croachments, GMD monetary and banking reforms proceeded with a vengeance, dispelling any illusions foreign bankers might have entertained about a letup in the campaign against their treaty-port prerogatives. To be sure, HSBC executives continued to express some skepticism about Chinese monetary unification, but were now more wary of the backlash they would face if the GMD accused them of obstructing the national agenda of state-building.

Nowhere was this attitude more evident than in the way the Bank reacted to GMD preparations for the demonetization of sycee in mid-1932. On July 1932, for example, the Head Office informed F. B. Winter, the submanager in Shanghai, that it was opposed to the attendant abolition of the tael unit of account, in all its multifarious forms, because of fears that government-minted dollars would be debased soon afterward.[89]

On March 16, 1933, shortly after the abolition of the tael had been proclaimed, HSBC's new political adviser, W. C. Cassels, wrote to the British consul-general in Shanghai, J. W. O. Davidson, that HSBC and other foreign banks viewed recent developments with apprehension, because of fears that it might foreshadow attempts to depreciate the silver contents of the Chinese currency.[90]

Nonetheless, by April 1933, Grayburn, the chief manager, conceded in a letter to A. S. Henchman (who had replaced A. B. Lowson as Shanghai manager in 1930) that the tael system had been "antiquated" and that if the Chinese government were "in earnest in [its] endeavor to work with one currency for China and will see that silver dollars are kept to standard, I do not think Foreign banks have a leg to stand on in opposing their wishes."[91] Grayburn's conciliatory tone toward the reform may have ensued from the resounding success of the abolition of the tael. But, perhaps more importantly, his wording reflected the astute manner in which GMD officials cajoled foreign banks into backing the reform by offering them seats on the Advisory Board that was to oversee its long-term implementation.[92]

The smooth abolition of the tael demonstrated in action rather than words the GMD resolve to work toward uniform national currency. The reform engendered an irreversible turnaround in quasi-foreign circulation volumes in Shanghai, which was then greatly compounded by rising world silver prices. In early 1934, the city's leading expert on currency, Edward Kann, estimated paper money circulation as set out in Table 5.4.

Kann's estimate for Shanghai dovetails with quantitative data compiled more recently. Sheehan's time series, for example, suggest that Chinese banknote circulation in Tianjin alone rose from $38.8 million in 1928 to $46.5 million in 1933.[93] Figures compiled by Cheng Linsun suggest that Chinese banknote circulation across the country totaled $452 million in 1931, as opposed to $578.5 million in 1933.[94] Cheng's time series also indicates that the largest annual percentage increase in the circulation of Chinese banknotes between 1920 and 1935 occurred right after *Wusa* 1925 (+35%).

Clearly, Chinese banknote circulation volume dwarfed the foreign one in 1933. But the monetary balance of power between the domestic and foreign banking sectors looked very different two decades prior. As late as 1913, China's first modern bank (IBC) claimed a total note circulation of merely $1.78 million. That year, HSBC's circulation volume in Shanghai alone reached $3.5 million.[95]

These figures bear out the growth of Chinese modern banking, but readers should still be aware that a total Chinese banknote circulation of $350.6 million in 1933 did not necessarily eclipse metallic currencies even at that stage.

Table 5.4 Paper Money Circulation in Shanghai (Unit: SH$ million)

	December 1931	December 1932	December 1933
Foreign Banks	3.7	3.3	2.4
Chinese Banks	271.3	284.7	350.6

Source: Article by Edward Kann in the Shanghainese English-language magazine *Finance and Commerce*, dated February 10, 1934, clipped in HSBC GA SH I–52.1.

Rather, the figures should be looked at in regional perspective: in Hong Kong *alone* British banknote circulation reached as much as HK$157.5 million in December 1933.[96] In other words, the comparison with Hong Kong lends support to the proposition that a large swathe of China was characterized by low monetization right up until the introduction of a uniform fiat currency in 1935.[97]

About a year after the abolition of tael, quasi-foreign note circulation volumes were yet again affected by an exogenous shock. Pressured by regional mining interests in Congress, the Roosevelt administration embarked on its Silver Purchase Policy, which was designed to lift America out of recession in 1934.[98] One of the immediate side effects of this policy was that China—now the only country in the world to cling to the silver standard—saw a rapid erosion in its terms of trade, which slashed exports and crippled the industrial base of the treaty-port economy.

Worse still, China's money supply was being depleted because the U.S. price of silver edged above the official exchange value of the Chinese silver dollar, resulting in incessant waves of sycee exports from Shanghai to America either directly or via London.[99] The implication for China's economy was double-pronged. First, after years of inflation and debasement, China's metallic currency was appreciating artificially on the cross rates. It made imports cheaper, thus dampening the relative price of agricultural produce and hitting living standards in the rural hinterland. But, much more importantly, it made simple business sense to buy silver dollars in Shanghai for U.S. dollars or other foreign currencies and then melt them into silver.

An upturn in world silver prices had already loomed on the horizon in 1931 when Britain came off the gold standard. Then, on June 19, 1934, the U.S. Congress passed the Silver Purchase Act in a bid to re-vitalize the silver mining industry and alleviate conditions in several Midwest states. The immediate impact was a drastic depletion of Chinese silver reserves in favor of much higher prices in the New York and London commodity exchanges. China was thus belatedly drawn into the whirlwind of the Great Depression.[100]

In such circumstances, maintaining a metallic silver reserve against notes outstanding in China (and Hong Kong) meant rising opportunity costs for domestic and foreign banks alike. Because no country but America could stem the rise in silver prices, China's economy was now facing an acute liquidity crisis, in which not only its exports were hit, but the very foundation of its money stock was also thrown into question.

After repeated Chinese representations to the Roosevelt administration to change course had failed through late 1934 and early 1935, a daring initiative took shape in discussions between Kong Xiangxi (H. H. Kung), Song Ziwen (T. V. Soong), and Jiang Jieshi (Chiang Kai-shek).[101] Though they were driven by different personal agenda, the three concurred that China should ride on the momentum afforded by U.S. policy to divorce Chinese currency of silver. This move, they hoped, would help the GMD government claw back greater latitude in the monetary realm and reap a windfall from the sell-off of the silver stock while prices were at their highest in decades.[102]

The initiative was fraught with theoretical and practical difficulties: implementation would require absolute secrecy to foil speculators' preemption and at least a semblance of wide international endorsement. Thus, when asked during a carefully orchestrated interview held in late 1934, whether China would resort to fiat currency to stem the flight of silver, Generalissimo Jiang replied: "A paper standard of currency is absolutely unsuitable for China . . . [T]he [Chinese] government does not attempt to adopt such a measure."[103]

Denials notwithstanding, the Chinese Ministry of Finance had already been bracing itself for the abolition of *all* silver-convertible notes. On the same day the interview with Jiang Jieshi was published, the Chinese press reported that the Ministry established a study group to examine the problems arising from quasi-foreign note issuance and make preparations for the full recovery of monetary sovereignty by government banks, in conformity with financial practices in other countries.[104]

Connected to the innermost circles of Chinese politics, the Bank soon got wind of the intense deliberations that Ministry officials were conducting. In a letter to Henchman dated October 1934, Grayburn was almost able to second-guess Chinese government intentions. He was convinced that "the Chinese cannot maintain a managed currency, while stocks of silver are still in the hands of the public"; but what disturbed Grayburn more than the choice of China's future currency was the government's "obvious determination to oust foreign banks."[105] Indeed, in December 1934, *Zhonghang yuekan* [The Bank of China Monthly Review] reported that the Ministry of Finance was planning to set up a special committee with the Ministry of Foreign Affairs to examine the implications of outlawing foreign banknote issuance.[106]

Unlike many of its competitors, HSBC seems to have bucked the trend to cash in on arbitrage in silver prices between China and world markets. In November 1934, Grayburn's newly appointed deputy, E. J. Davies, wrote begrudgingly to Henchman from the Head Office that foreign banks were busy transshipping large quantities of smuggled-in Mainland silver via Hong Kong—and that CBIAC was prominent among the offenders. But arbitrage resulted in increased profits for the Exchange Banks even if they had not been involved in overt smuggling. As Davies noted: "We continue to sell sterling and silver against it, which is very profitable, but one would wish to see profits from a less fortuitous source."[107]

The Chinese government tried to combat the flight of silver by imposing hefty export duties. However, several foreign banks, including CBIAC, continued to smuggle silver out of China right under the government's nose.[108] The high alternative cost of immobilizing silver reserves against the note issue in Shanghai during 1934–1935 may well have led foreign bank mangers to retire notes when presented for encashment. It is equally plausible that the smuggling of silver alarmed note bearers, who preferred to capitalize on the high price of silver themselves.

It was foreign bank smuggling that sparked a fresh wave of resistance against the prevalence of quasi-foreign notes and further spurred the GMD government to take on the foreign banks.[109] In spite of the fact that quasi-foreign circulation volumes were much less significant in early 1935 than had been the case in 1925, Chinese financiers were particularly vocal in demanding an end to foreign bank privileges.

On February 28, 1935, the Shanghai English-language daily *China Press* published, for example, an article under the heading "Native Bankers Renew Agitation against Note Issue by Foreign Banks." The article reported on several petitions that were presented to the Ministry of Finance against HSBC and other foreign banks. The foreign banks were said to be preparing to increase their note issuance in order to "absorb the silver reserves in the Chinese market" for export to America. In response to these allegations, a Ministry spokesman described the existence of quasi-foreign notes as "non beneficial to the country's economic fiber."[110]

The CBIAC and HSBC data presented above suggest that the petitions actually lagged behind market trends. The circulation volume of CBIAC Mainland branches had peaked in mid-1932, but was declining immediately thereafter. The Chinese petitions were even wider off the mark as regards HSBC, whose circulation volume on the Mainland declined some time after 1927 and whose managers had by then become insecure about their future prospects on the Mainland and reluctant to engage in massive silver trafficking for fears of antagonizing the Chinese and British authorities.

What underlay this insecurity was incipient recognition within the Bank that Chinese central banking was making impressive headway, thereby challenging the legitimacy of the foreign banks' long-standing treaty-port privileges. W. C. Cassels indicated in a letter to O. J. Barnes, manager of the London office, that the reserves held by Chinese banks against their note issue were on the whole more solid than in the past. In some cases the reserves "appeared to be up to the legal figure of 60 percent cash, while in others it was as low as 20 percent." Although this uneven percentage was deemed "unsatisfactory," the tenor of the letter bespoke an appreciation of the fact that Chinese note reserves were regularly supervised by the Chinese Ministry of Finance.[111]

But perhaps the most important factor that informed the Bank's downbeat prognosis of its Mainland business was Whitehall's increasingly close ties with the GMD. On January 14, 1935, Grayburn informed Henchman from Hong Kong that he was identifying signs of distrust toward the Bank in the Treasury.[112]

One of the questions that set the two parties on a collision course was how to deal with China's monetary reform momentum. Throughout the early 1930s, Charles Addis, the Bank's quintessential "Old China Hand," was working behind the scenes in London to revive the international bank Consortium and to float a loan on the order of GBP 20 million to remedy China's depleting money stock. In the Treasury's eyes, these maneuvers encapsulated the Bank's bias against the Nationalist regime, not least because the foreign bank medicine that Addis persistently prescribed had long since been anathema to the Chinese.[113]

By July 1935, differences between the Treasury and the British banks slid into full-blown conflict. Grayburn reported to Henchman that the Chinese government was whispering in the ears of Whitehall officials that the foreign banks were to blame for the shortage of cash in Shanghai, although he personally believed that only Japanese banks were seriously implicated in silver contraband.[114] Grayburn's anxiety over a burgeoning rift with the Chinese and Whitehall was profoundly compounded by signs that HSBC's HK$ note circulation figures were dropping on reports that the Colony might emulate the rumored Chinese plan to reduce the silver content of its currency.[115]

The souring of relations between the HSBC and Whitehall should also be seen in a global context: between 1920 and 1944 the Bank of England pushed for the creation of national central banks with note issue monopoly in all countries that did not have them yet. This was seen as an ideological foray promoting British soft power worldwide.[116]

The year 1935 was one of tense anticipation, at the end of which a *deus ex machina* for China's monetary crisis loomed large. The proclamation of the *fabi* reform in November saw the Chinese government offering its nationalized silver stock for sale in America—including silver that was yet to be advanced by foreign banks—in return for U.S. dollars.[117] The reform firmly put China's economy on a managed paper currency basis, thereby ending almost ninety years during which British and Chinese private banks issued notes on Chinese soil.

Thus, on November 5, 1935, the *North-China Daily News* could recount with much fanfare that "the decree of the Chinese government [regarding] the new currency policy and the decision to stabilize the dollar went into force yesterday and [were] generally well received."[118] The reform was affirmed concomitantly by the British ambassador to China, Sir Alexander Cadogan, a move that dealt the ultimate blow to the convertibility of British banknotes. Cadogan issued a special regulation under the China Order-in-Council 1925, which effectively prohibited payments in silver by British individuals or institutions and set out penalties for offenders. But he was not acting on his own authority—the Chinese government now had the full support of its British counterpart, with the latter having dispatched a special Mission to the region to lay the groundwork for future monetary arrangements between the two countries.

THE LEITH-ROSS MISSION (1935–1936)

Curiously enough, the initial success of the *fabi* reform has become almost synonymous in much of the pertinent literature in the West with the Leith-Ross Mission to China, conducted between September 21, 1935 and June 23, 1936.[119] As the following passages will demonstrate, Sir Frederick Leith-Ross was instrumental in pulling the British government, diplomatic corps, and Eastern Exchange Banks behind the reform. However, the archival material presented here will clearly show that it was the Chinese government, *not* Leith-Ross, who devised the particulars of the reform and determined its timing *without* pecuniary assistance from the British and *in the face of* British bank recalcitrance. Thus a number of scholars have missed the true historic significance of the Mission.[120] Rather than credit Leith-Ross with singlehandedly rescuing China from a monetary nemesis, or with inducting it into the new sterling zone, his Mission should be understood as the preface to a new British policy in East Asia. While primarily aimed at containing Japan, the new policy also sent a chilling wake-up call for British expatriates in China.

The second outcome, in particular, is not self-evident. Far from anticipating rebuke, the British business lobby in China had initially been one of the most vocal driving forces behind the launch of the Mission. Therefore, the Mission cannot be adequately understood without first considering the impetus that led to its formation, and the way in which its objectives were conceived of on the eve of Leith-Ross's arrival in the region.

By the early 1930s, most British businesses in China had felt less threatened by GMD ideology. At the same time, they became increasingly uneasy about Japanese ambitions for commercial dominance in the region. These sentiments came to the boil in early 1935, upping the ante for a Whitehall intervention. In a confidential memorandum dated March 15, for example, one of the most stalwart "China Hands," W. J. Keswick of Jardine Matheson & Co., was quoted as warning Bank of England officials:

> [Keswick] is much disturbed at the aggressive attitude of Japan, and is satisfied that if the British Government does not very soon announce firmly its intention of remaining in China and take steps to strengthen the British position and representation out there, Japan will in the near future dominate China and make it impossible for British people to trade there effectively . . . otherwise, although they are the biggest British firm in China . . . [Jardine Matheson & Co.] have made up their minds to leave the country.[121]

Whitehall and the Bank of England, however, were for the most part strictly averse to open confrontation with Japan. Rather, British policymakers favored a subtler gambit that would allow Britain to safeguard its China markets through courting better relations with the GMD, coupled with a willingness to cede more extraterritorial privileges.[122] Ironically, the Foreign Office had exuded more suspicion of Japanese intentions than either the Bank of England or the Treasury, but as soon as the Mission had begun work found fault with Leith-Ross for unduly provoking Tokyo's sensitivities.[123]

As already indicated, the decision to dispatch Leith-Ross to the region had to do in the first instance with mercantile concerns. However, the timing of the dispatch equally reflected concerns about U.S. foreign policy. In the course of 1934–1935, Kong Xiangxi, the Chinese finance minister, was thought to be playing Japan, the United States, and Britain against one another, as part of Chinese attempts to goad either one of the two Transatlantic Powers into granting China a large loan. Reports from the British Consulate in Shanghai warned the Foreign Office as early as December 18, 1934, that despite declarations to the contrary, Kong needed funds urgently in order to support a new fiat currency.[124] At the same time, Kong warned the British that if the Bank of England was not to facilitate a sterling loan to the Chinese government in London's capital market, it risked seeing the Communists taking over the country and reneging on all foreign debts.[125]

The British government was finally convinced of the seriousness of this Chinese demarche and was subsequently roused to action, only after its ambassador to Washington reported that sources in the State Department had told him that Nanjing was putting the final touches on a monetary plan of unprecedented magnitude. His ciphered telegram to the Foreign Office read:

> Some weeks ago the Department of State received from Chinese Minister at Washington the text of a message from Chinese Minister of Finance, containing the outline of a plan with regard to silver in which [it] was suggested that, in view of what China considered necessity of abandoning present silver basis and adopting a new currency system involving use of both silver and gold, the United States [will] extend to China a substantial loan in addition [to] a substantial credit.
>
> The Department made a reply that [the] American government did not deem it practicable for [the] United States to embark upon such an undertaking.[126]

It was the cold shoulder Washington had initially showed the Chinese in early 1935 that made hands-on British involvement all the more sensible.[127] As an overture, Whitehall suggested to the Chinese government that it send a high-ranking envoy in the image of Leith-Ross to study Chinese proposals for British government loans. From mid-1935 until Leith-Ross's arrival in Shanghai on September 21, 1935, Whitehall launched a concomitant diplomatic foray to cement international backing for China to join the newly established sterling zone.[128]

In a secret British Treasury memorandum issued on October 19, the principal objectives of the Mission were formally described as (1) to help stabilize a new Chinese currency with a loan from the "four Consortium Powers," that is, Britain, France, Japan, and the United States; (2) to prod the United States to barter gold reserves for the Chinese silver stock despite signs of objection in Washington to the pegging of the Chinese currency to the sterling; (3) to appease Japanese suspicion of British involvement in currency reform; (4) to consolidate debts incurred by successive Chinese governments; and (5) to ensure that, in return for British assistance, the GMD government appoint a British adviser to the Chinese Central Bank and that a British national continue to preside over the Chinese Maritime Customs.[129]

Ultimately, none of these ambitious objectives was to be fulfilled as planned. Over the next tumultuous decade China's currency *never* joined the sterling zone. Moreover, it is doubtful whether a sterling peg was ever seen as strategically compelling in British Treasury and Bank of England deliberations. As early as October 27, 1935, Leith-Ross cautioned, for example, that pegging China's currency to sterling would compromise Britain's relations with Japan; he suggested that from the British perspective the main purpose of any currency reform should be to promote British trade in China and settle debt defaults.[130]

From then on, and largely because of the views Leith-Ross formed, the role of the Eastern Exchange Banks in Anglo-Chinese relations loomed increasingly large in backroom Whitehall deliberations. The Mission's unexpected thrust became evident to HSBC about a month after Leith-Ross arrived in China. On October 22, 1935, Henchman wrote to Grayburn from Shanghai that Leith-Ross had summoned him to say that "he gathered the HSBC was not popular with the Chinese Government" because of allegations that the Bank had been involved in silver contraband.[131] The same sentiment resonated a few days earlier from a telegram, marked "strictly private," that the Hong Kong government sent to the Colonial Office, and where Leith-Ross was quoted as saying:

> You should know that Hong Kong and Shanghai Bank is regarded with considerable mistrust by Chinese. It is considered in Chinese Government circles that [Foreign] Banks have deliberately accentuated Chinese difficulties by pursuing excessive deflation policy and by unnecessarily exporting silver in order to escape possible [Chinese Government] embargo. It is stated that they so denuded themselves of silver here that they were obliged to borrow from [the New York-based] Chase to meet engagements. Further, they are regarded in Chinese banking circles as obstructive in their attitude both to [the formation of a Chinese] Central Bank and to institution of clearing. It is recognized that in recent management of exchange they have been most helpful but it is still feared that they cannot be relied upon to support [the] new [*fabi*] scheme even if they do not work for its breakdown.[132]

A ciphered telegram from Leith-Ross in Shanghai to the Treasury, dated November 1, 1935, suggests that the timing of the Chinese decision to move off silver caught him by surprise, but a request from Song Ziwen for his assistance in persuading the British banks to hand over silver did not.[133] Immediately after his meeting with Song, Leith-Ross communicated the Chinese government's intention to Henchman and Cockfarn, the respective Shanghai branch managers of the HSBC and CBIAC. Alarmed, the two bankers asked that a British government Order-in-Council be promptly issued to absolve them from paying out silver to depositors in light of the Chinese plan to nationalize silver stocks. Leith-Ross acceded, but insisted that British bank silver be handed over to the Chinese, to which Cockfarn agreed. However, Henchman "wished to exclude silver held against his own notes and to continue payment of silver against these notes. His object is to maintain the prestige of Hongkong and Shanghai banknotes (with Hongkong situation in mind) but of course any prestige they obtain involves prejudice to the Chinese notes."[134]

Despite Leith-Ross's facilitation of the desired Order-in-Council, HSBC held off the handover of silver. A month later, Henchman reported that it was the governor of the Bank of England, Montague Norman, who was behind Leith-Ross's firm line against the Bank and that the two devised a line "very little different from an ultimatum" to force HSBC to accommodate the *fabi* reform, by handing in all the silver in its possession in China to Chinese state banks, "or face the consequences."[135]

Hitherto, a voluntary handover of silver to the Chinese authorities would have been unthinkable. It meant in effect the surrender of much of the Bank's independence in China's monetary realm and, by implication, of its ability to issue local money to back up its exchange operations. Leith-Ross's demand was so far-reaching that Henchman concluded that the Mission had been designed for the benefit of the Chinese government, while the interests of the British banks and the expatriate community were in its "also ran" department.

Leith-Ross opposed Henchman's request to exempt HSBC's issue reserve from handover to the Chinese government because he feared it might be shipped out of China rather than be used to cash client liabilities. His colleagues at the Treasury conveyed these concerns when they wrote that "none of the foreign banks could afford to pay their deposits in silver" and that foreign banks "in principle should receive the same treatment as native banks *except in so far as their silver reserves are not held against liabilities expressed in Chinese currency* . . . It would be unfair and a source of grievance to the Chinese if foreign banks obtained a windfall profit on silver held against Chinese liabilities."[136]

This passage not only suggested that the British Treasury believed that quasi-foreign money had principally been held by Chinese bearers, but it also alluded to a widespread breach of confidence in foreign bank conduct: in compliance with Chinese requests, British banks disbursed Chinese banknotes rather than silver from as early as April 1935. Some banks, however, abused this "gentlemanly agreement" with the Chinese government to spirit away mandatory silver reserves overseas.[137]

The hard line, which Leith-Ross helped forge vis-à-vis the British banks, echoed a wider sea change in Whitehall. Hitherto, HSBC traditionally enjoyed good relations with British officialdom. As late as 1932, the Bank of England protected HSBC's position as the de facto central bank in Greater China by refusing a request from Song Ziwen, then Chinese finance minister, to nominate Lloyds Bank as the conduit for intergovernmental payment. A Bank of England official gave away the reason for the refusal in these terms: "the Hong Kong and Shanghai Bank [*sic*] are at present our bankers in London, and we naturally do not want to take action which is contrary to their interests."[138]

By late 1935, the Bank's senior management in London was beginning to receive very different messages. On November 5, for example, O. J. Barnes wrote to Henchman from London that the Treasury had intimated to him its position that all British banks in China should support the proposals put forth by the Chinese government and "hand in their stocks of silver against new currency notes."[139] Such was the Treasury's adamancy that the smaller banks—CBIAC and MBI—indicated as early as November 1 that they were likely to comply with the *fabi* reform, provided that all other foreign banks followed suit and that an Order-in-Council be issued in Shanghai to exempt them from paying silver over the counter to liability holders.[140]

HSBC did not cave in to the Treasury's pressure so easily. Henchman wrote to Grayburn on November 11—only twelve days before the Treasury's ultimatum was to expire—that he was trying to enlist Song Ziwen to mediate between the Bank and Kong Xiangxi, the incumbent finance minister, so that the latter would be forced to vouch for nonperforming Chinese debts in return for a smooth silver handover. If Kong was not to offer any concessions, Henchman indicated that he was prepared to mobilize the non-British foreign banks to obstruct the reform.[141]

But a month later, the Bank already had to retreat from its earlier demands, largely because the first month of the *fabi* reform was hailed a success even without its compliance. On December 10, Henchman expressed his disenchantment with the Mission's objectives in a letter he wrote to Grayburn, but was now forced to concede that the Chinese government possessed sufficient silver "to play with" and that this effectively dashed the Bank's hopes of clinching preferential terms for the handover of silver and of securing a role in future Chinese government loan floatation in London.[142] It was only on January 16, 1936 that Sir A. Cadogan, now British ambassador to Nanjing, could report back to the Foreign Office that due to the Mission's work the "surrender of [British bank] silver has been arranged."[143]

That Whitehall was not, however, fully attuned to the direction of Chinese policy at that stage is evidenced by a note Leith-Ross sent to Neville Chamberlain on July 31, 1935, only three months before the *fabi* currency was promulgated. In this note, Leith-Ross envisioned a broad international loan Consortium, including the Japanese, that would help support China's new legal tender in return for China's recognition of the Japanese occupation of Manchuria.[144] Once the Mission got underway, attempts at reconciling the GMD government, Japanese territorial ambitions, and British commercial concerns through holding out the prospect of an international loan proved futile.

Tokyo's suspicion of the Mission, and its refusal to partake in an international loan, disappointed Leith-Ross much more than Chinese adamancy over Manchuria had.[145] He frequently gave vent to his frustration with Japanese obstructionism, and to his warming up to Chinese national aspirations, in a flurry of correspondence with Whitehall shortly before the *fabi* reform was launched.[146]

Nonetheless, it would be a mistake to assume that the Chinese saw Leith-Ross as privy to the minutiae of the reform. In fact, the correspondence clearly shows that Kong Xiangxi and Song Ziwen pressed ahead with the reform *despite* impassioned pleas from Leith-Ross to defer any action until a British loan agreement was achieved. Instead, Kong and Song were working out an alternative agreement with the U.S. government to sell Chinese nationalized silver reserves via New York in return for American hard currency to support the *fabi*.[147] Extant records suggest that, if anything, the Mission played a minor role in securing American cooperation. In fact, the negotiations between Washington and Nanjing were kept under tight wraps over the course of October–November 1935, not least because the United States was suspicious of Britain's intentions.[148] From that moment and until 1949, Britain was to play second fiddle to the Americans when it came to supporting GMD government finances.

In the meantime, the initial success of the *fabi* reform paved the way for a swift demonetization of silver in Hong Kong too. Such a radical reform in the Colony could have, of course, much wider implications for the Bank's status as the semiofficial British bank in the region, because the lion's share of its notes had been issued from the Head Office and it was there that it kept most of its reserves. Once the Treasury instructed Hong Kong's government to opt out from the silver standard in favor of a fiat currency fully backed by sterling reserves, the fiduciary element and profit potential in the three Exchange banks' note issue became null and void. But since the Colony's government was not prepared to issue its own notes, a new formula had to be found for the continuation of the private bank issue, whereby the Hong Kong government would bear some of the administrative and printing costs involved.

In the process of negotiating a new arrangement with the Treasury and the Colony's government, HSBC quite naturally tried to overstate the costs it would have to shoulder if the private issue was to remain in effect. In a letter to the Treasury's Norman Young dated in early 1936, Grayburn maintained that the material and administrative costs of issuing HK$1 million amounted to no less than HK$115,000 annually, or 11.5 percent of the notes' face value.[149] It stands to reason that the ratio of production costs to face value was not critically different for HK$ notes than the ratio calculated for Shanghai dollar notes presented in Table 5.1, since the same print technology and safety precautions were used in both cases. The Shanghai ratio of production costs to face value (1.65 percent) was compounded by a 1 percent government tax imposed on local circulation volumes by the Colony's government. The resultant total (2.65 percent) is conspicuously smaller, however, than the one Grayburn advanced (11.5 percent), even when allowing for a miscellany of unaccounted expenses.

While intensive negotiations involving the Bank, Treasury, and the Colony's government over the future of the private issue in Hong Kong were moving ahead, the standoff between the Bank and the Chinese government remained unresolved. This was so much the case that on January 1, 1936 Leith-Ross sent the Bank a stern warning from his suite at the Cathay Hotel on the Bund. The warning was addressed to Henchman, the Bank's local branch manager, advising him that further delays in the handover of silver to the Chinese government would have grave consequences, especially in view of the fact that most other foreign banks—except the Japanese ones—had already endorsed these requisites.[150]

The determination and consistency that Leith-Ross demonstrated, seemingly on behalf of a foreign government, in bringing the Bank to heel left the Head Office nonplussed. On May 14, 1936, Grayburn divulged his growing concerns over the Mission. In a letter to A. C. Leith, the acting manager in

Shanghai, who was temporarily replacing Henchman at the helm, Grayburn confided that he thought Sir Frederick Leith-Ross would probably prefer to see British banks in China "vanish" altogether, and that he was indifferent to their pleas to recover Chinese debts in return for a smooth handover of silver.[151]

Leith-Ross, for his part, was not easily shaken by the litany of British expatriate rebuke. In addition to Bank of England and Treasury backing, he had some segments of the Foreign Office by his side. Wielding the clout and moral authority of a knighted professional, he was one of a select few in Whitehall who could challenge the Bank's China expertise and force it to renounce its silver reserves by mid-1936. Upon the conclusion of his Mission, the *Chicago Daily News* described Leith-Ross as "one of the leading members of that remarkable caste, whose job is to take the long-term, non-partisan view of British interests—the British Civil Service."[152]

In retrospect, it may well be argued that the Mission capped a slow shift in British foreign policy toward East Asia, which had begun a decade earlier; it saw Britain gradually relinquishing its hold on the Chinese treaty ports, so that the GMD could be wooed back into the Western fold and help contain Soviet and Japanese influence in the region. Leith-Ross was usually low key in his public pronouncements, so as not to antagonize those who could preempt those foreign policy objectives, be they Japanese diplomats in China, expatriate British bankers, or hostile GMD officials. Nonetheless, a confidential Treasury memorandum, compiled from Leith-Ross's notes for limited circulation within Whitehall ministries by one of his confidantes, divulged much of what he thought about Britain's role in the region. To borrow a Japanese popular term, this memorandum summed up Leith-Ross's *honne*, or all the things he wanted to say about some of his compatriots but could not afford to:

> In his note on British trade, Sir Frederick severely criticizes merchants, banks, the Purchasing Commission in London, The Exports Credits Guarantee Department, The Embassy and the Consular Service. Up to quite recent times the British merchants in China have had a sheltered and artificial existence. The Treaties and the timidity of the Chinese placed them in a privileged position in which by trading through a comprador they made easy profits without much effort or risk. In effect, the comprador, traded under the protection of the foreign merchants, and the more the latter, with the help of the Consul and the gunboat, asserted his privileges and rode rough-shod over Chinese rights and aspirations, the better for his business. The pent-up resentment of the Chinese exploded in 1925. They had been taught by the Russians not to agitate against all foreigners at once, but to concentrate their hate on the British, who were the chief upholders of the unequal

treaties and the gunboat policy. An eighteen-month boycott of British trade came as a rude shock and initiated a new era in Anglo-Chinese relations . . .

The British merchant found it very difficult to adapt himself to the new conditions especially as world economic causes had reduced his trade to a fraction of its former volume . . . [He] lacks with few exceptions the suppleness and patience necessary to make friendly contacts with Chinese business men [*sic*] or to deal with the exasperating difficulties of Chinese bureaucracy . . .

The British merchant in China instead of seeking friendly contacts and cooperation with the Chinese still trade[s] through a comprador and spend their time complaining of lack of support from the British government . . . to whose "weak policy" they affect to attribute all the ill that have befallen them . . . [although it was this policy that] really saved what was left of British interest in China from annihilation.

As regards the [British] Banks, evidence has been accumulating for some time that the present direction of the Hong Kong and Shanghai Bank is both narrow minded and short sighted. Here again the problems of the Bank (whose Head Office is in Hong Kong, not London) are affected to quite extra-ordinary degree by political considerations in regard to which the managers both in Shanghai and in Hong Kong are quite incapable of forming a sound judgment [by insisting on the international Consortium loan which aims to] . . . to bring China to heel.[153]

Another secret memorandum in which Leith-Ross expressed himself in the first person was circulated in Whitehall five days later. Though generally much more subdued in tenor, the second memorandum elaborated on some of the thornier issues raised in the previous memorandum:

The British merchants as a whole are reluctant to co-operate with Chinese firms and maintain less close and friendly contacts than merchants of other nationality. One British merchant told me that he had never received a Chinese in his house, and never would, and he believed that it was unsound policy to cultivate Chinese connections. Such firms leave the entire management of their Chinese business in the hands of their compradors, who undertake the responsibility for all deals with Chinese customers. The comprador system is perhaps inevitable but it increases the overheads of the firms concerned, as compared with German firms who do their business direct . . .

The Hong Kong Bank has hitherto made its profits out of exchange business and in most cases its managers appear to have no experience of, and little interest in, anything but exchange business. With the stabilization of the Chinese exchange, the profits to be obtained from such business will be greatly reduced, and the Bank will only be able to maintain its position in China by turning its attention to financing business instead of concentrating on exchange, co-operation with the

> Chinese is essential to the promotion of business in China. The Hong Kong Bank has not much goodwill in this matter. The Bank did assist in the management of the exchange during 1935 and the Chinese government recognized the assistance thus given very generously. But after the [*fabi*] reform was instituted, the Bank for two months opposed the surrender of its silver to the Chinese government, and for some time refused to enter into a clearing system with the central bank.[154]

Leith-Ross was careful to veil acerbic portions of his criticisms when engaging with HSBC stalwarts directly. On April 8, 1936, for example, Leith-Ross wrote a letter to enlist Charles Addis, the Bank's chairman in London, to his cause. In this letter, Leith-Ross tempered his satisfaction at the "astonishing speed" with which the *fabi* reform achieved price stability, with an admission that its ultimate success would depend on international good will. To that end, he pleaded with Addis to exert influence in the city to propitiate public opinion of China's progress and allay the concerns of Chinese government bondholders. Addis, for his part, indicated that he would oblige.[155]

How, then, are students of the period to account for Leith-Ross's backroom criticisms of HSBC? Tellingly, Leith-Ross, in unmistakable reference to the *Wusa* boycotts and subsequent GMD state-building efforts, acclaimed 1925 as the year in which Sino-British relations changed course.

London's view of the logic, affordability, and morality of defending the treaty-port paradigm gradually changed as a result of *Wusa*. One of the most succinct pronouncements that capture attitudinal change was perhaps Lloyd George's "Chinese nationalism is essentially a just cause."[156] In contrast, most British expatriates continued to harbor animosity toward the GMD and to live under the illusion of perpetual insularity and colonial grandeur. London observers came to sardonically label such attitudes as "The Shanghai Mind."[157]

Leith-Ross had had no substantive China experience before he arrived in the region and was therefore aligned with neither "Old China Hands" at the Foreign Office nor trading-house *taipans*. He seems to have primarily transmitted the winds of change blowing in London. It is otherwise difficult to determine how the personal chemistry between Leith-Ross and his hosts played out over the course of the Mission. Nevertheless, Cyril Rogers, who was Leith-Ross's closest aide, did not conceal how Chinese parleys had won him over:

> You must not smile if I confess that I have lost my heart to the Chinese. National characteristics as a rule do not lead me to enthusiasm. But the Chinese is so like a child (and therefore to be loved), so patient and full of good humor; so pathetic and yet very comic, that it is impossible not to like him. Of course in other (and

> higher) places the best is not seen. A gangster undercurrent exists here, in the best of Chicago tradition. Corruption acquires the garb of virtue because of its unavoidable necessity and everywhere one finds the foundations rotten. But even this attracts me. I get quite a lot [of] quiet satisfaction out of trying to understand the Chinese psychology and playing the "oriental game" for which there are no rules except that a smile must accompany everything and all must be genteel. But why do I tell you all this? You must have heard it all before.[158]

Leith-Ross exuded optimism upon his departure in June 1936.[159] This optimism had been predicated on the first few months in which China's new legal tender was taking root—arguably one of the most salient achievements of the Nanjing Decade. Nonetheless, the Japanese invasion of China proper (1937) and voracious demands subsequently put on the state treasury by Jiang Jieshi's generals, meant that the success of the *fabi* reform would not be an enduring one.

The hyperinflation that gripped China during 1937–1949 has been described at length elsewhere, and there is no pressing need to retell its effects in these pages. [160] The Guomindang's recourse to inflationary policy may have been an historic inevitability in view of the onset of the Sino-Japanese War.[161] Even so, some of the achievements of the *fabi* reform were irreversible: from a Nationalist perspective foreign banks had been reduced to a fraction of their former might in Shanghai, quasi-foreign banknotes were quickly disappearing from sight, and the international banking Consortium that had once dictated loan terms to the Chinese was pronounced "dead."[162]

The ravages of the second Sino-Japanese War eventually turned the *fabi* currency into worthless paper. Yet, the Sino-Japanese hostilities spared the foreign concessions in Shanghai between 1937 and 1941—a period during which the concession areas became known in Chinese as *gudao* 孤島 or "Solitary Haven." For a little while, the British banks could toy with the idea that hyperinflation would legitimize a renewed attempt to issue their notes and minimize their dependence on GMD-run banks. The British Treasury, however, promptly dashed any such hopes.[163] Moreover, all Western banks were now firmly committed to stop accepting deposits from Chinese nationals.[164]

Ironically, the fact that the Bank's latitude on the Mainland was constricted more than ever before turned HSBC, as from 1937, into one of the key advocates for the need to invigorate Chinese central banking. This was largely because the Bank was now totally dependent on Chinese currency for its remaining operations in Shanghai, and because it reemerged as a major underwriter for the

GMD government in the London capital market, after more than a decade of mutual suspicion over the aims of the Consortium.

By late 1938, the Bank's relations with the Nationalist government had come full circle. While the Nationalists took power on the back of popular abhorrence of the Consortium and foreign treaty-port privileges, they were now actively soliciting a loan on the order of GBP 5 million from HSBC for "currency stabilization," albeit without any Consortium involvement.[165] This convergence of interests notwithstanding, extant branch ledgers suggest that the China issue was well and truly on the road to oblivion by the early 1940s.[166] After Japan's surrender in 1946, the GMD continued to narrow down the foreign banks' operational latitude, even though it was heavily embroiled in civil war with the Communists. With the last powers of extraterritoriality finally ceded in 1942, HSBC was forced to submit to the Ministry of Finance data on branch balance sheets on a *daily* basis—a degree of subordination to "native" authority that would have been considered unthinkable before 1925.[167]

Along with other business ends, HSBC circulation figures in Shanghai became moribund. In August 1947, the branch reported to Nanjing that 281,521 *fabi* worth of old silver dollar notes had not been withdrawn yet, while overdrawn current accounts and nonperforming loans reached a whopping *fabi* 67.3 billion.[168] Clearly, the branch had by then become deadweight for the Head Office, and its days of glory were long gone.

But the worst was yet to come. During the early 1950s, Communist comptrollers placed HSBC notes outstanding, like all other prewar liabilities, under sedulous scrutiny. Their underlying strategy was to force the Head Office to remit to the authorities as much foreign currency as possible in return for the release of the Bank's Mainland staff, who had been effectively quarantined.[169]

In December 1954, the Bank's China circulation total was nominally made up of 336,176 demonetized, old silver dollars. The amount reflected either hoarded notes that were never presented for encashment and whose bearers' whereabouts were unknown, or notes defaced beyond repair in the course of war. Their real value in Renminbi units was infinitesimal.[170]

CONCLUSION

This chapter has examined in detail the vicissitudes of banknote issuance by the Hongkong and Shanghai Banking Corporation during the late-Republican period. It revealed how, in mid-1925, the China issue took a decisive—and from the Bank's standpoint—entirely *unexpected* battering as a result of nationalist agitation during the May Thirtieth and Shaji Incidents. Circulation volumes in Shanghai had recovered briefly by 1927 but, unlike the CBIAC case, the China aggregate did *not* peak in the early 1930s.

HSBC operations in China progressively diminished sometime after 1927 as a result of two principal factors: competition from government-backed banks of issue and the GMD's agenda of monetary unification. The second factor came to a head with the proclamation of the *fabi* reform (1935).

In Barlow's parlance, the May Thirtieth Movement presented the biggest challenge HSBC had faced over "many a long day." This chapter drew on correspondence by Barlow and his colleagues, as well as on Leith-Ross's observations and on the Bank's Mainland circulation figures, in an attempt to correct the scant attention paid to *Wusa* in the literature on the history of British business in Asia. Here, *Wusa* is framed as a critical link in a long chain of events, which helped the Guomindang seize power and eventually forge monetary unification. The *Wusa* boycott of British banks may not have been protracted, but its longer-term political, economic, and psychological ramifications cannot be understated.

As one would expect, the major economic junctures that China had traversed between 1912 and 1937 featured in this chapter sequentially. So, too, did a number of academic sticking points. These concerned the way in which the GMD-HSBC relationship had evolved; here the relationship was portrayed as shifting from festering hostility on the eve of the Nanjing Decade (1926–1927) to one of begrudging accommodation after the launch of the U.S. Silver Purchase Policy (1934). Although the appreciation of silver prices in the mid-1930s is shown to have hit China's economy very badly, the GMD managed to chart a solution course largely by itself. The Bank had almost invariably been privy to government economic policy in the late-Imperial and early-Republican eras. Hence, the *fabi* reform marked a considerable diminution of its standing in China.

Herein lies the significance of HSBC's China issue during the late-Republican period: because HSBC was by far the most important foreign bank in China, the highs and lows of its note circulation accurately capture not just its own performance, but also the transition from intensifying monetary fragmentation in the early-Republican period to effective central banking reforms during the Nanjing Decade.

Chapter 6 Conclusions

The following discussion aims to bind together the political, institutional, and technological threads emanating from the exposition of British banknote issuance in China. It begins by spelling out the ways in which the note circulation volumes presented in this book depart from previous estimates, and why this calls for a reassessment of the efficacy of antiforeign boycotts during the Republican era.

From clearly delimited issues where balance-sheet figures count most, the discussion will move to broader themes that bespeak the significance of British overseas banking in China. The last section will then explore whether quasi-foreign banknote issuance—being the aberrant monetary phenomenon that it was—can offer clues as to the historic development path of modern banking.

RETHINKING CIRCULATION VOLUMES

Previous estimates of foreign banknote circulation volumes in China were beset a priori by two limitations. First, European overseas banks had been under no obligation to disclose country-specific circulation volumes in their published annual reports. This allowed the British banks, whose banknote issues were truly multinational in nature, to withhold critical information especially during politically sensitive times. Second, most previous estimates did not adequately distinguish between banknotes denominated in colonial currency, which circulated mostly on China's periphery, to quasi-foreign banknotes, which had played a pivotal role in Shanghai and the outports.

As a result, most estimates of overseas banknote circulation in China proper reflected little more than guesswork. These estimates were particularly misleading as regards British banks, since they blurred links between the changing political climate and business performance. Thus, critical shifts in circulation volumes became entirely lost in overarching monetary aggregates spanning dominions, colonies, and nominally independent polities across the Asia-Pacific region.

This book offers a long-term reconstruction of British note circulation volumes in Shanghai that makes allowance for provincial and treaty-port particularities. Archival data gleaned from two leading British banks in East Asia, HSBC and CBIAC, provided the foundation for core arguments. By disaggregating these banks' HK$-denominated notes, whose spread contemporary observers had mostly confined to Guangdong province, from their SH Tls. and Mexican dollar (Mex$) notes, linkages between financial and political conditions in prewar Shanghai were revealed.

The circulation pattern that subsequently emerged was instructive in many ways. It corroborated desultory references made in secondary sources as to the toll that World War I and, a few years later, antiforeign agitation had taken on foreign banks in China. Equally importantly, the pattern suggested that the breakdown of central authority in China proper after 1911—accompanied as it was by the widespread debasement and overprinting of local currency—provided the single most important catalyst for the spread of quasi-foreign notes in the face of deeply rooted Chinese suspicion of fiduciary money.

More *indirect* findings emerged too. After examining British Treasury regulation and banknote production costs, evidence was presented to suggest that HSBC's quasi-foreign note issue was likely to have been very remunerative, particularly in the late-Imperial and early-Republican eras. Yet, the Bank's Head Office in Hong Kong was generally less enthusiastic about the growth of the China issue than were local branch managers. This was because of concerns that an unbridled expansion of quasi-foreign note circulation volumes would impinge on HSBC's role as de facto arbiter of Hong Kong's money supply.

As for the ubiquity of HK$ notes in Guangdong, the findings proved much less conclusive. Since the British banks were not party to border control arrangements between the Colony and China proper, and were unable to record banknote movements to and fro, scholars may never know the exact amount of HK$ actually used on the Mainland over time. Yet, building on balance-sheet figures for the CBIAC branch in Guangzhou, this book has shown that, at least insofar as this particular bank is concerned, previous estimates of HK$ circulation volumes in China proper contain a substantial upward bias. More generally, the high demand for notes in the Colony, as opposed to the relatively small volume of quasi-foreign notes, was shown to be the result of an institutional setting that had patently distinguished Hong Kong from the treaty-port mould.

Similar branch data and Inspector's Reports pointed, nevertheless, to the preponderance of both Shanghai and Hong Kong in the operations of British overseas banks in China. These records resonated with the sheer political and monetary fragmentation that characterized the rest of China. But wide variance in monetary conditions is shown to have existed not only between Hong Kong, Shanghai, and the rural hinterland, or between Shanghai and the outports in toto, but also between one outport and another. One important example, discussed in Chapter 5, was the fact that Chinese banknotes experienced wildly different degrees of receptivity in different HSBC branches across the Mainland.

THE EFFICACY OF CHINESE POPULAR BOYCOTTS

This book argues that the perception of Chinese boycotts in the early-Republican era as ineffectual in the long run (an idea entrenched largely through Remer's early work) is in need of serious revision.[1] This perception should be measured up, with the benefit of hindsight, against the cumulative evidence made available since Remer's time. One critical source of evidence, which Remer neglected, was the British Exchange Banks and their changing relationship with Chinese clientele. The case studies analyzed in these pages suggest that the ramifications of the *Wusa* Movement extended well beyond corporate boardrooms.

Evidence to that effect features throughout Chapter 5. Despite the fact that bilateral trade and British banknote circulation volumes had partly recovered by 1927, the *Wusa* upheaval resonated with Whitehall well into 1930s, as Leith-Ross's pronouncement clearly demonstrates. Britain's foreign policy in East Asia in the lead-up to World War II—its repudiation of hawkish expatriate views, its reconciliation with the GMD, its growing distrust of Japan, and its endorsement of the *fabi* reform—cannot be adequately explained without reference to the impact that the May Thirtieth Movement made on Whitehall's perception of Chinese nationalism and its long-term prospects. The GMD came to power on the hills of *Wusa*; it was against the backdrop of *Wusa* that the GMD won wide support for its economic agenda. Although not long-lasting in itself, the *Wusa* boycott was a critical link in a chain of events that paved the way for the rise of central banking and greater monetary integration in China.

Yet, the great majority of scholars who studied the antiforeign boycotts in China *after* Remer tended to skirt around economic analysis in favor of cultural, intellectual, journalistic, organizational, and political dimensions.[2] Perhaps this is why their work is heavily weighted toward the *Wusi* Movement (1919), which marked a historic turnaround in the Chinese sociopolitical consciousness but was—certainly for the Western Powers—of much less economic significance than the *Wusa* Movement six years later. More work needs to be done in the future to correct this imbalance.

STATECRAFT AND ECONOMIC POLICY IN PREWAR CHINA

The two previous conclusions were derived from, and largely supported by, balance-sheet figures. The following conclusions are of a more tentative nature.

One observation presented in this book, which accords with revisionist findings by notable China scholars in recent years, is the crucial role played by the GMD in reinforcing Chinese sovereignty and in pushing for national integration.[3] Long-held perceptions of the Nanjing government as weak, ineffectual, and corrupt may have formed in the West as a result of the Nationalists' poor performance after the Sino-Japanese War.[4] Nonetheless, when confined to the prewar era, GMD achievements at revitalizing central authority reverberate throughout Chapter 5, which describes Nanjing's adroit maneuvers in the lead-up to national currency unification and during the Leith-Ross Mission.

The Song Ziwen–Kong Xiangxi duo received particular attention in this book. The economic policy that the two men had jointly pursued as alternate finance ministers proved successful in stemming monetary fragmentation and in consolidating the Chinese banking sector. Concomitantly, they forestalled the recovery in quasi-foreign banknote circulation volumes during the early 1930s and brought foreign bank *taipans* to heel with their peculiar blend of humbug and belligerence. Later, they skillfully played off Whitehall, Tokyo, and Washington against one another to ultimately secure an American loan with which to back up the new Chinese currency. Although the value of the *fabi* nosedived shortly before Japan's invasion of China in 1937, at least one tenet of the Song–Kong legacy prevailed—namely, the rollback of foreign banking and overseas banknote issuance.

The spread of quasi-foreign banknotes in China proper during the first quarter of the twentieth century did not merely reflect a trivial idiosyncrasy of the treaty-port economy. It was also an issue directly affected by the performance of successive Republican governments in their attempts to reclaim China's prestige and sovereignty in the diplomatic arena. At the same time, it should be understood as a corollary of the breakdown of central authority and institutional trust beginning in the late-Imperial era.

Promulgated in 1935, currency unification per se entailed a fairly belated top-down writ that would have rung hollow unless the Nanjing government had ably mustered international backing and, in turn, demonstrated that its budget deficit and state-run banks were on the mend. The failure of the warlord-dominated Beiyang governments to reform Chinese banks along these lines before 1927 (their shared penchant being for overprinting and debasement) increased market insecurity to the extent that quasi-foreign banknotes traded at a considerable premium over Chinese banknotes.

It would be implausible to assume that this insecurity was any less endemic in China's agrarian sector or that it did not raise transaction costs in the hinterland in quite the same way as it did in the urban sector. In that sense, "optimistic" accounts of China's prewar economy are correct in drawing attention to the proliferation of paper money in the hinterland.[5] All the same, it should be remembered that quite often this was the result of warlord excesses rather than an indicator of growing market integration.

BRITISH BANKING IN CHINA

The failure of late-Qing and early-Republican governments to stem the breakdown of popular trust in state-issued currency was an experience not entirely removed from that of some European and colonial governments before the consolidation of central banking in the early twentieth century. As Chapters 1 and 2 have shown, however, the introduction of central banking in Europe had been preceded by almost two centuries during which private banknote issuance was receding, while in China the opposite trend persisted.

Despite the fact that paper money had been widely used in China long before Europe, it was largely British overseas banks that reintroduced this means of payment into the Chinese economy during the latter part of the nineteenth century. Why exactly, then, was there such a clear preference for quasi-foreign banknotes over domestic banknotes in China? It seems that more advanced European printing and counterforgery technology cannot adequately explain this preference. For, as indicated in Chapter 4, major Chinese banks like the IBC had ordered their notes from European printers too.

The immediate explanation for the popularity of British banknotes in China lies, of course, in the British banks' higher specie reserve ratios and their immunity from Chinese government diktat which, when foisted on local banks, often meant expropriation of silver reserves. But, more generally, the Treasury reserve principles that bound HSBC and CBIAC were just one by-product of the institutional environment, which had first emerged in London in the sixteenth century and eventually transformed the city into the world's largest financial clearing hub. Indeed, much of the regulatory framework underpinning these two banks carried over from, and was consistently refined by, earlier experience with monopolistic joint-stock trading companies like the EIC, or with failed chartered overseas banks like the OBC.

What this study might also offer, then, is some insight into the factors that had set the foreign corporate sector in the treaty ports apart from the domestic one. Differences here can be reduced to the enactment of charter provisions as the progenitors of economies of scale. Broadly based ownership is, in the final analysis, what distinguished large, publicly traded corporate entities like HSBC and CBIAC from China's fragmented and undercapitalized financial sector.

In other words, it was the scale of share capital that had set Shanghai's expatriate firms apart from domestic ones. Domestic firms were hamstrung by investor insecurity, which greatly reduced their ability to manage impersonal ties and militated British banks against engagement with Chinese industrialists. Banknote issuance was a much safer, albeit limited, means of tapping into the domestic sector. Not surprisingly, it was taken up by almost all the foreign banks operating in the treaty ports. However, the proceeds from quasi-foreign note issuance did not necessarily flow back into the domestic sector in the form of industrial credit. In that sense, foreign firms had a clear advantage over Chinese firms in Shanghai's capital market.

The Eastern Exchange Banks were predicated on Royal Charter stipulations or Colonial Ordinances. These were enacted only in the 1850s as rough-and-ready substitutes for limited liability. Financial institutions other than the Bank of England could be bestowed with statutory limited liability only in the following decade. Looked at from a purely temporal perspective, therefore, the institutional division between British and Chinese banks in Shanghai may not appear compelling. But the crucial point to remember is that what may seem like a fairly thin difference begot, in fact, one of the root causes for European economic primacy in the early modern age. This insight should become eminently clear, once "California School" scholars recognize the long continuum linking the establishment of Europe's early joint-stock trading companies (sixteenth–seventeenth centuries) with the emergence of nonchartered joint-stock companies (eighteenth century) and the consummation of limited liability and equity finance concepts by state regulators late in the nineteenth century.[6]

Put baldly, this book suggests that the occurrence (or absence) of joint-stock formations in China's long history is of secondary importance. What does matter is the unwillingness (or inability) of China's late-Imperial bureaucracy to enforce such arrangements as those that underpinned nonkin equity ownership in Europe and its satellites. Overwhelmed by the efficacy of Western technology in the treaty ports, the Qing Court was rightly convinced that drawing private capital to a government-led industrialization effort was the only way to catch up with the West. But the resultant mixed enterprise (*guandushangban* 官督商辦) failed precisely because, as Feuerwerker and Faure have shown, the Qing embraced the veneer rather than the substance of private ownership.[7]

DID QUASI-FOREIGN MONEY MATTER?

This book has focused on British banknote issuance in Shanghai as a key constituent of a wider, yet little-noticed, monetary phenomenon that, for want of a better description, was known as quasi-foreign money. The volumes of locally denominated notes that British banks put in circulation in Shanghai were found to be much lower than previously thought, but their qualitative contribution to the city's economy should by no means be underestimated.

By and large, the growth of Shanghai's economy between 1842 and 1937 derived from a distinct formula that set the city apart from the rest of China, turning it into "a gem on an elephant's back," to paraphrase Rhoads Murphey's famous trope.[8] While topography had made Shanghai a priori an ideal gateway to China's richest provinces, it was the implications of extraterritoriality that drew Chinese capital to the city en masse. The Chinese first flocked to the city in search of a safe haven from the Taiping rebellion, and then from warlord usurpation and central government coercion. Notwithstanding that the foreign concessions in Shanghai were often touted as a showcase of efficient Western governance in East Asia, Chapter 2 underscored the highly porous nature of their institutional foundations.

The importance of quasi-foreign money to Shanghai should be understood against this backdrop. Because of the global issue quotas imposed on CBIAC and HSBC by the British Treasury, even at the height of their popularity British banknotes were too small a component of the city's money supply to eclipse the plethora of metallic currencies in use or to eliminate shroffing costs. The SMC, for its part, was reluctant to introduce uniform metallic currency, in stark contrast to measures taken by the Hong Kong government. Quasi-foreign money therefore seems to have mattered most as a readily convertible store of value, as a resuscitator of Chinese banknote issuance, and as a touchstone for Chinese monetary reform. It was part of the formula that drew Chinese capital to the city—a liquid safeguard against one specific form of warlord and central government depredation, that is, debased coinage and inconvertible notes.

This observation may invoke recent debates about the historic merits or demerits of free banking. Generally, "free bankers" view modern central banks as government marionettes; they invariably believe that governments are recidivist sponsors of inflationary policy, that is, the printing of legal tender notes without proper backing. Drawing on a series of historic precedents, they argue that multiple commercial banks of issue would make more responsible arbiters of currency than central banks.[9] But, surprisingly, prewar Shanghai is one pertinent setting that "free bankers" have neglected to study. It lends at best very flimsy evidence for the ability of private banknotes to serve as *nationwide* medium of exchange or to withstand sunspot runs without intervention by incumbent governments.

Prewar Shanghai is a setting equally pertinent to, yet hardly noticed by, economic historians who work within the Gerschenkronian tradition. Alexander Gerschenkron (1904–1978) postulated that long-term bank credit had been a *necessary* condition for the industrialization of European emerging economies where equity markets had been underdeveloped in the nineteenth century. Yet Daniel Verdier has suggested, in turn, that European commercial banks that had been granted note issue prerogatives tended to steer clear of the industrial sector due to liquidity concerns.[10]

Frederick Leith-Ross's classified memoranda criticized HSBC—the largest foreign bank of issue in China—for relying on the short-term finance of trade to the neglect of Chinese business needs. This critique seems to lend support to Verdier's theory, albeit from a part of the world not originally included in his study. It gives a rather new perspective to the long-standing and often impassioned engagement of Chinese scholars with the theme of quasi-foreign banknote issuance.

Appendix: British Bank Note Circulation in Shanghai, 1881–1935

Unit: Silver Dollars (000). *Sources*: HSBC data compiled in the main from Figure 5.1 and from HSBC GA SHG I 51; SHG II-1044. Midyear figure for 1881 gleaned from HSBC GA SHG LEDG 46. For the 1889 midyear figure, see King (1987), vol. 1, p. 391, table 11.1. For the 1894 year-end figure, see ibid., p. 485, table 13.10. CBIAC data compiled from Figure 5.2 (SH Taels converted to SH$ based on a 0.715 parity).

MBI data compiled in the main from Green and Kinsey (1999), pp. 211–212. For the 1934 year-end figure, see PRO T160/648. Data for 1926–1929 added based on the average circulation volume between 1925 and 1930.

OBC aggregate circulation volumes (1881–1883) compiled from Wang Jingyu (1983a), pp. 273–275, table 1. Shanghai's share of the aggregate is estimated at 1 percent in accordance with early CBIAC data.

CMBILC aggregate circulation volumes (1881–1893) compiled from the *Bankers' Magazine* and Muirhead (1996), p. 251. Shanghai's share of the aggregate is estimated at 1 percent in accordance with early CBIAC data.

GBP figures have been converted to dollars throughout based on annual exchange rates featured in Hsiao Liang-lin (1974), pp. 190–192. The appendix is exclusive of British bank outport or Hong Kong–issued notes circulating in Shanghai.

Notes

CHAPTER 1: INTRODUCTION

1. See, for example, Hall (1921), p. 18; Morse (1921 [1967]), pp. 154–158. For two different translations of Marco Polo's impressions, see *The Travels of Marco Polo* [1987], pp. 147–148; cf. *The Book of Ser Marco Polo* [1903], vol. 1, pp. 423–430. (*Note*: Square brackets point to reprints or translations, while parentheses will henceforth indicate year of original publication.)
2. See Sheehan (2004). The "mini explosion" refers in the main to Cheng (2003); Ji (2003); and Sheehan (2003).
3. Katō (1959), vol. 1, pp. 395–411; Twitchett (1970), pp. 73–74.
4. Elvin (1973), pp. 150–161; Schifferli (1986); cf. Peng Xinwei (1958), pp. 280–291.
5. See Katō (1959), vol. 2, pp. 1–11, 56.
6. Elvin (1973), pp. 164–199; cf. Deng Gang (1999), pp. 301–324.
7. During much of the preceding Tang era, payment of silver was common in the Lingnan area, but otherwise quite restricted to ceremonial purposes. It was very rarely levied in land tax. See Katō (1944 [1970]), vol. 1, pp. 47–82.
8. Katō (1959), vol. 2, pp. 86–138.
9. Von Glahn (1996), pp. 48–50; Qi Xia (1987), vol. 2, pp. 557–565; "coin famine," or *qianhuang*, continued to haunt policymakers in late-Imperial China. For an illuminating description of how mid-Qing administrators perceived the flight of copper coins see, e.g., Dunstan (1996).

10. Von Glahn (1996), pp. 51–56; Qi Xia (1987), vol. 2, pp. 1188–1194.
11. Miyazaki (1977), vol. 2, pp. 418–422.
12. The Ming launched a rearguard attempt to revive note issuance between 1629 and 1644, but met with resounding failure. Large-scale note issuance was subsequently abandoned by Imperial governments until the late Qing. See Von Glahn (1996), pp. 197–206; cf. Tullock (1958) and Chen Chau-nan et al. (1995), pp. 273–279.
13. Schurtz (1959), pp. 1–32.
14. Flynn and Giraldez (1994), pp. 79–83; one source put the amount of silver dollars transported by the Spanish across the Pacific between 1571 and 1821 at 400 million, see Quan Hansheng (1972), p. 439.
15. Huang (1974), pp. 36–43, 118–122; the effects of the *lijia* reform have also been explained in detail by Yamane (1984). Nishijima Sadao has described how rapacious land taxes in fifteenth-century Songjiang spawned a thriving domestic cotton industry, which further expanded the monetization of silver. See Nishijima (1984), pp. 57–59.
16. The Ming tried to reintroduce paper money in the fourteenth century, but popular rejection of government notes at that stage was too difficult to overcome. Therafter, some Ming and Qing officials would occasionally revive the idea of issuing paper money in various memorials to the Throne, but a new Imperial issue was not implemented until the late-Qing. See Peng Xinwei (1958), pp. 429–433, 506–509; Yang Lien-sheng (1952), pp. 67–68.
17. Wang Yeh-chien (1973), pp. 59–61; Von Glahn (2007). For an overview of bimetallism in the late-Imperial era, see Kann (1927).
18. On the overriding importance of opium for British trading houses and early British financial institutions in China, see, e.g., Checkland (1953).
19. Davies (1994), pp. 278–282; Rondo Cameron proposed a more conservative estimate with specie still constituting half of Britain's means of payments in 1688–1689. See Cameron (1967), table II.2, pp. 42–46.
20. Baskin and Miranti (1997), pp. 34–63.
21. Heckscher (1954), pp. 91–92. There is some similarity between the circumstances in which banknotes had first emerged in China (Sichuan) and Sweden. The coinage of both economies had been based at the time on lower-value metals, i.e., copper in Sweden (seventeenth century) and iron in Sichuan (tenth century).
22. Mackenzie (1953), pp. 24–35; Coppieters (1955), pp. 13–20.
23. Helleiner (2003), pp. 57–58.
24. Ibid., pp. 58–59, 103.
25. Notable examples of countries which retained private banknote issues in the early twentieth century include Switzerland and Greece. Banknotes in Scotland are still issued by commercial banks. See Schuler (1992).
26. On the evolution of Hong Kong's unique monetary system, see Jao and King (1990).
27. Spalding (1924), pp. 272–273.
28. For currency substitution between local currency and HK$ in South China, see Li Taichu (1936), pp. 3–21; Schenk (2000). Banknotes issued by the British Chartered Mercantile Bank in Melaka, which amounted to 70,000 Straits Settlement dollars (S$) in 1882, were

crucial for the survival of its branch there. These banknotes were commonly used in neighboring Malay states; see Muirhead (1996), pp. 224–225.

29. France's predominant financial organ in East Asia, the Banque de l'Indochine, seems to have issued Rouble notes with Cyrillic script in Vladivostok during the Allied intervention against the Red Army between 1919 and 1920; see Kolsky and Muszynski (1996), pp. 303–306. The Bank of Abyssinia, a subsidiary of the British-owned National Bank of Egypt, opened its first offices in Addis Ababa and Harare on February 15, 1906. It had pioneered banknotes in Ethiopia in 1915 and was subsequently nationalized by Haile Sellassie in 1931; see Marcus (2002), pp. 130–146. On the notes issued by the Franco-British owned Imperial Ottoman Bank, see Eldem (1998), pp. 75–110.
30. Bowen and Cottrell (1997), pp. 107–108.
31. Cassis (1994), p. 78.
32. Jones (1990), pp. 33–34.
33. On the evolution of British legislation as regards overseas note issues by private banks, see Chalmers (1893), pp. 27–32; Jones (1993), p. 19; cf. Nishimura (2003), part 1, p. 8.
34. Grossman (2001), p. 111.
35. Jones (1990), p. 40.
36. Gonjō (1993), pp. 178–182, 267–271; Müller-Jabusch (1940), pp. 215–219.
37. Jones (1990), p. 36.
38. Joslin (1963), pp. 137–138. Private note issuance in Latin America was ultimately phased out through government-backed issues in the early 1920s; see Bulmer-Thomas (1994), pp. 179–180.
39. The Siamese government decided to replace HSBC, CBIAC, and Banque de l'Indochine notes circulating in Bangkok with an issue of its own in 1902; see Ingram (1971), pp. 150–155. Between 1889 and 1894, HSBC's circulation in Yokohama and Kobe slumped from the yen equivalent of HK$86,517 to HK$5,675. Japan's share of the Bank's total circulation volume thereby dropped from approximately 1.5 percent to 0.057 percent; see King (1987), vol. 1, pp. 39, 485.
40. Because of their lead position in issuing exchange bills, the larger British trading houses—headed by Jardine Matheson & Co.—had tried to resist the establishment of Anglo-Indian banks in Guangzhou [Canton] and Shanghai. But when the transition to specialized banking appeared irreversible, these trading houses worked in conjunction with other merchant groups to set up their own bank, i.e., the Hongkong and Shanghai Banking Corporation (est. 1865). Eventually, even Jardine Matheson & Co. took up a share in HSBC. See Checkland (1953). See also Le Fevour (1968), pp. 136–140.
41. Late British entrants into the Chinese market include the P&O Banking Corp., the Eastern Bank, the National Bank of India, and the National Bank of China. On the history of these banks in China, see Tyson (1963), pp. 32–33, 92, 108; Jones (1993), pp. 77–78, 158–159; Orbell and Turton (2001), pp. 203–204, 425.
42. For a few of the most comprehensive numismatic listings, see Pick (1990), vol. 1, pp. 253–288; Huang and Wang (2004), vol. 1, pp. 14–54; Mao (1977), vol. 2; Ma Chuande et al. (2000), pp. 23–60; *Zhongguo zhibi biaozhun tulu* (1994), pp. 567–644; *Ziben zhuyi*

guojia zai jiu Zhongguo faxing he liutong de huobi (1992); Cribb (1987); see also Notar (2002). On free banking see, e.g., the article compilations by Dowd (1992) and White (1993).

43. Selgin (1992), p. 104.
44. Ibid., p. 120.
45. The word *sycee* is a derivative of the Cantonese pronunciation for pure silk (细丝), the equivalent in Mandarin being *dingzi* (錠子) or *yuanbao* (元寶). In South China, good-quality silver bullion was thought to possess a shiny veneer reminiscent of silk.
46. For an overview of Qing and early-Republican monetary fragmentation, and of how novel foreign banknote designs were emulated by Chinese financial institutions, see *Zhongguo jindai zhibi shi* (2001); Hsu Yih-tzong (1997 and 1998); Zhang Zhizhong (1997). On underground Communist currency, see, for example, Wu Ping (1994); Ding Guoliang and Zhang Yuncai (1993).
47. The best-known work in this vein is Xian Ke's influential monograph (1958).
48. The specter of foreign exploitation pervades much of the research on Chinese economic history. For a methodological survey of pertinent literature see, e.g., Wright (1986).
49. Consider, for example, the uneven performance of Yan Xishan's Shanxi Provincial Bank and Liu Xiang's financial excesses in Sichuan with the relative stability of the Provincial Bank of Guangdong under warlord Chen Jitang between 1931 and 1936. On Yan Xishan see Gillin (1967), pp. 99–116, 134–139; on Liu Xiang see Kapp (1973), pp. 93, 113–114; on Chen Jitang see Fitzgerald (1990), pp. 764–766.
50. Even implacable critics of GMD policies concede that the scale of the *fabi* reform was unprecedented. See, e.g., Zhong Xiangcai's detailed study (1995), p. 30; cf. Lin Wei-Ying (1936).
51. The most notable examples being King (1987), vol. 3; Mackenzie (1954), pp. 248–253; cf. Jones (1993), pp. 191–192.
52. Weber's influential treatise *The Religion of China* was first published in German in 1922.
53. Rawski (1989), pp. 329–337; Brandt (1989), pp. 133–134, 179–180. For a representative dismal appraisal, see Ash (1976).
54. See, e.g., Esherick (1991) and Little (1992).
55. Fox (1994), for example, explicitly argues against the notion of fast equilibrating interprovincial labor and commodity markets that Brandt and Rawski propose for early twentieth-century China. Though broadly of the same school as Rawski, Wright (2000) also observed that Chinese factor markets did not function well in the hinterland. In her newly published monumental work, Lillian Li (2007, pp. 196–220) clearly observes a considerable *decline* in intraprovincial market integration across North China from the eighteenth to the nineteenth century.
56. For useful summaries of the main protagonists in this debate and of their respective arguments, see Myers (1991) and Richardson (1999), pp. 77–83; for an earlier overview, see Myers (1970), pp. 211–214, 292–295.
57. Elvin (1981), pp. 254–255; based on extensive fieldwork in Sichuan, Skinner (1993, p. 40) pointed to another facet of microvariation in prewar China: some local markets in the same marketing area used different weights and measurements until the 1950s.

58. For representative arguments, see Weber (1922 [1951]); Wittfogel (1957), pp. 101–103; Balazs (1964), pp. 28–32; Balazs and Wittfogel, in particular, view the rapacity of Chinese state organs as the main brake on urban regeneration and mechanization.
59. Since Mao's legacy has lost much of its appeal on the Mainland, Chinese and other social scientists have mobilized Confucius onto the CCP reformist bandwagon to explain China's pursuit of economic prominence in the twenty-first century. For an overview of this trend, see De Bary (1991), pp. 103–109.
60. For an overview of PRC theoretical trends in economic history, see Zelin (1998).
61. Cf. Chang Chung-li (1962), pp. 149–195; Chan (1977), pp. 187–195.
62. See, e.g., Elvin (1973), pp. 285–316.
63. Low taxation and self-sufficiency were implicit in Ming and Qing neo-Confucian indoctrination. See Wong (1997), p. 102; cf. Skinner (1993), p. 11.
64. Kiser and Tong (1992), p. 311; cf. Wagel (1914 [1980]), pp. 325–329.
65. Vries (2003), pp. 27–28.
66. See, e.g., North and Thomas (1973), pp. 154–157.
67. On the Netherlands see North and Thomas (1973), pp. 132–142; see also De Vries (1976), pp. 116–128, 251–252; Mokyr (1976), pp. 83–132, 221–230. On the United States, see Davis and North (1971), pp. 105–134.
68. For a survey of current trends in Asian economic history, see Van der Eng (2004).
69. Greif (2005).
70. For work broadly associated with the "California School," see Wong (1997); Li Bozhong (1998); Frank (1998); Pomeranz (2000); and Hobson (2004).
71. Pomeranz (2000), pp. 66–68, 281–283.
72. On retarded industrialization in Spain *despite* the inflow of colonial bullion and rich domestic mineral deposits (particularly iron ore) see, e.g., Tortella Casares (2000), pp. 73–114; Harvey and Taylor (1987). On the "Great Divergence" across Europe and between Northwestern Europe, South Asia, and China, see also Broadberry and Gupta (2006).
73. Landes (2003), pp. 41–42, 74–75, 77–76, 98–99.
74. Pomeranz (1993), pp. 30–40; on exorbitant interest rates in late-Imperial China, see also Isett (2007), pp. 266–273. Interestingly, Isett posits that "California School" scholars *overemphasize* the importance of institutions in modern economic development (pp. 299–304), whereas Northian scholars would probably argue the opposite.
75. Shiue and Keller (2004); cf. Shiue (2002).
76. See Shiue and Keller (2004), data appendix pp. 32–37, table 3.
77. For this critique of Pomeranz's *Great Divergence,* see Elvin (2001).
78. Goldstone (2002), pp. 339–353.
79. Goldstone (2002), p. 374; the "engine science" is a concept that radically departs from Goldstone's earlier analytical framework, which was essentially culturalist. See, e.g., Goldstone (1996); on the diverging trajectories of scientific exploration between Europe and China, see Elvin (2004).
80. This notion is largely based on William Rowe's magisterial study of Hankou and Madeleine Zelin's work on the Furong Salt Yard in Sichuan. These two scholars have pointed to the occurrence of joint-stock enterprise in early modern China, but whether

their respective case studies substantiated nonkin participation in stock-holding is open to question. See Rowe (1984), pp. 72–73; Zelin (1988). On kinship networks in Chinese enterprise, see also Faure (2006), pp. 42–43, 53.

81. See, for example, Shiba (1968), pp. 117–120, 458–461.
82. William Scott's monumental work *The Constitution and Finance of English, Scottish and Irish Joint-Stock Companies to 1720* (3 vols.) was first published in 1912.
83. On chartered overseas trading companies as precursors of the Western corporate model, see Carlos and Nicholas (1988). On the evolution of the London stock exchange, see Michie (1999), pp. 15–36.
84. Taylor (2006); on joint-stock banks, see also Cameron (1967), pp. 27–29.
85. See Chen Shao-teh (1932 [1982]), pp. 303–305; Yang Yinpu (1930 [1972]), pp. 195–197; Guo Xiaoxian (1935 [2005]), pp. 103–104.
86. Hong Jiaguan (2004), p. 193.
87. Huang (1991), pp. 313, 316–317.

CHAPTER 2: THE SINO-FOREIGN FINANCIAL GRID IN PREWAR SHANGHAI

1. See, e.g., Murphey (1953) and *Zhongguo ziben zhuyi gongshangye de shehui zhuyi gaizao* (1993).
2. For pioneering studies that have begun addressing some of these aspects see Wasserstrom (1991); Wright (1991); Roux (1993); Perry (1993); Wakeman (1996); Takahashi and Furumaya (1995); Yeh Wen-Hsin (1995); Goodman (1995); Martin (1996); Bickers (1999); Lu Hanchao (1999); Fogel (2000); Ristaino (2001); Yeh (2002); Meyer (2003).
3. Aldous Huxley, for example, depicted Shanghai as timeless, but, in fact, the origins of significant Chinese settlement in its immediate environs can be traced back to the eighth century at the very earliest. See Huxley (1926 [1991]), pp. 271–273. On Shanghai before the arrival of Europeans see, e.g., Elvin (1977) and Johnson (1995); for a detailed chronology of Shanghai's development see Tang Zhenchang (1989), pp. 963–994.
4. Henriot (2001), p. 6; see also Miller (1937).
5. Dong (2001); Sergeant (1990); Wei (1987).
6. Barber (1979), pp. 144–159; Bergère (2002), pp. 359–362.
7. See a copy of the dispatch from Hong Kong's governor, Sir Hercules Robinson, to the Duke of Newcastle dated March 9, 1861, in *Hong Kong: Copy of Correspondence between the Secretary of State for the Colonies and the Governor of Hong Kong upon the Subject of the Currency of the Colony* (1863).
8. The British contemplated minting tael coinage in 1867 specifically for use in Shanghai, but the plan fell through due to Chinese suspicion. See, e.g., Cribb (1987), p. 11. In 1925, another attempt to introduce municipal subsidiary coinage was similarly aborted. See the notes on currency in *Gongbuju dongshihui huiyilu*, vols. 23–24 (1925–1926); cf. *Dongfang zazhi* 22.12 (June 25, 1925): 46–51; *Shen bao*, April 11, 1925, p. 14; *Shen bao*, September 6, 1925, p. 15; *Shen bao*, December 2, 1926, p. 10; Xu Jiqing (1932 [1970]), p. 233. On the import of Hong Kong currency in Shanghai, see, e.g., Goodman (1995), pp. 241–242. On the incremental expansion of the British Settlement, see Kotenev (1927), pp. 27–71; Bickers (1999), pp. 123–131; Takahashi and Furumaya (1995), pp. 79–

85; Osterhammel (1999), pp. 146–115. For a perspective on the institutional underpinning of the neighboring French Concession, see Marybon (1929).

9. Murphey (1953), pp. 57–61.
10. See "Notes on Chinese Currency," dated March 22, 1866, in School of Oriental and African Studies Archive [hereafter SOAS], Charles Addis Papers, PP MS 14/380.
11. Yang Yinpu (1930 [1972]), pp. 194–195; Lee (1926 [1982]), p. 32; Baba (1922), vol. 2, pp. 1432–1433; Chen Shao-teh (1932 [1982]), pp. 292, 300–301.
12. Hanna, Conant, and Jenks (1904), pp. 47–49. These paragraphs were part of the report submitted by the Jenks advisory mission to China, referred to below.
13. In SOAS, Charles Addis Papers, PP MS 14/380. This subsequent memorandum is not dated but reference to "the late Manchu Dynasty" suggests that it was entered not long after the 1911 Revolution; for near-contemporary surveys that reached much the same conclusion, see Wei Wen Pin (1914), p. 50 and Arnold (1919), p. 591.
14. Ho Hon-wai (1993), pp. 389–391.
15. See *Diplomatic and Consular Reports: China*, "Report for the Year 1897 on the Trade of Foochow," p. 11.
16. See *Diplomatic and Consular Reports: China*, "Report for the Year 1897 on the Trade of Shashih," p. 27; the rarity of silver dollars or notes as media of payment in the interior is also attested to in Hanna, Conant, and Jenks (1904), p. 14. On copper and copper-cash notes, see also Kuroda (2005), pp. 107–113.
17. In National Library of Australia [hereafter NLA], Braga Papers, MS 4371; on the millions of dollars worth of inconvertible notes that had inundated other parts of China by then, see, e.g., report in the *Chinese Economic Bulletin*, June 4, 1927, pp. 304–306.
18. Darwent (1920), pp. v–vii.
19. King (1965), p. 104.
20. The *Times*, July 3, 1928, p. 16.
21. These foreign advisers left behind a fairly large body of literature on China's economic problems. The principal foreign adviser to the Qing was Jeremiah Jenks. For details on his mission, see Wagel (1915), p. 86; Hanna, Conant, and Jenks (1904). Another principal adviser, Dutchman G. Vissering, completed his work on China after the fall of the Qing—see Vissering (1914); Wagel (1915), pp. 111–112, 124–126. In 1928, the GMD government invited E. W. Kemmerer, a Princeton University professor, to overhaul China's silver currencies. For details on his mission, see Ji Zhaojin (2003), p. 171. Toward the end of the Nanjing Decade, Sir Frederick Leith-Ross and American envoy Arthur Young were intimately involved in Chinese monetary reforms. For background details on their mission, see Ji Zhaojin (2003), pp. 190–194 and Young (1971).
22. On the GMD's banknote reserve policy, see Cheng Linsun (2003), p. 160; on central bank reforms, see, e.g., Chinese press reports from Guangzhou quoted in *Zhonghua minguo huobishi ziliao* (1989), vol. 2, pp. 74–78.
23. On the Customs Gold Unit, see Shen Lyn Yu (1941 [1980]), pp. 70–75; King (1965), p. 210.
24. For background details on the abolition of the tael in 1933 and the *fabi* reform of 1935, see, e.g., Ji Zhaojin (2003), pp. 182–185, 194–203.

25. See *Diplomatic and Consular Reports: China*, "Report on the Treaty-Port of Nanning 1909," p. 8.
26. Jones (1972), pp. 48–51; *Shanghai qianzhuang shiliao* (1960), pp. 752–756; Du Xuncheng (2002), pp. 56–57; Zhang Guohui (1989), pp. 1–14.
27. Jones (1972), p. 61.
28. McElderry (1976), pp. 68–69; *Shanghai qianzhuang shiliao* (1960), pp. 3–7; Cheng Linsun (2003), p. 38.
29. *Shanghai qianzhuang shiliao* (1960), pp. 29–30; McElderry (1976), p. 21; Pan Liangui (2004), p. 105.
30. McElderry (1976), pp. 18–19; Hamashita (1984), pp. 409–424.
31. McElderry (1976), pp. 1–25; *Shanghai qianzhuang shiliao* (1960), pp. 557–595.
32. See, e.g., Zhang Guohui (1963).
33. Nishimura (2005).
34. McElderry (1976), pp. 111–115; Du Xuncheng (2002), pp. 85–87; Thomas (2001), pp. 145–169; Bergère (1964), pp. 1–11.
35. Elvin (1967), pp. 221–229.
36. *Diplomatic and Consular Reports: China*, "Report for the Year 1913 on the Foreign Trade of China," p. 10.
37. On the compradors, see Wagel (1914 [1980]), pp. 114–118; Sha Weikai (1927); Ji Zhaojin (2003), pp. 54–57.
38. Sha Weikai (1927), pp. 46, 49–50; cf. Negishi (1948), pp. 251–262 and Motono (2000), pp. 22–23.
39. See, e.g., Zhang Naiqi (1936), pp. 330–331.
40. Ji Zhaojin (2003), pp. 141–147.
41. Bergère (1992), pp. 17–20.
42. Cited in Dai Jianbing (2005), pp. 184–185.
43. Yang Yinpu (1930 [1972]), pp. 385–386; Hong Jiaguan (1989), pp. 69–71.
44. Xu Jiqing (1932 [1970]), pp. 138–140; Ding Richu (1994), vol. 2, pp. 67–68, 101.
45. On the Chinese-American Bank of Commerce, see Pugach (1997).
46. Chen Shao-teh (1932 [1982]), pp. 293–296; Bergère (1989b), pp. 240–242. See also contemporary observations quoted in *Zhonghua minguo huobishi ziliao* (1989), vol. 1, pp. 894–897.
47. Du Xuncheng (2002), pp. 82–83; Cheng Linsun (2003), p. 75.
48. See "Notes on Chinese Currency," dated March 22, 1866. In SOAS, Charles Addis Papers PP MS 14/380.
49. *Nanshi* denoted the district comprising what had been walled Shanghai until 1914 and its environs. Lying beyond foreign jurisdiction, this area was often rendered into English as the "Chinese" or "Native" city. The geographical term Nantao (in pinyin transliteration—*Nandao* 南島) originated in the Chinese for "South Island." Strictly speaking, it denoted an island-like stretch of *Nanshi* that was outside the wall perimeters, running along the Huangpu. It was sometimes rendered as the "Chinese Bund." See *Lao Shanghai ditu* (2001), maps 29, 33.
50. Yang Yinpu (1930 [1972]), p. 110.
51. Hong Jiaguan (2003), pp. 112–113.

52. This estimate is based on the customary 0.25 percent shroffing commission charged by both the *yinlu* and *gonggu ju*. See Hong Jiaguan (2003), pp. 113–115.
53. Carroll (2005), pp. 126–129; Barnett (1984), pp. 36–40; on July 1, 1912, the *South China Morning Post* reported rather laconically (p. 2): "Chinese copper cents are no use in Hongkong as of to-day. It will be interesting to watch developments." The following day, a Chinese throng converged on the Colony's main post office where, for the last time, Mainland copper cents could be exchanged at a discount for Hong Kong currency. See *South China Morning Post*, July 2, 1912, p. 2.
54. For an overview of early Hong Kong banknote issuance, see Pennell (1961), p. 47.
55. Lee (1926 [1982)], p. 38.
56. McElderry (2001), pp. 4–7; see also Goetzmann and Köll (2004), p. 48, figure 1.
57. Hong Jiaguan (1989), pp. 147–148; see also Xu Xiaoqun (2001), pp. 30–32.
58. *Jindai Shanghai chengshi yanjiu* (1990), pp. 580–585.
59. Thomas (2001), pp. 252–264.
60. McElderry (2001), pp. 9–10; Liu Ta-Chun (1936), p. 158.
61. In 1893, the British commissioner of customs in Shanghai observed that "at least 40 per cent of the shares of some foreign companies are held by Chinese . . . [as well as] a considerable portion of deposits in local banks." See Murphey (1953), pp. 6–7. See also Hong Jiaguan (1989), pp. 136–137; Thomas (2001), pp. 86–91.
62. Hong Jiaguan (1989), pp. 136–137; Thomas (2001), pp. 35–38.
63. As early as 1856, the largest single contribution to SMC revenue (SH$18,275) was attributed to tax collected from Chinese residents (SH$5,400). See Jernigan (1904), p. 399; on Chinese ratepayers' campaign for representation on SMC, see Kotenev (1925 [1968]), pp. 40–44, and Justice Richard Feetham's report to the SMC on the future of Shanghai (1932), vol. 2. In NLA, Braga Papers, MS 2826; on Chinese representation on the MCFC, see Martin (1996), pp. 74–76; cf. Johnstone (1937 [1973]), pp. 226–243.
64. Keeton (1928), vol. 2, pp. 78–79. See also Ch'en (1992).
65. Morse (1921 [1967]), pp. 195–197.
66. Keeton (1928), vol. 2, pp. 94–102. Cf. Kotenev (1925 [1968]), pp. 45–68.
67. Moulder (1977), pp. 112–114; Wang Jingyu (1965), p. 56.
68. Keeton (1928), vol. 2, pp. 106–109; cf. Lee (1926 [1982]), pp. 102–105.
69. On Likin contingencies, see Morse (1921 [1967]), pp. 208–211; Hanna, Conant, and Jenks (1904), pp. 45–47; Motono (2000), pp. 37–39.
70. Keeton (1928), vol. 2, pp. 123–126; cf. Goodman (2004), pp. 78–79.
71. On the jurisdiction of Mixed Courts, see, e.g., Jernigan (1904), pp. 224–228.
72. Kirby (1995).
73. Wang Jingyu (1965), pp. 39–74; cf. Lin Man-houng (2001), pp. 994–998.
74. Motono (2000), pp. 69–72.
75. Feuerwerker (1980).
76. Sheehan (2003), pp. 54–60; Cheng Linsun (2003), pp. 61–62; Du Xuncheng (2002), p. 128; Chen Shao-teh (1932 [1982]), p. 294; Mickey (2004), pp. 193–255.
77. Coble (1980), pp. 43–65; cf. Martin (1996), pp. 93–112, and Smith (2000), pp. 200–205.
78. Sheehan (2003), pp. 164–165; Coble (1980), pp. 172–192.
79. Cheng Linsun (2003), pp. 67–68.

80. Cheng Linsun (2003), pp. 42–45.
81. See, e.g., Wood (1998).
82. For a representative "world system" analysis, see Moulder (1977).
83. Gallagher and Robinson (1953), p. 13.
84. O'Brien and Pigman (1992).
85. Koehn (1994), pp. 62–72, 104; cf. Semmel (1970), pp. 130–157.
86. O'Brien (1988), p. 167; Van der Eng (1998).
87. Platt (1968), pp. 10–11, 266, 288–289.
88. Platt (1968), p. 323.
89. Platt (1968), pp. 331–333, 346–351.
90. Lieu (1929); Remer (1933 [1968]).
91. Lieu (1929), pp. 115–116, table 39.
92. Remer (1933 [1968]), p. 397, table 14.
93. Remer (1933 [1968]), p. 403, table 15; for 1914 see p. 361, table 4.
94. Lieu (1929), p. 37, table 14; for corroboration purposes, it is worth noting that Douglass Paauw estimated total Chinese foreign debt, including railway bond repayments, at C$1.72 billion—or approximately GBP 98.8 million—in 1937. See Paauw (1950), table 7.
95. Rippy (1959), p. 25, table 3.
96. Rippy (1959), pp. 67–68; for corroboration purposes, it should be noted that Randall estimated British investment in Argentina alone at GBP 22.6 million circa 1875. By 1913, however, total British investment in Argentina had shot up to GBP 479.7 million, with railways accounting for 46 percent and manufacturing for only 4 percent thereof. See Randall (1977), vol. 2, p. 215, table 7.17.
97. Another tentative explanation for Britain's heavier military presence in East Asia may, of course, be the fact that China had traditionally been promoted as a huge untapped market. In reality, predictions about the commercial potential of the China trade proved overly optimistic.
98. Unlike Eastern Exchange practices, many Latin American nationals sat on London-registered company boards, and European overseas banks often owned a controlling interest in local banks. See Rippy (1959), pp. 23–24, 99. In addition, Latin Americans had more direct access to the London capital market than Chinese firms; see Jones (1977), pp. 22–25.
99. On banking profitability in Latin America, see Rippy (1959), pp. 171–184; on China, see Remer (1933 [1968]), pp. 339–407.
100. On deposits with British banks in Latin America, see Jones (1977), pp. 18, 27, 49; on China, see Hou Chi-ming (1965), pp. 52–58.
101. On China, see Chapter 5; on British banknote issuance in Latin America, see Jones (1977), pp. 28–30, 32, 38.
102. In his classic study of German banking, Alexander Gerschenkron was the first to spell out an inexorable linkage between industrialization and bank credit across Continental Europe. He stressed that the later the drive to industrialization started, the more important the role of banks and the state in facilitating credit became. See Gerschenkron (1966), pp. 353–364.

103. For proponents of this view see, e.g., Zhang Naiqi (1936), pp. 315–317; for a critical view, see Cheng Linsun (2003), pp. 82–84; cf. Wright (1984), pp. 18–23.
104. Verdier (2003), pp. 31–32. For similar though much less explicit interpretations, see Da Rin and Hellman (2002), pp. 383–385; Burhop (2006), pp. 55–58.
105. The closest thing to such juxtaposition is W. A. Thomas's review of HSBC share register data; see Thomas (2001), pp. 78–83. His findings suggest that most of HSBC's major shareholders in 1870s Shanghai were European.
106. *Shanghai minzu jiqi gongye* (1979), vol. 1, pp. 459–466; *Shanghai minzu xiangjiao gongye* (1979), pp. 85–114.
107. Chen Zhen (1957), vol. 1, pp. 38–53.
108. Cochran (2000), pp. 118–146.
109. Kwan Man Bun (2001), pp. 138–144.
110. Wright (1984), pp. 122, 124–125.
111. Huang Jianhui (1994), p. 87; on Chinese bank loans to expatriate firms, see also *Zhongguo di yi jia yinhang* (1982), p. 142.
112. Ishii Kanji (2002), pp. 122–124.
113. *Meiguo Huaqi yinhang zai Hua shiliao* (1990), pp. 590–559; Cleveland and Huertas (1985), p. 208.
114. Nishimura found that by 1913 HSBC fixed deposits in Tianjin and Shanghai had made up as much as 82.9 percent and 69.2 percent of the local balance sheets, respectively. In Tianjin, much of these deposits had been drawn from Chinese firms and individuals. See Nishimura (1994), pp. 25–27.
115. Between 1925 and 1934, total loan advances by the twenty-eight Chinese-run banks in Shanghai increased by 195 percent; deposits by 251 percent; the combined note issue by 196 percent; cash reserve by 143 percent and capitalization by 123 percent. See Liu Ta-Chun (1936), p. 156.
116. See Remer (1933); for more recent analyses that are still heavily reliant on Remer, see, e.g., Hou Chi-ming (1965), pp. 150–152; Kikuchi (1966); Fewsmith (1985), pp. 80–81; Jordan (1991). A notable exception is perhaps Daniel Meissner's (2005) study of Sino-American competition in the Shanghai flour milling industry.
117. Remer (1933), pp. 25–26.
118. Wang Guanghua (2001); Wong Sin Kiong, (2002).
119. Wong Sin Kiong (2002), pp. 134–137; it should be noted that the antiforeign imagery that was often instigated during the Republican era did by no means preclude expressions of admiration for Western aesthetics in the popular media. See, e.g., Ho (1991).
120. Wasserstrom (1991), photo addendum to chapter 4. Images of "foreign turtles" in the same addendum pun on the homonymous expletive "foreign devils" (*yanggui* 洋鬼); Cochran (1980); Jordan (1991); Goto-Shibata (1995); Gerth (2003). On student antiforeign activism in Shanghai, see also Perry (1993), pp. 81–87. On the evolution of student consciousness in Shanghai from nonviolent cosmopolitanism prior to 1919 into pronounced antiforeignism during 1925, see Schwarcz (1986), pp. 145–176. See also Banno (1989) for a cursory survey of Chinese boycotts from a distinctly Japanese perspective.

CHAPTER 3: THE CHARTERED BANK AND ITS NOTE ISSUE

1. The CBIAC local branch balance sheets on which this chapter is based have only recently been opened to public scrutiny, as part of a much wider collection deposited in the Guildhall Library, London, in 1989. More qualitative materials from this collection are not expected to be released soon. On the fate of other Chartered Bank historical records, see Freeth (1991).
2. CBIAC's first three supplemental charters were granted in 1861, 1874, and 1884. See United Kingdom Public Record office [hereafter PRO] TS 18/434.
3. Mackenzie (1954), p. 25; Jones (1993), p. 22; Kawamura (2005), pp. 42–43.
4. Greenberg (1951), pp. 179–184; Philips (1961), pp. 276–280; cf. Kawamura (2005), pp. 25–39.
5. Baster (1934), pp. 140–141; Jain (1929), pp. 140–142; cf. McGuire (2004), pp. 2–4.
6. On EIC opposition to new exchange banking ventures in the 1840s, see, e.g., King (1979), pp. 150–177.
7. Limited-liability provisions were enacted in India only in 1860; see Jain (1929), pp. 142–146; on the evolution of the Agra Bank's legal status, see summary by Orbell and Turton (2001), pp. 48–49. The Bank of Western India opened its Hong Kong and Guangzhou branch as early as 1845, closely followed by its Shanghai branch (est. 1847). See Ding Richu (1994), vol. 2, p. 62.
8. Baster (1934), pp. 143–145; Davenport-Hines and Jones (1989), pp. 11–12.
9. Baster (1934), p. 147. The Bank of India may have not actually commenced business at all. See Orbell and Turton (2001), pp. 70–71,
10. Jones (1993), pp. 23–24.
11. On the liquidation proceedings of Overend Gurney, see the *Bankers' Magazine* 26.2 (1866): 848–863, 1132–1138; King (1936), pp. 238–256.
12. See "The Failure of the Oriental Bank," *Bankers' Magazine* 44 (1884): 613–616; for a somewhat different analysis for the reasons behind the Oriental Bank's failure, see McGuire (2004), pp. 14–15.
13. The Oriental Bank's total liabilities in December 1883 amounted to 11.25 million pounds, of which the note issue made up more than 6 percent. See *Bankers' Magazine* 44 (1884): 664–670.
14. Mackenzie (1954), p. 146.
15. Triffin (1985); Van der Eng (1999); Yokouchi (1996), pp. 171–173; for CBIAC's perspective on currency fluctuations, see Mackenzie (1954), pp. 110–112.
16. Mackenzie (1954), pp. 160–161; Nishimura (1997), p. 2. Similar misjudgment with respect to silver prices blighted the Oriental Bank Corporation; see McGuire (2004), p. 12.
17. Cassis (1994), pp. 229–231.
18. For two somewhat different interpretations of the Bimetallists' political agenda, see Green (1988) and Howe (1990).
19. For a concise overview of contemporary bullion movements, see Triffin (1985); for the CBIAC perspective on currency fluctuations, see Mackenzie (1954), pp. 110–112.
20. Davenport-Hines and Jones (1989), pp. 13–14.

21. In the late nineteenth century, nearly half of HSBC's shares were traded in the Shanghai and Hong Kong bourses. See Jones (1990), p. 32.
22. China's tax revenue was, during that period, largely extracted through the Maritime Customs. This establishment was administered for the Chinese Imperial Court by British subjects, who were generally on good terms with HSBC executives. See, e.g., King, (1987), vol. 1, pp. 86–87, 538–541, 547–553.
23. Mackenzie (1954), pp. 205–207; Jones (1993), pp. 121–126.
24. King (1987), vol. 1, p. 400.
25. King (1987), vol. 1, pp. 277–278; cf. Collis (1965), pp. 61–67.
26. Edwards (1987), pp. 15–16.
27. Edwards (1987), pp. 26–27, 95–96, 167.
28. Between 1887 and 1913, CBIAC total liabilities averaged GBP 1.28 million in Singapore alone, compared with 1.22 and 1.12 million in Hong Kong and Shanghai, respectively. See CBIAC GL Ms 31519/5-30; cf. Nishimura (2004), Part 2, pp. 9–11, 15–19.
29. In contrast to Hong Kong, HSBC and CBIAC had an equal share of colonial government business in the Straits Settlements. See, e.g., Collis (1965), p. 93.
30. Export of tin from Southeast Asia to India probably began in the fifth century by *Orang Asli* prospectors and was taken over by Chinese migrant labor in the early nineteenth century under colonial auspices. See Drabble (1989), pp. 12–17, 107–111.
31. Brown (1994), pp. 123–126.
32. In December 1926, for example, up to 61 percent of the current account balance CBIAC's Penang branch kept with other financial institutions derived from Overseas Chinese banks. CBIAC interbank credit balances were much less dominated by Chinese banks elsewhere during the same period. This ratio stood at 8.5 percent in Hong Kong and 6 percent in Hankou, for example. See CBIAC GL Ms (31519), 84–89; cf. Brown (1990), p. 179.
33. Brown (1994), pp. 133–134, 152, 155.
34. Brown (1994), pp. 158–159, 188.
35. U.S. overseas banking was effectively blocked by Senate legislation before the 1920s. See Cleveland and Huertas (1985), pp. 76–79; Dayer (1981), pp. 1–3; Jones (1990), pp. 33–34; Pugach (1997), pp. 32–33; Wilkins (1986), pp. 281–282.
36. Davenport-Hines and Jones (1989), pp. 1–4.
37. Short-term interest rates in Europe at the time were close to 8 percent per year, whereas call loans in East Asian entrepôts could fetch upwards of 10 percent. See, e.g., Baster (1929), pp. 10–13; on the lucrative credit market in Guangzhou [Canton] shortly before the onset of overseas banking, see Greenberg (1951), pp. 152–156 and Van Dyke (2005), pp. 97–99, 150–160.
38. The Presidency Banks were closely aligned with the colonial government of British India. They enjoyed exclusive custody of government balances but, unlike the Eastern Exchange Banks, were denied the right to raise capital in London. On their note issue see Bagchi (1989), pp. 96–98.
39. Baster (1929), pp. 46–48; Hickson and Turner (2004).
40. Baster (1929), pp. 23–24; see also Grossman (2001).

41. A colonial issue was initially considered less desirable than a private one because it entailed higher reserve requirements by law; see, e.g., King (1987), vol. 1, pp. 374–376.
42. Ironically, Wilson, who had advocated free banking in Britain, was later the main driving force behind the abolition of private banknote issuance in India. This was in his capacity as financial secretary to HM Treasury. See Chalmers (1893), p. 346; White (1984), pp. 79–90. For a biographical sketch of Wilson's flamboyant career as businessman, journalist, and politician, see Cortney (2004).
43. This principle is likely to have derived from the Peel Act of 1844, which required the Bank of England and Scottish joint-stock banks to maintain 100 percent bullion reserve against excess issue. Concomitantly, the Act clamped down on the smaller country banks of issue in England and Wales. See White (1984), pp. 76–78.
44. HSBC enjoyed special relationships with the Hong Kong government, and was expected in return to issue notes as a gratuitous service to the colony. As a result, the difference in circulation patterns between HSBC and the smaller CBIAC and MBI became increasingly pronounced in the twentieth century. HSBC's total note circulation as a proportion of paid-up capital shot up from 2.4 in 1928 to 7.3 in 1933, whereas the corresponding ratio for CBIAC and MBI declined, respectively, from 0.56 and 0.21 in 1928 to 0.43 and 0.09 in 1933. For a general analysis, see "Comparative Studies of Some Recent Bank Reports," *Bankers' Magazine* 137 (1934): 917–919.
45. See page 9 of the original charter in PRO TS 18/434; cf. Mackenzie (1954), pp. 21–22, 171–172. Since 1890, HSBC's note issue prerogative had been subjected to far more stringent reserve requirements generally equivalent to two-thirds of its authorized circulation volume. In addition, HSBC notes had been designated from the outset as unlimited liability on shareholders in case of liquidation. Cf. King (1987), vol. 1, pp. 112–114, 122, 391–397, and vol. 2, pp. 67–69.
46. In Shanghai, for example, the midyear ratio of liquid cash reserves to notes in circulation averaged 2.3 between 1900 and 1909, while the ratio between liquid cash reserves to notes and current accounts averaged 0.51. Calculated from CBIAC GL Ms 31519/13–24.
47. See, e.g., letter dated October 8, 1910, from CBIAC to Treasury specifying the securities deposited with the Bank of England against one-third of the maximum note issue—PRO T1/11225 (F15108).
48. On the abandonment of the Silver standard and subsequent monetary evolution in the Straits Settlements, see Nelson (1983); Van der Eng (1999), pp. 71–71; Drake (2004), pp. 102–104.
49. See a letter dated August 20, 1910, from the Treasury to the Undersecretary of State in the Colonial Office indicating that the Treasury had no objection to "the proposed reallocation [of the CBIAC] authorized note issue between several branches in the East"—PRO T1/11225 (F 15126); cf. King (1987), vol. 2, pp. 226–229.
50. HSBC statistics reveal an opposite trend because, as the paramount bank in the Crown Colony, it was expected to engage in unprofitable excess issues: in December 1903, the HSBC total note circulation (equivalent to HK$13.3 million) constituted 5 percent of total liabilities, whereas in 1935 it made up 11.3 percent (HK$119 million). See King (1987), vol. 2, pp. 56–57 and vol. 3, p. 182; cf. CBIAC GL Ms 31519 and Jones (1993), table A5.1.

51. According to Imperial Maritime Customs statistics, there had been approximately a 24 percent rise in Anglo-Chinese trade (excluding Hong Kong) between 1864 and 1900, whereas trade between China and Annam (French Indochina) registered a tenfold increase. Comparison in the following period is even more striking: between 1901 and 1932 Anglo-Chinese trade had trebled, while trade with French Indochina grew by 33 times. Notwithstanding accounting inconsistencies throughout the period, these figures trace out a phenomenal upward trend. See time series in Hsiao Liang-lin (1974), pp. 144–150; cf. Sugihara (1996); on the limitations of Maritime Customs data, see, e.g., Lyons (2003), pp. 69–72.
52. Wagel (1915), p. 240.
53. Jones (1993), pp. 84–85, 90–92; Bostock and Jones (1989), pp. 40–41.
54. Muirhead (1996), pp. 141–143, 153, 169.
55. Jones (1990), p. 41.
56. See, e.g., early-Republican gazetteer fragment presented in *Jindai Shanghai diqu fangzhi jingji shiliao xuanji* (1984), p. 111.
57. In the 1850, Overseas Chinese associated Australia—and Victoria in particular—with new gold discoveries, hence "New Gold Mountain." The older Gold Mountain was the title reserved for San Francisco, whose gold rush had broken out only a year earlier. Other banks like the Oriental Bank and the U.S.-based International Banking Corporations were known by different Chinese names across Greater China. See, e.g., Ji Zhaojin (2003), pp. 76–77; Xu Jiqing (1932 [1970]), pp. 77–79.
58. Peng Xinwei (1958), pp. 556–559.
59. For a detailed analysis of Xianfeng monetary policies, see Hamashita (1989), pp. 57–61. Unlike foreign banknote design, Xianfeng notes were upright, woodblock-printed, and largely devoid of realistic watermark imagery. See, e.g., Huang Hengjun (2001), pp. 77–101.
60. Mackenzie (1954), p. 59; CBIAC Shanghai balance sheets put note circulation figures in mid-1864 at Tls. 18,890, swiftly plummeting to Tls. 30 by 1870. See CBIAC GL Ms 31519/1–4.
61. The second issue in Shanghai gained a circulation of Tls. 12,500 in mid-1886, but dropped to Tls. 7,500 the following year. The circulation steadily picked up thereafter. See CBIAC GL Ms (31519), 5–6; cf. Pan Liangui (2004), pp. 74–75.
62. Mackenzie (1954), p. 61.
63. Late-Qing Imperial and private banks in the provinces over-relied on note circulation and sidelined deposit acceptances. See Wagel (1915), p. 165 and Peng Xinwei (1958), pp. 673–675.
64. Cf. CBIAC GL Ms 31519/111—this 1930 Beijing balance sheet shows that Chinese notes were seldom included in the bank's cash reserves even after the political unification of the country. Earlier, the only exception may have been notes issued by the Imperial Bank of China circa 1909; see Tamagna (1942), pp. 36–37.
65. Hao Yen-p'ing (1970), pp. 109–112.
66. Feuerwerker (1958), pp. 54–56. British foreign policymakers were, in fact, averse to calls by the expatriate mercantile community in the treaty ports to use military force in order to establish effective control over the Chinese hinterland. As was precociously

stated in the Mitchell Report (1852), the Foreign Office could not be led to believe that military intervention would make appreciable headway for British exports, because it perceived of the Chinese economy as self-sufficient. See Pelcovits (1948), pp. 15–18; Moulder (1977), pp. 107–109.

67. Huang (1990), pp. 305–314.
68. Arrighi et al. (2003), pp. 294–295.
69. On the rise of homegrown banks in the 1920s, see, e.g., Cheng Linsun (2003).
70. Lee En-han (1981), pp. 1445–1450; Wood (1998), pp. 181–183.
71. As part of this accommodation, HSBC refrained, for example, from accepting more deposits from Chinese nationals through the 1930s by a "gentlemanly agreement" with GMD officials. See King (1987), vol. 3, p. 355–362.
72. Extraterritoriality in China was formally abrogated only in January 1943, as a wartime gesture of the Allies. See Bickers (1998), p. 162; Lee En-han (1981), p. 1464.
73. For the belligerent British attitudes toward the GMD before the thaw in relations see, e.g., dispatch from the Hong Kong government to the Colonial Office—PRO FO 371/12417 (F1120 folios 265–271), dated November 5, 1926.
74. On British bank compliance with the *fabi* reform, see, e.g., a report in the *Bankers' Magazine* 141 (1936): 250.
75. See Tamagna (1942), p. 106; Rawski (1989), pp. 376–378.
76. For the mid-1920s, see King (1990), p. 26 and King (1987), vol. 3, p. 63; for the early 1930s, see King (1987), vol. 3, p. 365.
77. Xian Ke (1958). Xian's estimates exerted profound influence on other important English-language publications. See, e.g., Feuerwerker (1983), p. 198.
78. See Xian Ke (1958), pp. 52, 154–161. Rawski erroneously stated in his book that Xian had attributed 100 percent of the Banque de l'Indochine note circulation volume to China proper. In fact, the ratio advanced by Xian was one-third; the highest ratio of Banque de l'Indochine notes circulating in China proper that was suggested by Chinese scholars seems to be two-thirds. See Ding Richu (1994), vol. 2, pp. 85–86.
79. Zheng Jiadu (1981), pp. 152–163.
80. Lee (1926 [1982]), pp. 26–27.
81. See *Yunnan jindai huobishi ziliao huibian* (1984), pp. 93, 96, 170–177; Xian Ke (1958), p. 55, table 6.
82. Faure (1989), pp. 59–60. A 1903 guide for Western visitors to the city of Guangzhou suggests that money primarily implied silver dollar coins there, but "any of the [banknotes] circulating in Hongkong" were also current. See Hurley (1903), p. 22. A 1919 handbook for American businessmen similarly reported that "among the Chinese" in Guangzhou the unit of currency was provincial subsidiary coinage, while "between foreigners" and in the import-export business "Hongkong notes" were used. See Arnold (1919), vol. 1, p. 111; for more contemporary observations in that vein, see *Zhonghua minguo huobishi ziliao* (1989), vol. 1, pp. 910–911.
83. Schenk (2000), pp. 746–750.
84. King (1987), vol. 3, p. 64.
85. See Leith-Ross to H. H. Kung, dated May 6, 1936, in SOAS Maritime Customs Files [Maze Papers] Ms 285232.

86. Given the fact that local cash reserves did not include sycee, it is very likely that at least some CBIAC Guangzhou agency loans were disbursed and paid back in HK$ notes; on the silk industry in Guangzhou, see Eng (1984), pp. 353–370, 354–355. Eng estimated that silk had contributed 63 percent of value of Guangzhou exports between 1912 and 1929. However, his assumption that Western capital was not introduced to this industry (p. 359) is qualified by the balance sheet in question. It seems that British bank-lending policy in 1920s Guangzhou was, in this sense, very different from that in Shanghai.
87. On Hong Kong as transshipment center for Guangdong exports, see, e.g., Orchard (1930), p. 258; Fung (1991), pp. 44–45.
88. The cash reserve for December 1920 consisted of HK$85,000 in CBIAC-issued notes and HK$124,318 in other banknotes. Subsidiary coins merely amounted to HK$0.88. See CBIAC GL Ms 3159/53.
89. See CBIAC GL Ms 31519/54.
90. Interestingly, the Shanghai ratio (0.51) was closer to that of Tianjin than Hong Kong's.
91. Since it is plausible that part of the notes issued in Hong Kong crossed the border, the CBIAC note/cash ratio for the Crown Colony is in itself biased upward and can only serve as a rough guide.
92. King (1990), p. 31.

CHAPTER 4: HSBC AND ITS NOTE ISSUE IN SHANGHAI, 1866–1925

1. Allen and Donnithorne (1954), pp. 107–108.
2. See Hamashita (1983), pp. 321–349.
3. HSBC was first of the three European banks that issued banknotes in Siam. Its role in that capacity began on November 15, 1888, when the Bank's agent in Bangkok, J. R. M. Smith, tipped off the Head Office that the Siamese government would be prepared to experiment with paper notes "on a small scale." See HSBC Group Archives [hereafter HSBC GA] CLASSIFIEDS C-G F1.1, "The Note Issue." The CBIAC and Banque de l'Indochine followed HSBC's lead only a decade later; cf. Conant (1927), pp. 604–605; on HSBC as adviser to the Chinese governments, see, e.g., Coble (1980), pp. 126–127.
4. See, e.g., a letter from J. O. P. Bland to the Hong Kong Chamber of Commerce, dated February 19, 1916, in which this controversial "Old China Hand" demanded that the Chamber secretary apply pressure on HSBC to dispel concerns among British expatriates concerning the Bank's ties with the Deutsch-Asiatische Bank, and to "eliminate German Business"—in HSBC GA SHG II 183; for an incisive biographical sketch of Bland (1863–1945), see Bickers (2004).
5. See, e.g., Wang Hongbin (2001), pp. 396–400; on the economic nexus that propelled the opium trade with China, and on its opponents, see Blue (2000), pp. 31–54; cf. Moulder (1977), pp. 98–105.
6. Clarence Davis (1982, p. 254) has described the Consortium as a foreign bank mechanism "to guard against Chinese initiatives to improve the terms under which loans might be issued, to secure access to additional sources of capital, to improve a

competitive stance or transform a rival into a partner, and ostensibly, to protect China from unsound loans." It should be noted, in this context, that the total value of loans that HSBC had floated for successive Chinese governments was staggering—GBP 110 million. See J. R. Jones, "Brief Notes on the History of the Bank," in HSBC GA J11-16, folio 13; cf. Chen (1965), pp. 107–120; Baster (1935 [1977]), pp. 184–189.

7. The defeat of Germany in 1918 and the liquidation of Banque Russo-Asiatique in 1926 effectively left HSBC as the sole foreign depository of Chinese Maritime Customs revenue, which had financed indemnity payments incurred after the Boxer Rebellion (1901). See "Historical Notes," in HSBC GA J11-3-7.
8. Chen Guangfu 陳光甫, a leading Chinese banker and government adviser, was the most vociferous critic of HSBC's predominance in the foreign exchange market in Shanghai. In the mid-1920s, he claimed that the Bank periodically dampened silver prices in the city to synchronize with China's government foreign debt repayment schedule, thus unduly netting a profit of Tls 1.9 million. See Gao Yang (1981), p. 226; cf. Yang Yinpu (1930 [1972]), p. 184.
9. Zhang Guohui (2002), pp. 391–392.
10. Recent notable contributions by Japanese scholars to the research of foreign banking in prewar China include Nishimura (2005); Yokouchi (1996); Hamashita (1994); Gonjō (1993); and Yasutomi (2003).
11. King (1987); for reviews in this vein see, e.g., Thomas (1989) and Coble (1991).
12. The term *digressive* was used by Andrea McElderry in a review she wrote for the *Journal of Asian Studies*; see McElderry (1991), p. 915. Her assessment of King's work was otherwise positive; Marie-Claire Bergère commended King for observing "strict academic standards" in a commissioned work, but pointed to the "missing perspective" in King's analysis, that is, how the Bank is depicted in Chinese sources. See Bergère (1989a).
13. Xian Ke was the first Chinese scholar to address foreign note issuance in a full-length monograph. His main thesis was that foreign banks in China duped undiscerning Chinese note bearers because they kept only threadbare reserves against their note issue. See Xian Ke (1958), pp. 22–61; for similar tirades see, e.g., Wei Jianyou (1955), pp. 207–213.
14. Zhang Guohui (2002), p. 238.
15. *Zhongguo jindai zhibi shi* (2001), p. 1036.
16. See, e.g., King (1990), pp. 26–27.
17. Although it had a longer history in the region, CBIAC became the second-largest British bank in East Asia after the establishment of HSBC. Nonetheless, both banks operated on much the same principles and were regulated by the same Whitehall ministries. More quantitative data on the China branches of the Chartered Bank are available because, unlike HSBC, its Head Office has always been located in London. Consequently, records sent thereto from China branches escaped the sort of degradation that local HSBC branches underwent during World War II.
18. Albert Pick's famous numismatic catalogue suggests that the earliest note HSBC circulated in China was denominated 1 Shanghai Tael and printed by Barclays & Fry in London. See Pick (1990), vol. 1, p. 269.

19. Nelson (1984), pp. 202–205.
20. See Jones (1990), pp. 33–34; the note issue was independent of the Bank's role as underwriter for Chinese government loans floated in London or, indeed, the volume of trade between Britain and China.
21. A similar conjuncture of a fairly free note circulation and deposit agglomeration lay at the heart of joint-stock bank ascendancy in the British Isles between 1830 and 1870. See Collins (1988), pp. 93–97.
22. Because they were considered more stable, Scottish joint-stock banks retained many of the issue prerogatives that their English counterparts had lost by the mid-1840s; on the Scottish model of note issuance, see Conant (1927), pp. 142–170, 590–593; Checkland (1975), pp. 381–384, 435–439; White (1984), pp. 38–49.
23. King (1987), vol. 1, pp. 74–77, 158–160; on Hong Kong's short-lived Mint, see Tom (1964), pp. 38–41.
24. For a general survey of late-Qing economic reforms, see Ch'en (1980), pp. 120–123; on Zhang Zhidong's economic standpoint, see Li Xizhu (2003), pp. 176–192. One of Zhang Jian's most formative experiences as an entrepreneur was his inability to raise sufficient capital for his first textile mill in 1898, which persuaded him of the urgent need to set up new financial institutions; see Zhu Zhiqian (1972), pp. 20–23.
25. Ye Shichang (2002), pp. 599–604.
26. Jiang Hongye (1991), pp. 3–17; Huang Jianhui (1994), pp. 96–104.
27. On the statistical pitfalls confronting Chinese banking historians, see Tang and Huang (1985), pp. 57, 61–62.
28. Figure 4.1 draws on data recently compiled by Cheng Linsun on the capital of early Chinese banks (see the source note on the figure). Readers should nonetheless be aware that Cheng's figures on Chinese bank capital are substantially higher than, for example, the ones presented in Hirase (1942), pp. 361–362. In addition, the data do not seem to incorporate Chinese provincial banks, where overprinting of notes was endemic; see, e.g., Huang Jianhui (1994), pp. 97–100. Whereas Cheng estimates total Chinese bank note circulation in 1911 at $20 million, Huang places his late-Qing estimate in the vicinity of $48 million.
29. The first note issuance period of the Chartered Bank in Shanghai had begun in 1859 but was withdrawn a decade later due to lack of demand. The issue resumed in 1886. See CBIAC GL Ms 31519/1–26.
30. In the treaty ports, foreign banks were protected from Chinese government intervention by virtue of their extraterritorial status. Foreign banks rarely opened branches elsewhere, with the exception of politically sensitive Beijing.
31. Xia Dongyuan (1981), pp. 73–75; Zheng Guanying (1982), vol. 1, p. 685.
32. Within the Imperial bureaucracy, the chief proponents of banknote issuance between the 1810s and the 1830s had been Cai Zhiding 蔡之定, Wang Liu 王鎏, and Xu Mei 许楣, but their views were rejected by mainstream critics. More cautious policies were proposed by Wang Maoyin in 1851, resulting in a botched issue of Imperial paper money between 1853 and 1862. See Yang Duanliu (1962), pp. 104–113; Ye Shichang (1963), pp. 36–43; Lin Man-houng (1991). By the turn of the century, Zheng Guanying and several other Qing officials argued that China needed to abandon the silver standard in favor of

a more stable gold-pegged currency. See, e.g., Zheng Guanying (1921 [1969]), pp. 921–927; Huang Jianhui (1994), pp. 90–91.

33. Zheng Guanying (1982), vol. 1, pp. 19–22, 71–75.
34. Ibid., pp. 192–193.
35. Ibid., pp. 680–681, 683–690.
36. See Elvin (1999).
37. McLean (1976), pp. 292–293, 300–304.
38. Foreign banks in China habitually complained about the chaotic state of China's currency, but the silver-convertible notes they issued were nothing more than a palliative designed for use within specific treaty ports and *not* between them. That the foreign banks were in fact ambivalent about monetary unification is evidenced by the fact that they used to discount their very own notes by 5 percent when presented for encashment in another treaty port. See, e.g., Conant (1927), pp. 598–599.
39. See classified report from Jordan to Grey, dated December 11, 1908, in PRO FO 371/435, folios 561–562, 570; cf. Cheng Linsun (2003), pp. 162, 168.
40. Jordan to Grey, dated December 11, 1908, in PRO FO 371/435, folios 561–562, 570.
41. See Feuerwerker (1958), pp. 228, 232; Chen Limao (2003); cf. Hamashita (1980), p. 459.
42. *Zhongguo di yi jia yinhang* (1982), p. 157; on Chinese banknotes produced by foreign printers see, e.g., Huang and Wang (2004).
43. Feuerwerker (1958), pp. 230–231, 233, 240 (table 24); *Zhongguo di yi jia yinhang* (1982), pp. 28–29.
44. Huang Jianhui (1994), pp. 100–104.
45. Wagel (1915), p. 83; Hall (1921), pp. 20–23.
46. See *Diplomatic and Consular Reports: China*, "Report for the Year 1908 on the Trade of China," pp. 10–11.
47. *Waijiao bao* 24.255 (September 28, 1909): 21–22.
48. See *Guofeng bao* 1.16 (July 17, 1910): 103–104.
49. See Little to the Shanghai Consul-General, Sir Pelham Warren, February 7, 1910, and Müller to Grey, May 6, 1910, in PRO FO 371/856, folios 240–241, 227–228; Qing reformers tried to enforce a sweeping 40 percent cash reserve requirement against all private Chinese banknote issues. This percentage was higher than the reserve the British Treasury nominally required of British banks in China (33 percent). Unlike British banks, however, domestic banks did not keep government bonds as additional security at that period.
50. See pamphlet dated June 22, 1910 in HSBC GA SHG I 53; on the Imperial Bank of China, which was established in 1897 and partly modeled on the HSBC, see Feuerwerker (1958), pp. 225–241.
51. See translation of Imperial Edict dated June 22, 1910 in HSBC GA SHG I 53.
52. CBIAC, for example, designated a note reserve in Shanghai only in 1928. Until then, there was only one metallic reserve to support local liabilities, but its ratio was effectively at the branch managers' discretion. See HSBC GA Ms 31519/1–101. Neither do early HSBC records from Shanghai attest to the existence of a special note reserve. By the same token, the overall metallic branch reserve was not to fall below one-third of the value of local current accounts; see, e.g., Allen and Donnithorne (1954), p. 112. The

CBIAC Shanghai balance sheets suggest, however, that this guideline was not applied uniformly. On light regulation, see also King (1987), vol. 4, Preface, pp. xl–xli.

53. Treaty-port notes had to be readily redeemable in Hong Kong too—hence the implicit overlap relative to all British banks except HSBC; figures published in the *Straits Settlements Government Gazette* 32.33 (June 10, 1898): 665 suggest that, at least until the turn of the century, CBIAC was expected to maintain locally a bullion reserve of up to one-fourth of its notes outstanding in Singapore and Penang, while HSBC drew on its Hong Kong reserve to cover its note issue there; cf. King (1987), vol. 1, pp. 120–122.
54. Helleiner (2003), pp. 55–57, 71–75.
55. White (1984), pp. 28–30, 38–44.
56. On the collapse of Ceylon's coffee plantations, which brought down the Oriental Bank Corporation, see Bandarage (1983), pp. 77–79.
57. Chiang Hai Ding (1963), pp. 356–360.
58. See HSBC Chief Manager G. E. Noble to J. Stewart, the Hong Kong Colonial Secretary, dated June 8, 1889, in PRO CO 129/241, folios 621–624.
59. See Treasury letter to Undersecretary of State for the Colonies, dated February 22, 1890, in PRO CO 129/248, folio 273; as from the 1900s, similar bond purchases were imposed to secure the note issues of all the other British banks in Asia. Nonetheless, since the bonds bore interest, the new reserve of securities was different from the unremunerative metallic one.
60. See Treasury to Undersecretary of State for the Colonies, dated July 18, 1890, in PRO CO 129/248, folios 295–296.
61. See Treasury to Undersecretary of State for the Colonies, dated August 4, 1890, in PRO CO 129/248, folios 99–300.
62. Nelson (1984), pp. 157–159; Tom (1964), pp. 50–56. On the deep-seated suspicion of paper money in late-Imperial China, see, e.g., Cheng Linsun (2003), pp. 160–161.
63. Frank King argued that HSBC had opposed the introduction of the Straits legal tender because of concerns that its notes could not be withdrawn quickly enough there to satisfy the demand for notes in Greater China; see King (1987), vol. 1, p. 487. This explanation overlooks the considerable profits made by HSBC on the Straits issue, as well as its proportionate volume, as compared with the transient Lunar New Year demand for notes in Hong Kong. The opposite may have been true: HSBC worried that slack demand in Hong Kong and the Chinese treaty ports might not be appropriate recompense for the loss of its Straits issue. For a detailed analysis of the Eastern Exchange Banks' opposition to the monetary reforms in Straits, see Chiang Hai Ding (1963), pp. 355–357 and Nelson (1984), pp. 190–197, 223–229.
64. Exactly how the different shades of governance in Hong Kong and the Straits Settlements played out in the monetary sphere is an understudied question.
65. See *Straits Settlements Government Gazette* 32.33 (August 10, 1898): 665.
66. Ibid.; for CBIAC, the *Gazette* provides a breakdown of the reserve: S$830,000 in silver dollars deposited with the Straits government, S$237,000 worth of Japanese government bonds at 5 percent per year stored in Singapore, and S$266,000 worth of British dominion bonds at 2.5 percent per year held by Crown Agents in London.
67. CBIAC's net published profits are listed chronologically in Jones (1993), table A5.I.

68. See laconic reference to the Bank's Bangkok notes in HSBC GA F1.1, "The Note Issue"; CBIAC notes in Bangkok were first introduced in 1898, and this bank's local circulation volume was about Tical 400,000 by 1902—see CBIAC GL Ms 31519/15; the substantial issue of Banque de l'Indochine in the city began a year later but declined immediately thereafter. Local circulation figures in 1902 were given as FF 865,000, which were then equivalent to about Tical 430,000. See Gonjō (1993), pp. 181–182.
69. See S/O ("semiofficial") memorandum from Head Office to Shanghai, dated November 3, 1899, in HSBC GA SHG I 51.
70. The Cantonese population in the colony increasingly resorted to notes rather than traditional silver ingots for the traditional debt settlement that accompanied the Lunar New Year.
71. See, e.g., King (1987), vol. 1, p. 68.
72. S/O from Head Office to Shanghai, dated November 17, 1904, in HSBC GA SHG I 51.
73. See Shanghai branch to Peter Smith in Head Office, dated March 12, 1908, in HSBC GA London II—670; "Notes Outstanding" in HSBC GA SHG I 51.
74. See S/O from Head Office to Shanghai Branch, dated December 30, 1911, in HSBC GA SHG I 51.
75. See S/O from Head Office to Shanghai Branch, dated December 30, 1911, in HSBC GA SHG I 51; notably, private bank note issuance in Australia incurred a state tax of 2 percent before 1910. Yet, banks of issue were still thought to have enjoyed a 2.5 to 3 percent margin of profit there. See Vort-Ronald (1982), pp. 35, 253.
76. See SOAS, Charles Addis Papers, PP MS 14/21 dated March 7, 1903.
77. See entry in "Notes Received and Issued," HSBC GA SHG I 51 dated October 24, 1901; the increasing number of attempted forgeries of foreign banknotes in China is also attested to in a short reference by the *Times* correspondent (September 22, 1908, p. 6): "Of trade questions with Japan, the most important for foreigners in China is the infringement of trade-marks, the forgery of foreign bank-notes, and the importation into China of Japanese imitations of Chinese provincial notes."
78. See HSBC GA SHG LEDG 51.
79. Ibid.; Chinese scholars trace the Bank's first-issued notes in Shanghai to 1867. See, e.g., Pan Liangui (2004), pp. 77–78. However, the record cited above shows that HSBC notes had already been circulating in Shanghai by late 1866.
80. The global percentage is calculated from King (1987), vol. 1, table 6.6, pp. 196–197.
81. Ibid.
82. Baster (1935 [1977]), pp. 160–178; cf. Conant (1927), p. 598; Allen and Donnithorne (1954), pp. 110–111. W. E. Nelson described the Eastern Exchange banks as financial institutions whose "real business [was] exchange operations, note issue, and services to government." See Nelson (1984), p. 37. He is one of the few commentators who recognized fiduciary note issuance and colonial government backing as enduring constituents of British bank strategy in prewar East Asia.
83. Addis to Leith, dated June 11, 1866, in SOAS Addis Papers PP MS 14/64/58.
84. Chinese Imperial Maritime Customs statistics clearly indicate that China sustained a chronic trade deficit with India right until 1948. During the 1870s, the deficit averaged

Tls. 17 million per year. With Great Britain, China's trade was at least twice as big until the turn of the twentieth century. China was a net exporter to Great Britain until the mid-1880s, but its position reversed thereafter. See Hsiao Liang-lin (1974), pp. 148–150.

85. Although most of HSBC's initial public offering had been taken up in Asia, demand for HSBC shares in Shanghai was relatively weak. Shanghai-based investors may have preferred to buy shares in the Bank via Hong Kong due to a better legal infrastructure in the colony. Throughout the nineteenth century, the Shanghainese bourse was nonetheless dominated by banking sector shares. See Thomas (2001), pp. 38–41, 72.

86. Overall, the Bank's total assets grew by 23 percent from $39 million in 1876 to $48 million in 1881; the Shanghai branch thus accounted for about 20 percent of the global aggregate during that period—calculated from the Shanghai balance sheet and King (1987), vol. 1, pp. 196, 269.

87. Hsiao Liang-lin (1974), pp. 148–150.

88. Wang Jingyu (1983a), pp. 244–245, 257; a more raw version of the same observation appeared in an earlier article—see Wang Jingyu (1963) pp. 58, 62–63. Yokouchi Masao has broadly described how, similarly, Asian branch fixed deposits became increasingly important as a proportion of liabilities for MBI, the third-largest British Eastern exchange bank, between 1900 and 1913. See Yokouchi (1990), pp. 86–88, 95–96; Shanghai's leading Chinese newspaper, *Shen bao*, commented favorably on HSBC's active pursuit of deposits from ethnic Chinese in the city in editorials dated April 23, 1881 and May 23, 1884.

89. Zhang Guohui (2002), p. 239. Zhang's estimate was seemingly based on perusal of an article in the *Shanghai Evening Courier*, dated March 17, 1874. Curiously, Wang Jingyu (1983b, p. 292) had used this source much earlier but was not duly cited in Zhang's article. Two years later, Pan Liangui (2004, p. 79) did address himself to Wang's earlier article but ignored Zhang's. In yet another case of overstatement, Cheng Linsun cited Tang Chuansi and Huang Hanmin, who had estimated foreign banknote circulation in China proper circa 1911 at $35 million, although HSBC's *global* circulation cap at the time was only $15 million, most of which was allocated for Hong Kong. See Cheng Linsun (2003), p. 162; Tang and Huang (1980), pp. 45–50.

90. Much of China's customs revenue after 1860 was channeled through foreign rather than Chinese bank deposits to pay off international loans and war indemnities. See, e.g., Hamashita (1989), pp. 68–74. Between 1904 and 1909 at least Tls. 55 million in war indemnities had been remitted through HSBC; see data presented in Huang Jianhui (1994), p. 84; for references to the flow of Chinese deposits into foreign bank coffers see, e.g., Gao Yang (1981), pp. 221–222; Baster (1935 [1977]), pp. 160, 180; Ding Richu (1994), vol. 2, p. 66. A more illuminating, near-contemporary indication of the importance of local deposits is provided by D. K. Lieu: "Deposits of Chinese and foreign customers, especially savings and long term deposits, are invested by [the foreign banks] in [China] or other countries . . . although we are able to obtain their condensed balance sheets for all branches, it is impossible with a few exceptions to secure data concerning their China branches alone. As to the way they invest the

deposits of their customers, detailed particulars for our purpose are also unavailable." See Lieu (1929), p. 86.

91. Hao Yen-p'ing (1970), pp. 120–136.
92. See, e.g., Huang and Lu (2002), pp. 137–140; Liu Ta-Chun (1936), pp. 91–98.
93. Jones (1994), p. 153.
94. For a useful overview of various definitions of the term *junfa* from Song times onward, see *Beiyang junfa shi* (2002), vol. 1, pp. 7–18.
95. See, e.g., Sheridan (1966); Pye (1971); Kapp (1973); Gillin (1967). See also Eastman's (1974 [1990]) classic study.
96. See, e.g., Goldstone (1991), pp. 368–375.
97. The repayment of debt to the European Powers and Japan took up at least one-third of the central government budget between 1911 and 1916, whereas figures before 1890 were at around 2 percent. The three largest sources of government revenue throughout the Republican period were excise on opium, alcohol, and gambling; salt gabelle duties, and the Maritime Customs receipts—the last two having been, of course, under foreign tutelage. See Van de Ven (1996). Warlord regimes had an inherited public debt problem resulting from mass acquisitions of Western weaponry, as well as from the Shimonoseki and Boxer indemnity incurred by the Qing. See, e.g., Lin (2002), pp. 179, 189–203; Fitzgerald (1990), pp. 752–759.
98. Cheng Linsun (2003), pp. 75–78; Du Xuncheng (2003).
99. See report in *Yanyong* 1.21 (October 1, 1913): 8–9. cf. Pinnick (1930), pp. 37–38.
100. See, e.g., a letter to the Treasury, dated December 5, 1913, by H. L. Read, an aide to the undersecretary of state at the Colonial Office, indicating that the latter had no objection to the proposed reallocation of HSBC note issue volumes, and preferred the first of two reallocation alternatives offered by CBIAC. The letter also stated that the correspondence regarding the new allocation quotas would be communicated to the governors of the Straits Settlements and Hong Kong, as well as to the Crown Agents for the Colonies in London. In PRO T 1/11590.
101. See correspondence dated June 13, 1914 in HSBC GA MB HIST 1215.
102. In reply to MBI's request that its note issuance requirements be relaxed to allow a circulation volume parallel with the bank's paid-up capital, and with only one-third of the amount in metallic reserve, the Secretary of State for the Colonies, Viscount Harcourt, reiterated the Treasury's position opposing the equalization of MBI reserve requirements with those of HSBC and CBIAC because of the former bank's recent insolvency; see also Green and Kinsey (1999), pp. 211–212.
103. N. J. Stabb to A. G. Stephen, dated October 19, 1917, in HSBC GA Currency F2.3.
104. Stephen to Addis, dated October 6, 1919, in HSBC GA SHG I 764.1, folios 81–83.
105. *Yuan da tou*—literally translated Yuan's Big Head—in reference to China's first president of the Republic, Yuan Shikai (1859–1916), whose portrait was inscribed on the coin.
106. See, e.g., E. G. Hillier in Beijing to A. G. Stephen in Shanghai, dated November 14, 1919, in which Hillier praised the China Maritime Customs inspector, Arthur Aglen, for prodding the Chinese government to adopt currency reform while sounding a guarded note on the government's previous reform record: "Aglen is wrong in saying that there is no standard dollar. A perfectly good standard was fixed by the currency

regulations issued a few years ago, and these actually provided for the free coinage of silver, but the trouble is that they have never been carried out." In HSBC GA London II—Box 2, Item 33.

107. See copy of a letter from J. N. Jordan to the Chinese Foreign Ministry, dated December 20, 1919, which recapitulated the British Chambers of Commerce plea "that the Chinese government be strongly urged to take steps to discontinue the use of Sycee and establish a uniform currency of Dollars and subsidiary silver and copper coinage throughout the country; [d]uring the [Chambers'] discussion of this resolution in Shanghai, a reference was made to the several memorials on Currency Reform which were submitted to the Imperial Court in 1911. But it was shown that no real reform has occurred; that the present issues of banknotes are largely discredited; that enormous quantities of subsidiary silver and copper coins have been put on the market by various provincial mints, and have rapidly depreciated, thus destroying the confidence of the people in those coins; and that the present state of coinage inflicts great hardship on the Chinese people and on the traders of all nations." In HSBC GA London II—Box 2, Item 33.

108. Djang Siao-mei (1936 [1968]), p. 1149; cf. *Shanghai qianzhuang shiliao* (1960), pp. 593–605; cf. McElderry (1976), p. 9.

109. The CBIAC Shanghai branch balance sheet for June 1916 shows note circulation at $1.5 million, bullion holdings at $3 million, and liquid cash reserves at $2.9 million. See CBIAC GL Ms31519/36–7.

110. Huang Jianhui (1994), pp. 136–137.

111. For background details on the role of inspectors in British overseas banking, see Jones (1993), pp. 49–50.

112. See, e.g., Perkins (1969), pp. 29–32, 151–155; Murphey (1974), pp. 17–22, 39; Ma Debin (2005).

113. Not just foreign bank paper note holdings, but also the types of silver coinages commonly used, varied from province to province and from one treaty port to another. An American business handbook (Arnold, 1919) reported, for example, that while Hubei provincial dollars were the only "legal tender" in Hankou (p. 161), currency conditions in Mukden [Shenyang] were "chaotic" (p. 228). In Shanghai, the "actual" currency in circulation was Mexican silver dollar coins (p. 265). But in Tianjin copper cash was most popular, while Mexican dollar coins were "now seldom seen" (p. 322). In Amoy [Xiamen] "[the] many currencies in circulation make it difficult to give definite statements on exchange" (p. 363). And in Nanjing there were no less than "10 [types of] silver dollars, with their respective subsidiary coins, current" (p. 591).

114. See Inspector's Report on Qingdao, dated July 24, 1915, in HSBC GA L II 8.123.

115. See Inspector's Report on Harbin, dated October 12, 1914; on Dalian, dated November 18, 1914; on Tianjin, dated February 11, 1915, in HSBC GA L II 8.123. For a general account of monetary fragmentation in Northeast China at the time, see, e.g., *Nongshang gongbao* 3.4 (November 15, 1916): 34–35.

116. See Inspector's Report on Hankou, dated April 9, 1915, where the local balance is uniquely divided into Hankou-issued, Shanghai-issued, and Beijing-issued notes—suggesting a discount on, or at least a different view of, quasi-foreign notes from other treaty ports. In contrast to the large amount of Hubei provincial banknotes,

no Chinese bank appears in the branch's interbank clearance account. In HSBC GA L II 8.123.

117. See Inspector's Report on Beijing, dated March 4, 1915, in HSBC GA L II 8.123; although Beijing was not a treaty port par excellence, the figures suggest that the early Beiyang government did not block the Bank's issue even in China's capital.
118. See, e.g., *Dongfang zazhi* 9.1 (July 1, 1912): 9–13; *Dongfang zazhi* 15.8 (1918): 189–194.
119. The foreign banks' joint statement was attached to a report sent by A. G. Stephen (Shanghai) to Charles Addis (London), dated March 15, 1920, in HSBC GA Currency F2.3.
120. On Baker's career and his role as the Bank's ultimate auditor, see King (1987), vol. 1, pp. 97, 162–163; vol. 2, pp. 38, 105–106.
121. The General Inspector's Report on China was submitted by Baker to the Hong Kong Head Office on September 29, 1922. In HSBC GA SHG I 327.
122. McCord (1993), pp. 272–276, 285–297.
123. See Inspector's General Report on China, submitted by Baker to the chief manager on September 29, 1922, in HSBC GA SHG I 327, folios 15–16; cf. Du Xuncheng (2003), pp. 20–23.
124. *The Foreign Trade of China 1925* (1926), pp. 8–9.
125. See Inspector's General Report on China, submitted by Baker to the chief manager on September 29, 1922, in HSBC GA SHG I 327, folios 16–17. Incidentally, the General Report also estimated that total deposits in Chinese modern banks amounted to $469 million, while the face value of their notes outstanding reached $96.3 million. Assuming that Baker's data were credible, we may infer a notes to deposit ratio of 20 percent for Chinese banks, while the Shanghai branch balance sheet for CBIAC put the same ratio in June 1922 at only 9 percent. See CBIAC GL Ms 31519/67.
126. Inspector's Report on Yantai, dated September 2, 1922, in HSBC GA SHG I 329; Baker observed that in this small outport, HSBC notes were mostly in demand by U.S. Navy personnel, by the local branch of the Russo-Asiatic Bank, and by some "native banks"; contrary to Baker's recommendation in this Report, on May 19, 1926 the Head Office instructed the manager of the Shanghai branch, G. H. Stitt, to phase out local Yantai notes and instead disburse Shanghai-issued notes to U.S. Navy personnel. In HSBC GA GHO 13.3.
127. Ibid. Baker was concerned about the legal complexity that a local issue might pose because he was informed shortly before his arrival that an attempt by the U.S.-owned International Banking Corporation to issue notes in Yantai had not materialized due to opposition from the local Chinese authorities; the inspector was equally concerned about the stability of local Chinese banks and therefore recommended strict adherence to metallic money where possible. He estimated Chinese bank note circulation in Yantai at $425,000 against a "trifling" metallic reserve of $97,000.
128. See Inspector's Report on Shanghai (1922) in HSBC GA CLASSIFIEDS H–K SHG 343.1 folio 6.
129. See Inspector's Report on Qingdao, dated June 22, 1922 in HSBC GA CLASSIFIEDS H–K SHG 349.

130. During the early 1920s, HSBC had been increasingly involved in financing groups opposing the GMD in South China, culminating in the 1924 merchant militia uprising led by the Bank's one-time comprador, Chen Lianbo (Chan Lin-pak). See Bergère (1986), pp. 234–236; Tsin (1999), pp. 109–110.
131. Barlow to Stabb, dated September 15, 1922, in HSBC GA SHG II 576.
132. On Hillier, see King (2004).
133. Barlow to Hillier, dated January 6, 1922, in HSBC GA SHG II 576; Barlow indicated that circulation in Xiamen amounted then to only $2,187, while in Fuzhou it totaled a few hundred dollars. The withdrawal of these local issues, therefore, could not have significantly alleviated demand pressures and an attendant reserve crunch on the Bank's Hong Kong issue, which had reached HK$40 million by then.
134. Ibid. For a near contemporary article in the financial Chinese press openly condemning the spread of quasi-foreign banknotes as a drain on the nation's resources, see, e.g., *Dalu yinhang yuekan*, January 3, 1923, pp. 58–62; cf. Beiyang Ministry of Finance records quoted in *Zhonghua minguo huobishi ziliao* (1989), vol. 1, pp. 1293–1308.
135. Barlow to Hillier, dated July 21, 1923, in HSBC GA SHG II 576; on Song Hanzhang, his deputy and close associate, Zhang Jia'ao [Chang Kia-ngau] 張嘉璈, and their attitudes toward nationalism and Chinese business cooperation with foreign firms, see Cheng Linsun (2003), pp. 233–239; Bergère (1986), pp. 138–140. A short biography of both bankers appears in Boorman (1967–1979), vol. 1, pp. 26–30 (Zhang) and vol. 3, pp. 195–196 (Song); see also *Zhongguo yinhang hangshi* (1995), pp. 73–83, 897–900.
136. See *North-China Herald*, June 30, 1923, p. 860.
137. Barlow to Hillier, dated February 28, 1924, in HSBC GA SHG II 576.
138. This point of view is finally becoming recognized by younger scholars in the People's Republic. See, e.g., Zhang Ning (2002), pp. 307–312.

CHAPTER 5: HSBC AND ITS CHINA NOTE ISSUE IN THE LATE-REPUBLICAN ERA, 1925–1937

1. See, e.g., King (1983), pp. 283–284; King (1987), vol. 3, pp. 406–416. Collis (1965), Mackenzie (1954), and Tamagna (1942) barely mention the May Thirtieth Movement. Roberta Dayer's (1988, pp. 259–263) account of the implications of the May Thirtieth Movement is rather laconic. Curiously, the volumes on the Republican era in the *Cambridge History of China* (vols. 12, 13) have little to say on *Wusa*, let alone on its economic implications. See, e.g., Feuerwerker (1983).
2. On the antiforeign flux unleashed in 1925, see primarily Rigby (1980), pp. 38–56. Cf. Borg (1947), pp. 39–40; Wou (1989); Frazier (1994); Waldron (1995), pp. 241–244, 255–256; and Osterhammel (1997), pp. 1–22.
3. Some Chinese bankers demanded, for example, that customs surplus be deposited only with Chinese banks. See, e.g., *North-China Herald*, September 19, 1925, p. 338.
4. See report in *Shishi xinbao* 时事新报, June 4, 1925, quoted in *Wusa yundong shiliao* (1981), p. 199.
5. Wright (1984), p. 130.

6. In the long haul, invisible CBIAC liabilities in Shanghai, like fixed deposits, were not as vulnerable to antiforeign agitation as the bank's local note circulation. In fact, total liabilities grew from Tls. 16.2 million in June 1925 to 18.3 million in June 1926. See CBIAC GL Ms 31519/83 and 86.
7. On the *Herald* as mouthpiece of expatriate disdain for Chinese national aspirations and for racialist commentary on the "Chinese character," see Clifford (1991), pp. 117–118, 241, 278–279.
8. On June 8, 1925, the *Gongli ribao* 公理日报 reported that a sudden run on HSBC in Shanghai exhausted its cash reserves and that Chinese bearers of CBIAC notes were now anxious to redeem them. The two British banks were allegedly saved from collapse only when two moneyshops had decided to honor their notes for an exorbitant commission. Quoted in *Wusa yundong shiliao* (1981), pp. 200–201. Although front-page advertisements promoting substitutes for British cigarette brands and reports on student demands for the boycott of quasi-foreign notes started appearing in *Shen bao* as early as June 4, 1925 (pp. 2–4, 13–15), the newspaper's editorial line remained relatively subdued. On *Shen bao* reporting during *Wusa*, see also Mittler (2004), pp. 390–397.
9. See report in *Minguo ribao*, June 3, 1925, quoted in *Wusa yundong shiliao* (1981), p. 214; cf. pp. 184–185; Gerth (2003), pp. 171–185.
10. *Yinhang zhoubao* 9.29 (August 4, 1925): 410; for background information on the Shanghai Commercial and Savings Bank in the 1920s, see Zeng Xianming (2002).
11. See extensive correspondence between the Colonial Office and the Eastern Exchange Bank through 1925–1926 in PRO CO 129/510/1.
12. Mackenzie (1954), pp. 236–237. The *China Press* reported on June 25, 1925 (p. 1) that "some of the office-boys of the Hongkong and Shanghai bank have walked out."
13. Calculated from Jones (1993), table A5.I; based on the adjusting-account entry in the Shanghai balance sheet, it can be plausibly inferred that at least 30 percent of the drop in overall CBIAC profits during 1925 was attributable to underperformance at this branch. See CBIAC GL Ms 31519/83. Despite the superior performance of HSBC in 1925, its executives were equally alarmed by the long-term implications of the boycott. See report in the *Economist*, April 17, 1926, pp. 791–792.
14. Calculated from Green and Kinsey (1999), pp. 199–212.
15. Osterhammel (1989), pp. 193–194; British-owned department stores in Shanghai's International Concession catered almost exclusively for the foreign community. The leading Chinese chains, Wing On and Sincere, had been set up with Overseas Chinese joint-stock capital. They did not seem to have borrowed foreign bank capital on a large scale until the 1930s. See Chan (1996).
16. Cochran (1980), pp. 177–178; cf. Remer (1933), pp. 101–112, 121.
17. Cochran (1980), pp. 182, 230; Nicholas Clifford (1991, p. 132) reached a similar conclusion.
18. Rigby (1980), pp. 142–146; see also Clifford (1991), p. 137 and Cox (2000), p. 181.
19. Hong estimated total deposits in principal Chinese banks at 1.4 billion silver dollars in late 1924. By late 1926, the total is said to have reached 2.4 billion silver dollars. See Hong Jiaguan (1989), pp. 18–19.
20. See CBIAC GL Ms 31519/78 to 83.

21. See Bills of Lading, dated October 8, 1924, to February 11, 1925, in HSBC GA SHG LEDG 294; the notes were ordered from Waterlow & Sons, arriving in Shanghai about forty days later. In the late-Imperial period, HSBC ordered notes from Barclays & Fry, another London printer.
22. See, e.g., King (1990), pp. 22–23, 32–34.
23. See entries for December 31, 1924 and March 6, 1925 in "Tientsin Market Conditions," HSBC GA SHG II 28.1.
24. See entry for December 29, 1922 in HSBC GA SHG I 764, folio 606; interestingly, an earlier Shanghai entry in the same file, dated July 11, 1919 [folio 65], suggested that there was no need to order a new batch since "we have good supply of unsigned notes in hand." The difference between the two entries provides clear indication that, as HSBC notes became more popular in the early 1920s, attempts at forgeries grew more numerous.
25. This point is made eminently clear in a letter, titled "Peking Agency Note Issue," that A. H. Barlow sent to A. E. Baker of the Shanghai branch on April 16, 1924 (in HSBC GA SHG II 576). In essence, Barlow explained to Baker how the Mainland issue offset the Bank's issue capacity in Hong Kong. He then told Baker that it was "unadvisable" for the Bank to increase its Beijing issue beyond $600,000 because the prevailing political uncertainty in the capital made HSBC notes extremely popular to the extent that additional issues would be immediately hoarded, thus narrowing the Bank's ability to balance off circulation volumes between the Mainland and the Colony; the premium on HSBC notes in Hong Kong was often the theme of discussions between the Colony's government and the Treasury in London during the 1920s–1930s, but there are much fewer references to a similar premium over metallic currencies on the Mainland. See, e.g., Barlow to Hillier, dated January 6, 1922, in HSBC GA SHG II 576. In that correspondence, Barlow recounted *en passant* that many deposits had been withdrawn from the Bank's Mainland branches upon the outbreak of World War I, but that often the clients insisted on payment in HSBC notes rather than in silver.
26. Share prices in Shanghai and London are based on the *North-China Herald* and the *Financial Times,* respectively. Interestingly, CBIAC and MBI shares, which traded exclusively in London, sustained a smaller price decline during the same period.
27. Hong Kong share prices are based on the *South China Morning Post.* Trading in the colony was suspended between July and November 1925 as a result of the spreading disturbances; cf. Ku Hung-ting (1984), p. 863.
28. See Chinese press reports from Guangzhou quoted in *Zhonghua minguo huobishi ziliao* (1989), vol. 2, pp. 3–33.
29. For Sun Yixian's vehement criticism of foreign banks, see his collected works (1989), vol. 1 (*San min zhuyi*), pp. 17–19, 44; on Sun's complex attitude toward the Powers, see Bergère (1994), pp. 409–420.
30. Miners (1987), pp. 16–19; Waldron (1995), p. 244.
31. Ku Hung-ting (1984), pp. 866–868; Tsin (1999), pp. 143–144, 153–160.
32. Whereas the drop in the CBIAC Shanghai circulation volume between June 1925 and June 1926 reached 47.9 percent, Hong Kong registered a mere 2.2 percent dip during the same period. See CBIAC GL Ms 31519/ 80, 84.

33. The first measures of martial law had been declared as early as July 19 (four days before the Shaji Incident broke out); see Ku Hung-ting (1984), p. 851. See also *Sheng Gang da bagong ziliao* (1980), p. 316.
34. Fung (1991), p. 49.
35. See *Huazi ribao*, November 16, 1925, p. 3; Qian Yizhang (1987), p. 39.
36. See Qian Yizhang (1987), pp. 134–137; Ku Hung-ting (1984), p. 857. On June 21, 1925, the *China Press* (p. 1) reported on the appearance Guangzhou circulars calling for the boycott of HK$ notes.
37. Li Hong (1988), pp. 66–67; Orchard (1930), pp. 257–258.
38. See Qian Yizhang (1987), pp. 40–44.
39. *North-China Herald*, June 27, 1925, p. 486; Tsang (2004), pp. 97–100.
40. Fung (1991), pp. 50–53; on the par value of GMD-issued currency against HK$ banknotes, see *North-China Herald*, May 15, 1926, p. 327.
41. Quoted in Tsin (1999), p. 159.
42. See CBIAC GL Ms 31519/80 and Ms 31519/87.
43. See *North-China Herald*, August 15, 1925, pp. 155–156. By December 19, 1925, however, the *Economist* correspondent described Hong Kong's plight as "desperate" (p. 1043). He also complained that British trade in Hong Kong was "slowly being strangled," while Japanese businessmen were slipping through the boycott by buying off the Chinese strike committee (pp. 155–156). Four years later, Dorothy Orchard still maintained that the *Shaji* strike and the Guangzhou blockade had been "disastrous" for Hong Kong's economy. See Orchard (1930), p. 259; see also Carroll (2005), pp. 133–135.
44. See anonymous report under the title "The Position of Hong Kong," *The Economist*, May 22, 1926, p. 984.
45. Throughout 1916, for example, Shanghai's pro-German prefect attempted to destabilize HSBC and probably other British banks by spreading rumors that German battleships had scuttled Shanghai-bound vessels freighting bullion from England. Then the prefect misinformed the Chinese government that HSBC's managers in Shanghai and Hong Kong had absconded and that their branches were forced to shut down, resulting in a run on HSBC banknotes. See King (1987), vol. 2, pp. 575–576.
46. See CBIAC GL Ms (31519) 80, 85.
47. Borg (1947), pp. 40–41; Sheehan (2003), pp. 110–125, 152. The stark differences between the CBIAC and HSBC circulation patterns in Tianjin *after* 1925 is most likely a reflection of HSBC's policy of retiring China notes following the *Wusa* upset. CBIAC, on the other hand, seems to have harnessed greater demand for quasi-foreign notes in the North, where residual warlordism and Japanese encroachment destabilized domestic banks, in order to offset the shrinking of its Shanghai issue.
48. Barlow to Stitt, dated June 19, 1925, in HSBC GA GHO 13.2, folio 28. Stitt resigned from the Bank in 1926 after thirty-six years of service. See King (1987), vol. 3, p. 300. The lack of reliable data on the foreign financial sector obscured the few contemporary reports that emerged in the Chinese press on the impact of the boycott of quasi-foreign notes. On October 10, 1926, the *Jingji xuebao* [Journal of Economics] briefly addressed the issue with these words (vol. 2, no. 2, p. 271): "HSBC banknotes had been popular in China ever since the use of paper money was [reintroduced] to the country. Following

the tragic events of *Wusa* last year, Chinese [activists] have called for the severing of economic ties [with Britain]. The circulation of HSBC notes in the Chinese sector [diminished] somewhat thereafter, but was entirely unfazed in the foreign sector."

49. For this view see King (1987), vol. 3, pp. 62–63.
50. Addis to Stephen, dated June 15, 1921, in HSBC GA F1.1 ("The Note Issue/Extracts from Sundries File Kept in the Chief Accountant's Office").
51. Undersecretary of State at Colonial Office to the Foreign Office, dated June 2, 1921, in PRO FO 371/6650, folio 154.
52. Hong Kong Colonial Treasurer to Barlow, dated June 25, 1925, in HSBC GA GHO 13.2, folio 45; Stitt to Barlow, dated June 32, 1925, in HSBC GA GHO 13.2, folio 52.
53. Barlow to Stitt, dated July 3, 1925, in HSBC GA GHO 13.2, folio 50.
54. Cited in Pan Liangui (2004), pp. 126–127; the Chinese bank implicated was rumored to be Yu's *Siming yinhang* 四明銀行, but it promptly denied the allegations. Yu Qiaqing is also known as Yu Xiaqing or Yu Ya-ching. See Du Xuncheng (2002), p. 84; cf. Du Xuncheng (2003), pp. 85–86.
55. See *Rexue ribao*, June 7, 1925, p. 2.
56. Barlow to Stitt, dated July 3, 1925, in HSBC GA GHO 13.2, folio 50.
57. In fact, the Bank's HK$ circulation volume rose through 1925–1926 because of the moratorium on coin withdrawals and concurrent run on "native banks." For background details, see *South China Morning Post*, dated July 2, 1925, p. 2.
58. Stitt to Barlow, dated July 2, 1925, in HSBC GA GHO 13.2, folio 54; the wording of Stitt's telegram suggests that notes were more vulnerable to popular runs than current accounts or fixed deposits because they were redeemable on demand.
59. Stitt to Barlow, dated July 8–9, 1925, in HSBC GA GHO 13.2, folio 69.
60. Stitt to Barlow, dated July 13, 1925, in HSBC GA GHO 13.2, folio 71.
61. Stitt to Barlow, dated July 16, 1925, in HSBC GA GHO 13.2, folio 81.
62. Barlow to Stitt, dated August 5, 1925, in HSBC GA GHO 13.2, folio 111.
63. Barlow to Stitt, dated August 17, 1925, in HSBC GA GHO 13.2, folios 121–122.
64. Barlow to Stitt, dated July 24, 1925, in HSBC GA GHO 13.2, folio 83.
65. Barlow to Stitt, dated June 23, 1925, in HSBC GA GHO 13.2, folio 43; in this telegram, Barlow indicated, among other things, that the "Head Office note issue [in Hong Kong] has so heavily increased that it is probable we shall require at least $2 million of our [Consular note reserve] deposit in Shanghai retained as cover. For background details on the situation in Hong Kong and unusual demand for HK$ notes at that time, see the *Times*, June 23, 1925, p. 16; see also Sinn (1994), pp. 33–35. In all, however, HSBC's global circulation volume fell from the equivalent of HK$49.6 million in December 1924 to HK$45.2 million in December 1925, see *Bankers' Magazine* 121 (1924): 643–644; 121 (1925): 768–777. CBIAC circulation patterns in Shanghai and Hong Kong through 1925–1926 are negatively correlated in much the same way.
66. Barlow to Stitt, dated October 5, 1925, in HSBC GA GHO 13.2, folios 225–226.
67. *The Foreign Trade of China 1925* (1926), p. 1. The China Association Annual Report for 1925–1926 also noted that anti-British sentiments were largely "abating"; see SOAS CHAS/A8.
68. Barlow to Lowson, dated June 4, 1926, in HSBC GA GHO 13.3.

69. Head Office to Lowson, dated August 24, 1926, in HSBC GA GHO 13.3.
70. See, e.g., King (1987), vol. 3, pp. 62–63. Surprisingly, the May Thirtieth Incident does not appear in the index to volume 3 of King's *History*. Similarly, volume 3 does not discuss the evolution of circulation volumes in China before 1927.
71. On *Wusa* as a movement that paved the way for the GMD's takeover of China, see, e.g., Van de Ven (2003), p. 85. Over the Nanjing Decade, the GMD government refrained almost completely from borrowing money through foreign banks to the detriment of HSBC in particular. See, e.g., Paauw (1950), pp. 332–333, 336.
72. See Yasutomi (2003), figure 2, p. 29 and table 10, p. 40.
73. HSBC posted a net published profit of GBP 1,503,000 in 1924 compared with just GBP 786,000 in 1935, the year quasi-foreign banknote issuance was abolished. The comparison is even more striking when it comes to CBIAC's global real profits: these measured GBP 800,000 in 1924, but merely GBP 166,000 in 1935. Comparison figures are based on Jones (1993), appendix 5.
74. Isaacs (1961), pp. 175–185; Dayer (1988), pp. 266–269.
75. See HSBC GA F1.1 ("The Note Issue," based on an article in the *Canton Gazette*, March 11, 1927); Li Jianmin (1986), pp. 207–208; see also GMD Provincial Government and Chinese Strike Committee reports in *Sheng Gang da bagong ziliao* (1980), pp. 681–687, 731–732.
76. See anonymous handwritten remark in a Shanghai banknote ledger, which made reference to a semiofficial letter that had apparently been sent from the Head Office on August 10, 1927, advising the branch that the Mainland circulation cap was placed at $2.5 million—in HSBC GA SHG LEDG 294.
77. See Head Office to Lowson, dated September 20, 1927, in HSBC GA GHO 13.4, folio 274. Once again, the Head Office resisted the pressure from Lowson to increase the China issue because it was wary of the hoarding of new notes, which was likened to "pouring water into a bottomless well." The Head Office then added that "in these disturbed times we want to keep our note issue as low as possible outside Hongkong."
78. A. Eugenes at Head Office to Lowson in Shanghai, dated January 4, 1928, in HSBC GA GHO 13.4, folios 376–379; see also closely related letter from the Foreign Office to the Chief Manager of MBI, dated March 1, 1928, in HSBC GA F1.1 ("The Note Issue").
79. A. Eugenes at Head Office to Lowson in Shanghai, dated January 4, 1928, in HSBC GA GHO 13.4, folios 376–379.
80. King (1987), vol. 3, pp. 61–65, 246–250.
81. See article by Jin Lüqin 金侶琴 (Deputy General Manager of the Bank of Communications) in *Yinhang zhoubao* 11.13 (April 12, 1927): 1–19.
82. Head Office to Lowson, dated January 4, 1930, in HSBC GA GHO 13.6.
83. Head Office to Lowson, dated February 10, 1930, in HSBC GA GHO 13.6, folios 236–237. The author of the letter may seem to have been oblivious to the rise CBIAC's China circulation volume.
84. Hubbard to Grayburn, dated January 26, 1931, in HSBC GA SHG I 52.1.
85. Ibid. As regards banknote reserves, Hubbard observed that Chinese law now "requires a minimum of 60 percent in sycee" and that the circulation was administered by five principal banks.

86. See Sheehan (2005).
87. On the spread of Chinese banknotes and foreign bank oversight, see, e.g., *Gongshang banyuekan*, March 19, 1931, p. 12.
88. Hubbard to Grayburn, dated January 11, 1932, in HSBC GA GHO 98. Nishihara Kamezō was Japan's special envoy to China. In 1917–1918 he negotiated a controversial 145 million yen loan agreement with the Beiyang government in return for Chinese territorial concessions in Shandong. See, e.g., *Beiyang junfa shi*, vol. 1, pp. 509–552. Hubbard's stance reflected British official policy of appeasing both Chinese nationalists and the Japanese. However, it was out of touch since one of the immutable pillars of Nanjing government policy was the refusal to recognize warlord-era debts to the Japanese. See, e.g., Paauw (1950), pp. 283, 294–295.
89. Head Office to Winter, dated July 18, 1932, in HSBC GA GHO 13.8, folios 58–59.
90. Cassels to Davidson, dated March 16, 1933, in HSBC GA SHG I 52.1.
91. Grayburn to Henchman, dated April 10, 1933, in HSBC GA GHO 13.8, folios 333–334. In this letter, Garyburn expressed his concern that overt foreign bank opposition to Chinese reforms might escalate their unpopularity. He made these comments in response to a telegram from Henchman, dated April 7, 1933, indicating that the British-appointed Maritime Customs inspector, Frederick Maze, was trying to rally the foreign banks to obstruct the abolition of the tael. In HSBC GA GHO 13.8, folios 336–337; on foreign bank attitudes toward the abolition of the tael, see also *China Press* clipping, dated March 10, 1933 in HSBC GA SHG I 52.1; Dai Jianbing (2005), pp. 180–182.
92. On the involvement of HSBC and other leading foreign bankers in Chinese government deliberations on monetary reform, particularly with regard to new minting quality safeguards, see *China Press* clipping, dated May 11, 1933, in HSBC GA SHG I 52.1. See also Chinese Central Mint Advisory Committee report, dated August 8, 1933, in HSBC GA SHG I 61.
93. Sheehan (2003), p. 189.
94. Cheng Linsun (2003), pp. 252–253.
95. For Imperial Bank of China data, see Feuerwerker (1958), p. 240. For HSBC data, see Figure 5.1 in this volume.
96. See *Hong Kong Blue Book*, December 1933 issue, section R1.
97. This proposition is supported by what British envoy, Sir Frederick Leith-Ross, heard from Chinese Finance Ministry officials upon his arrival in the region in late 1935: "They assured me that the experience of the *past two years* [emphasis added] during which the Bank of China had been gradually putting notes into circulation in place of silver in Shantung [Shandong] and other up-country districts showed that the public soon got accustomed to notes." In PRO FO 371/20218, folio 154. On the strategic entry of the Bank of China into the Chinese rural hinterland during the early 1930s, see also Yeh Wen-Hsin (1995), pp. 114–119.
98. Friedman and Schwartz (1963), pp. 483–492.
99. See *China Press* report entitled "Silver Rush Begins," dated August 22, 1934, in HSBC GA SHG I 52.1. The report warned that "unusual banking activity has been witnessed over the week-end . . . [the banking district was crowded with] coolies carrying boxes and bars of precious metal . . . ports from Shanghai reached 90 million dollars [since introduction of the new American silver policy]." See also Salter (1934), pp. 20–27; Lin (1936), pp. 11–16.

100. See Salter (1934), pp. 3–14; Sheehan (2003), p. 163; Shiroyama (2008), pp. 91–167. Some scholars have argued that U.S. silver policy did not affect China's economy radically. See the debate between Friedman (1992) and Burdekin (2008), on one end of the spectrum, and Brandt and Sargent (1989) and Rawski (1993) on the other. For a middle-ground interpretation, see Lai and Gau (2003).
101. On February 20, 1934, Henchman reported to Grayburn that H. H. Kung, the Chinese finance minister, and other high-ranking Chinese officials had sent a "strongly-worded" message to Roosevelt in an attempt to persuade him to abrogate the Silver Purchase Policy (in HSBC GA SHG I 52.1). See also article in the *North-China Daily News*, dated January 8, 1935, reporting that Alfred Sze, China's minister in Washington, was seeking from the U.S. administration a promise to lower the silver content of the U.S. dollar so that world prices of silver would stabilize. These overtures had been paralleled by a rumored Chinese proposal to sell the Americans silver in return for gold, which Secretary of State Cordell Hull subsequently denied. On the Chinese government's frantic attempts to stem the outflow of silver from China by imposing a surcharge on silver exports, see, e.g., report by the Kuo Min News Agency, dated October 24, 1934, clipped in HSBC GA SHG I 52.1.
102. On the different support bases and varying motives driving Jiang, Kong, and Song, see Coble (1980), pp. 109–115; Fewsmith (1985), pp. 187–195. For a short biography of Kong and Song, see Boorman (1967–1979), vol. 2, pp. 263–269 and vol. 3, pp. 149–153.
103. See Kuo Min News Agency Brief ("Translated Interview with Chiang Kai-shek"), dated December 26, 1934, in HSBC GA SHG I 52.1.
104. English translation from *Xinwen bao* [Sin Wan Pao], December 26, 1934, clipped in HSBC GA SHG I 52.1
105. Grayburn to Henchman, dated October 22, 1934, in HSBC GA GHO 13.9.
106. *Zhonghang yuekan* 9.6 (December 1934): 63.
107. Davies to Henchman, dated November 22, 1934, in HSBC GA GHO 13.9; on foreign bank shipment of silver from China during 1933–1935, see also Dai Jianbing (2005), pp. 295–304, 311.
108. See, e.g., Department of Overseas Trade Memorandum, dated December 13, 1934, in PRO FO 371-18138, folio 210.
109. On the linkage between the outflow of silver and Chinese alarm at the continued prevalence of quasi-foreign banknotes, see article in the *Zhonghang yuekan* 10.4 (April 1935): 86–67; see also Mao Chih-Li (1996), pp. 444–447.
110. See *China Press* article, dated February 28, 1935, clipped in HSBC GA SHG I 52.1. A similar story was published by the Chinese-language daily *Shehui wanbao* 社會晚報 on February 22, 1935, and translated into English for executive perusal (in HSBC GA SHG I 52.1). See also article in the February 25 issue of *Shen bao* (1935, p. 7), which suggested that extraterritoriality in the treaty ports enabled foreigners to smuggle out silver from China, thus exacerbating the monetary crisis and the precarious state of Chinese banknote reserves. Nonetheless, *Shen bao*'s anonymous reporter conceded that quasi-foreign money volumes began decreasing right after *Wusa*, 1925.
111. Cassels to Barnes, dated February 6, 1935, in HSBC GA SHG I 52.1.
112. Grayburn to Henchman, dated January 14, 1935, in HSBC GA GHO 13.10.

113. On Addis and the Consortium, see Bergère (1986), pp. 264–266; King (1987), vol. 3, pp. 392–393; Dayer (1988), pp. 274–288. Addis's espousal of the International Consortium and Japanese bank participation was blatantly inconsistent with his otherwise anti-Japanese stance on Manchuria. The Foreign Office accused him of senility, and he was subsequently removed from his influential position in the Bank's London office
114. Grayburn to Henchman, dated July 3, 1935, in HSBC GA GHO 13.10; Grayburn's view suggests that he was largely oblivious of the accusations that E. J. Davies leveled at CBIAC in November 1934 with respect to silver smuggling (see note 107 above).
115. Grayburn to Henchman, dated August 19, 1935, in HSBC GA GHO 13.10.
116. Helleiner (2003), pp. 146–151.
117. On this and other aspects of the *fabi* reform, see *Zhonghua minguo huobishi ziliao* (1989), vol. 2, pp. 240–263; the initial amount of silver pledged for sale in the United States was 100 million ounces.
118. See *North-China Daily News* article, dated November 5, 1935, clipped in HSBC GA SHG I 52.2.
119. For background details on the Mission, see Leith-Ross (1968), pp. 195–227. In this autobiography, Leith-Ross himself did not go so far as claiming the credit for devising the reform.
120. For accounts that tend to play down the Chinese role in the *fabi* reform, see, in particular, Cain and Hopkins (1993), pp. 251–259. Cain and Hopkins erroneously stated that Frederick Leith-Ross had "devised" the reform in an attempt to draw China into the sterling zone. A similar approach is advanced by Dayer (1988), pp. 292–296. Firsthand accounts that frame Leith-Ross's contribution to the reform as auxiliary include Young (1971), pp. 230–233; Endicott (1973–1974), pp. 488–490; Trotter (1975), pp. 148–167; Rothwell (1975); and Shiroyama (2008), pp. 168–199. For criticism of Cain and Hopkins, see, e.g., Akita (1995), pp. 10–18.
121. Confidential Memorandum, dated March 13, 1935, in the Bank of England Archives [hereafter BoE] G1/298.
122. Osterhammel (1984), pp. 261–263, 277–279.
123. Medlicott (1981); see also article titled "Sir F. Leith-Ross Criticized" in the *Times*, November 26, 1935, p. 13.
124. See, e.g., A. H. George, Commercial Counselor for the British Consulate in Shanghai, to Sir Alexander Cadogan, Head of the British Legation in Beijing, dated December 18, 1934, in PRO FO 371/19239, folios 3–12.
125. Ibid.
126. Sir R. Lindsay in Washington to the Foreign Office, dated March 1, 1935, in PRO FO 371/19239, folio 159; cf. Coble (1980), pp. 192–197.
127. On the American cold shoulder to Chinese pleas, see, e.g., *Foreign Relations of the United States: Diplomatic Papers* (1935 [1950]), vol. 3, pp. 539–540.
128. On the British diplomatic foray see, e.g., French Foreign Ministry letter to the British Embassy in Paris, dated March 18, 1935, and similar correspondence in PRO FO 371/19240. For the American perspective, see Young (1971), pp. 372–376; *Zhonghua minguo hubishi ziliao* (1989), vol. 2, pp. 119–127.

129. See "Note of a Meeting Held at the Treasury," dated October 19, 1935, in BoE OV 104/63.
130. See ciphered telegram from Leith-Ross to the Foreign Office, dated October 27, 1935, in BoE OV 104/63.
131. Henchman to Grayburn, dated October 22, 1935, in HSBC GA K1.13.
132. Hong Kong Government to Colonial Office, dated October 15, 1935, in BoE OV 104/63.
133. Ciphered telegram from Leith-Ross in Shanghai to the Foreign Office, dated November 1, 1935, in BoE OV 104/63.
134. Leith-Ross from Shanghai to the Foreign Office, dated November 2, 1935, in BoE OV 104/63. See also telegram from A. Cadogan, the British consul-general in Shanghai, to the Foreign Office, dated November 3, 1935, in BoE OV 104/63. Cadogan supported Leith-Ross's suggestion that an Order-in-Council be issued to protect British banks from silver claims in return for the latter's handover of silver to the Chinese government.
135. Henchman to Grayburn, dated November 23, 1935, in HSBC GA K1.13. In this letter, Henchman opined that HSBC ought to have sought compensation for complying with silver nationalization and that the only plausible compensation could be Chinese government intervention to force a payoff of outstanding debts to the Bank. See also Bank of China telegram, dated November 4, 1935, demanding that HSBC immediately hand over its silver in return for *fabi* notes—in HSBC GA K1.14.
136. Memorandum entitled "Silver Reserves," dated November 5, 1935 in BoE 104/63 (emphasis in the original).
137. For a reference to this "gentlemanly agreement," see ciphered telegram from Leith-Ross to the Foreign Office, dated November 2, 1935, in BoE OV 104/63.
138. Blackley (?) to Rodd, dated September 7, 1932, in BoE OV 104/53.
139. Barnes to Henchman, dated November 5, 1935, in HSBC GA K1.13.
140. See copy of a statement to that effect by CBIAC and MBI, dated November 1, 1935, in HSBC GA K1.13.
141. Henchman to Grayburn, dated November 13, 1935, in HSBC GA K1.13.
142. Henchman to Grayburn, dated December 10, 1935, in HSBC GA K1.13. Henchman was also embittered about the distance the Mission kept from British bankers: "I don't suppose my opinion will be sought, and if so, very little notice will be taken of it."
143. A. Cadogan to the Foreign Office, dated January 16, 1936, in BoE OV 104/63.
144. See enclosure in a letter from Leith-Ross to Sir R.Vansittart of the Treasury, dated July 31, 1935, in PRO F 5081/6/10. This document is reproduced in *Documents on British Foreign Policy* (1981), pp. 568–571.
145. Ironically, Japanese right-wingers came to believe that the Mission and attendant currency reform disguised a British plot to destabilize occupied Manchuria. On Japanese perceptions of Leith-Ross's aims, see archival documents compiled in *Senryōchi tsūka kōsaku* (1983), pp. 63–107.
146. See letter from Leith-Ross in Shanghai to Sir S. Hoare, dated October 9, 1935, in PRO F 6415/66/10. Reproduced in *Documents on British Foreign Policy* (1981), pp. 614–617.
147. See letter from Leith-Ross in Shanghai to Sir S. Hoare, dated October 29, 1935, in PRO F 6767/6/10. Reproduced in *Documents on British Foreign Policy* (1981), pp. 647–648.

148. See Memorandum dated December 24, 1935 in BoE OV 104/63; cf. *Foreign Relations of the United States: Diplomatic Papers* (1935 [1950]), vol. 3, pp. 631–650; Friedman (1940), pp. 65–66.
149. Grayburn to Young, dated January 9 and March 12, 1936, in HSBC GA F1.1. Grayburn's costing included "printing, signing, cancelling [of notes] and other expenses." It was exclusive, however, of the annual 1 percent duty, which the Hong Kong government imposed on circulation volumes.
150. Leith-Ross to Henchman, dated January 6, 1936, in HSBC GA K1.14.
151. Grayburn to Leith, dated January 6, 1936, in HSBC GA K1.14.
152. See *Chicago Daily News* article, dated June 24, 1936, clipped in PRO FO 371/20218.
153. See Treasury Notes for limited circulation, dated July 23, 1936, in PRO FO 371/20218, folios 129–136.
154. See "Notes by Sir F. Leith-Ross on His Mission to China," dated July 28, 1936, in PRO FO 371/20218, folios 139–167.
155. See Leith-Ross to Addis, dated April 8, 1936, and Addis to Leith-Ross, dated June 3, 1936, in SOAS Addis Papers PP Ms 14/437.
156. Lloyd George (1927), p. 10.
157. Ransome (1927), pp. 28–32. For British expatriate attitudes, see also Woodhead (1929).
158. Rogers to Siepmann, the British consul-general in Shanghai, dated November 11, 1935, in BoE OV 104/53.
159. See, e.g., *China Press* article entitled "Leith-Ross Optimistic about China in Farewell Interview," dated June 24, 1936, in HSBC GA SHG I 52.2; Leith-Ross continued to sound upbeat pronouncements on the *fabi* reform achievements overseas. The *China Press* reported on December 2, 1936, that the eminent economist had told a group of leading City bankers in London that the success "with which managed paper currency was working in china . . . recalled [that] paper currency circulated throughout the country in the time of Kublai Khan."
160. See in particular Chou Shun-hsin (1963); Chang Kia-ngau (1958); Young (1971).
161. On March 17, 1937, for example, Henchman reported to Grayburn that Jiang Jieshi was resorting to provincial banknote issuance and subsidiary coin debasement as a means to increase government revenue, thereby sacrificing the monetary stability that the *fabi* reform had achieved. In HSBC GA K1.15.
162. On April 15, 1937, Grayburn wrote to Barnes that the International Consortium was an ineffectual entity because of infighting among its constituent Powers. Grayburn then exclaimed "I will be quite glad to see [the Consortium] dead and buried, and I cannot see the good of a partnership where the partners do not keep to the rules." In HSBC GA K1.15. On British Foreign Office opposition to the Consortium, see Dayer (1988), pp. 303–306.
163. On October 7, 1937, R. E. N. Padfield, co-manager of HSBC's London Office, wrote to Grayburn that the Treasury was not inclined to accept pleas from CBIAC, MBI, and the P&O Banking Corporation to allow British banks to reissue notes in war-ravaged Shanghai. In HSBC GA K1.15.
164. See "Statement of the Current Position of Foreign Banks in Shanghai," dated August 1937, in HSBC GA London II, Box 13, Item 156.

165. Barnes to Grayburn, dated October 31, 1938, in HSBC GA K1.16.
166. See ledgers in HSBC GA SHG LEDG 1220.
167. HSBC Shanghai branch report to Chinese Ministry of Finance in Nanjing, dated December 10, 1947, in HSBC GA SHG I 138.1.
168. HSBC Shanghai branch balance sheet, dated August 20, 1947, submitted to the Chinese Ministry of Finance, in HSBC GA SHG I 138.1.
169. See correspondence in HSBC GA SHG II 610; cf. Shai (1996), pp. 36–38; Clayton (1997), pp. 123–138.
170. See report from HSBC Shanghai branch manager to the Communist government Ta Hwa holding company, dated December 20, 1954, in HSBC GA SHG I 49. On CCP monetary policy in the early 1950s see, e.g., Burdekin and Wang (1999).

CHAPTER 6: CONCLUSIONS

1. See Remer (1933).
2. See, e.g., Chen (1971).
3. See, e.g., Strauss (1998), pp. 184–192; Kirby (2000).
4. See, e.g., the highly critical monographs written by Fewsmith (1985) and Sheridan (1975).
5. See, e.g., Rawski (1989).
6. This institutional continuum has been explained with particular cogency by Rosenberg and Birdzell (1985), pp. 189–210 and Alborn (1998), pp. 257–260. It stretched from Western Europe to its former colonies, coalescing into "managerial capitalism" in the United States by the early twentieth century; Alfred Chandler has shown, in turn, that the formation of salaried corporate management in the United States during the early twentieth century had been closely linked to the consistent flow of British and Scottish accounting skills as from the 1880s. See Chandler (1977), pp. 464–465.
7. Feuerwerker (1958), pp. 16–28; Faure (1994), pp. 86–87; see also Goetzmann and Köll (2004), pp. 13–19. Studies documenting closely related attributes of the Chinese early-modern economy are wide-ranging and on the rise. These include articles on deliberate opaqueness in Chinese accounting practices to avoid state interference; see, e.g., Gardella (1992). On the perfunctory emulation of Western corporate law in the early 1900s see, e.g., Kirby (1995); and on the massive flight of Chinese private capital to safe havens in the treaty ports, see, e.g., Ma Debin (2004).
8. Murphey's original metaphor (1974, p. 39) cast Shanghai as "a fly on elephant's back," but such articulation overlooks the overriding concentration of Chinese wealth there. Ironically, Murphey exaggerated in the same article the impact of quasi-foreign money on the Chinese economy as a whole: "By the end of the twentieth century . . . notes issued by foreign banks in the treaty-ports circulated *all over China* at face value . . . they constituted an important element in the system of currency and had *largely displaced the traditional notes of credit and transfer previously associated with this trade*" (1974, p. 53; emphasis added).
9. See, e.g., Von Hayek (1976); Selgin (1988).
10. Verdier (2003); cf. Gerschenkron (1966).

Glossary

Capital Market refers to the market for stocks or bonds offered either by companies or by the government as a means of raising long-term funds. The term is not to be confused with the "money market," which refers to trade in liquid assets like bank drafts or foreign currency.

Debased Currency refers to coins whose metallic content has been improperly alloyed, while its external features and nominal value markers remain intact.

Dollars ($) refers to the silver unit of account—known in Chinese as *yuan* 圓—that was customary throughout the trading ports of East Asia in the prewar era, unless otherwise stated. In 1920s Shanghai, goods priced in dollar units (termed here SH$) usually involved payment in ubiquitous Mexican silver dollar (Mex$) coins. Similarly, paper money denominated in dollar units was converted into Mex$ coins, although other foreign and Chinese silver coins were also current.

Fiat Currency refers to paper money that is not convertible into precious metal. It is accepted as a medium of payment in business transactions solely by virtue of a government decree.

Fiduciary Currency refers to convertible paper money denominated in precious metal units, but only partly backed by a metallic or bond reserve. Strictly speaking, the fiduciary issue of a bank is that part of its note issue that is not covered by gold or silver assets.

Free Banking refers to the theory advocating free issue of currency by multiple commercial banks and the abolition of central banks as an enduring remedy for inflation.

Reserve Ratio refers to government regulation stipulating a minimum ratio of precious metal and/or securities to be held by banks in their vaults against the total amount of their customer deposits and the notes that they issue.

Seigniorage refers to the difference between the nominal value of coins or notes and their actual cost of production. This difference embodies profits accruing to the *seigneur*, or ruler, who monopolizes the issue of currency in any given polity.

Shroff is a term that was used by British bankers throughout Asia to describe indigenous currency experts. Shroffs were hired to detect debased coinage, ascertain the quality of paid-in bullion, or guarantee draft and notes issued by domestic financial institutions.

Taels [Tls.] are disparate silver units of account, known collectively in Chinese as *liang* 兩 and often rendered as "ounce" by Westerners. The Shanghainese variant of the tael [SH Tls.] was roughly equivalent to 1.4 silver dollars, but the exchange rate fluctuated in accordance with the supply of Mex$ coins. Commodities priced in SH Tls. were usually paid for in sycee bullion. In 1933, the GMD government phased out all tael units.

References

PRIMARY SOURCE ACRONYMS

BoE	Bank of England, Archives, London
CBIAC GL	Chartered Bank of India Australia and China Balance Sheet, Guildhall Library Manuscript Collection, London
HSBC GA	Hongkong and Shanghai Banking Corp., Group Archives, London
NLA	National Library of Australia, Braga Papers, Feetham Report, Canberra
PRO	United Kingdom Public Records Office, Treasury Files, Foreign Office Files, Colonial Office Files, London
SOAS	Archive of the School of Oriental and African Studies, Charles Addis Papers, Maritime Customs Files, China Association Files, London

NEWSPAPERS AND PERIODICALS CONSULTED (PRE-1937 EDITIONS)

Note: Bracketed titles indicate English translations.

Bankers' Magazine
The China Press
Chinese Economic Bulletin
Dalu yinhang yuekan 大陸銀行月刊 [Mainland Banking Monthly]

Diplomatic and Consular Reports: China		
Dongfang zazhi	東方雜誌	[Eastern Miscellany]
The Economist		
The Financial Times		
Gongshang banyuekan	工商半月刊	[Commercial Biweekly]
Guofeng bao	國風報	[Country News]
Hong Kong Blue Book		
Huazi ribao	華字日報	[The Chinese Mail, Hong Kong]
Jingji xuebao	經濟學報	[Journal of Economics]
Minguo ribao	民國日報	[GMD Daily, Shanghai]
Nongshang gongbao	農商公報	[Farming and Trading Gazette]
North-China Daily News		
North-China Herald		
Quanguo yinhang nianjian	全國銀行年鑑	[All-China Banking Yearbook]
Rexue ribao	熱血日報	[Hot-Blooded Daily]
Shen bao	申報	[Shun Pao Daily News]
South China Morning Post		
Straits Settlements Government Gazette		
The Times (London)		
Waijiao bao	外交報	[Foreign Affairs Bulletin]
Xinwen bao	新聞報	[Sin Wan Pao]
Yanyong	言庸	[The Justice]
Yinhang zhoubao	銀行周報	[The Bankers Weekly]
Zhongyang yinhang yuebao	中央銀行月報	[Central Bank Monthly]
Zhonghang yuekan	中行月刊	[Bank of China Monthly Review]

BOOKS, BOOK CHAPTERS, AND ARTICLES

Akita, Shigeru. 1995. "British Informal Empire in East Asia 1880s–1930s: A Japanese Perspective." In Susan C. Townsend, ed., *Japanese Perspectives on Imperialism in Asia*, 1–25. London: London School of Economics and Political Science.

Alborn, Timothy L. 1998. *Conceiving Companies: Joint-Stock Politics in Victorian England*. London: Routledge.

Allen, G. C., and Audrey G. Donnithorne. 1954. *Western Enterprise in Far Eastern Economic Development*. London: George Allen and Unwin.

Arnold, Julean. 1919. *Commercial Handbook of China*. 2 vols. Washington, D.C.: U.S. Government Printing Office.

Arrighi, Giovanni, Po-keung Hui, Ho-fung Hung, and Mark Selden. 2003. "Historical Capitalism, East and West." In Giovanni Arrighi, Takeshi Hamashita, and Mark Selden, eds., *The Resurgence of East Asia: 500, 150 and 50 Year Perspectives*, 259–333. London: Routledge.

Ash, Robert. 1976. *Land Tenure in Pre-revolutionary China: Kiangsu Province in the 1920s and 1930s*. Research Notes and Studies No. 1. London: University of London, School of Oriental and African Studies, Contemporary China Institute.

Baba Kuwatarō 馬場鍬太郎. 1922. *Shina keizai chirishi* 支那經濟地理誌 [Handbook for China's Regional Economy]. Shanghai: Uiki gakkai.

Bagchi, Amiya Kumar. 1989. *The Presidency Banks and the Indian Economy, 1876–1914*. Calcutta: Oxford University Press.

Balazs, Etienne. 1964. *Chinese Civilization and Bureaucracies: Variations on a Theme*. Arthur F. Wright, ed. Trans. from the French by H. M. Wright. New Haven, Conn.: Yale University Press.

Bandarage, Asoka. 1983. *Colonialism in Sri Lanka: The Political Economy of the Kandyan Highlands, 1833–1886*. New York: Mouton.

Banno Junji. 1989. "Japanese Industrialists and Merchants and the Anti-Japanese Boycotts in China, 1919–1928." In Peter Duus, Ramon H. Myers, and Mark R. Peattie, eds., *The Japanese Informal Empire in China, 1895–1937*, 314–329. Princeton, N.J.: Princeton University Press.

Barber, Noël. 1979. *The Fall of Shanghai*. New York: Coward, McCann and Geoghegan.

Barnett, Martin. 1984. *Tramlines: The Story of the Hong Kong Tramway System*. Hong Kong: South China Morning Post.

Baskin, Jonathan Barron, and Paul J. Miranti Jr. 1997. *A History of Corporate Finance*. New York: Cambridge University Press.

Baster, A. S. J. 1929. *The Imperial Banks*. London: P. S. King and Son.

———. 1934. "The Origins of the British Exchange Banks in China." *Economic History* (Supplement to the *Economic Journal*) 3.9: 140–151.

———. 1935 [Rep. 1977]. *The International Banks*. New York: Arno Press.

Beiyang junfa shi 北洋軍閥史 [The History of Beiyang Warlords]. 2002. 2 vols. Lai Xinxia 來新夏, comp. Tianjin: Nankai daxue chubanshe.

Bergère, Marie-Claire. 1964. *Une crise financière à shanghai à la fin de l'ancien régime*. Paris: Mouton.

———. 1986. *L'âge d'or de la bourgeoisie chinoise, 1911–1937*. Paris: Flammarion.

———. 1989a. Book Review of *The History of the Hongkong and Shanghai Banking Corporation* (King 1987). *Business History Review* 63.2: 465–466.

———. 1989b. "The Consequences of the Post First World War Depression for the China Treaty-Port Economy, 1921–3." In Ian Brown, ed., *The Economies of Africa and Asia in the Inter-war Depression*, 221–252. London: Routledge.

———. 1992. "The Shanghai Bankers' Association, 1915–1927: Modernization and the Institutionalization of Local Solidarities." In Frederic Wakeman Jr. and Wen-hsin Yeh, eds., *Shanghai Sojourners*, 15–34. Berkeley: University of California Press.

———. 1994. *Sun Yat-Sen*. Paris: Fayard.

———. 2002. *Histoire de Shanghai*. Paris: Fayard.

Bickers, Robert A. 1998. "Shanghailanders: The Formation and Identity of the British Settler Community in Shanghai 1843–1937." *Past and Present* 159: 161–211.

———. 1999. *Britain in China: Community Culture and Colonialism, 1900–1949*. Manchester: Manchester University Press.

———. 2004. "Bland, John Otway Percy (1863–1945)." In the British Academy, comp., *Oxford Dictionary of National Biography*, vol. 6, 162–164. Oxford: Oxford University Press.

Blue, Gregory. 2000. "Opium for China: The British Connection." In Timothy Brook and Bob Tadahashi Wakabayashi, eds., *Opium Regimes: China, Britain and Japan, 1839–1952*, 31–54. Berkeley: University of California Press.

Boorman, Howard L. 1967–1979. *Biographical Dictionary of Republican China*. 5 vols. New York: Columbia University Press.

Borg, Dorothy. 1947. *American Policy and the Chinese Revolution*. New York: Macmillan.

Bostock, Frances, and Geoffrey Jones. 1989. "British Business in Iran, 1860–1970." In Frances Bostock and Geoffrey Jones, eds., *British Business in Asia since 1860*, 31–67. Cambridge: Cambridge University Press.

Bowen, H. V., and P. L. Cottrell. 1997. "Banking and the Evolution of the British Economy." In Alice Teichova, Ginette Kurgan-Van Hentenryk, and Dieter Ziegler, eds., *Banking, Trade and Industry: Europe, America and Asia from the Thirteenth to the Twentieth Century*, 89–112. Cambridge: Cambridge University Press.

Brandt, Loren. 1989. *Commercialization and Agricultural Development: Central and Eastern China, 1870–1937*. New York: Cambridge University Press.

Brandt, Loren, and Thomas J. Sargent. 1989. "Interpreting New Evidence about China and US Silver Purchases." *Journal of Monetary Economics* 23: 31–51.

Broadberry, Stephen, and Bishnupriya Gupta. 2006. "The Early Modern Great Divergence: Wages, Prices and Economic Development in Europe and Asia, 1500–1800." *Economic History Review* 59.1: 2–31.

Brown, Rajeswary. 1990. "Chinese Business and Banking in South-East Asia since 1870." In Geoffrey Jones, ed., *Banks as Multinationals*, 173–190. London: Routledge.

———. 1994. *Capital and Entrepreneurship in South-East Asia*. New York: St. Martin's Press.

Bulmer-Thomas, Victor. 1994. *The Economic History of Latin America since Independence*. Cambridge: Cambridge University Press.

Burdekin, Richard C. K. 2008. "US Pressure on China: Silver Flows, Deflation, and the 1934 Shanghai Credit Crunch." *China Economic Review* 19.2: 170–182.

Burdekin, Richard C. K., and Fang Wang. 1999. "A Novel End to the Big Inflation in China in 1950." *Economics of Planning* 32.3: 211–229.

Burhop, Carsten. 2006. "Did Banks Cause the German Industrialization?" *Explorations in Economic History* 43: 39–63.

Cain, P. J., and H. G. Hopkins. 1993. *British Imperialism: Crisis and Deconstruction, 1914–1990*. London: Longman.

The Cambridge History of China: Republican China 1912–1949. 1983–1986. Vols. 12 and 13. John K. Fairbank and Albert Feuerwerker, eds. Cambridge: Cambridge University Press.

Cameron, Rondo. 1967. "England, 1750–1844." In Rondo Cameron, Olga Crisp, Hugh T. Patrick, and Richard Tilly, eds., *Banking in the Early Stages of Industrialization: A Study in Comparative Economic History*, 15–59. New York: Oxford University Press.

Carlos, Ann M., and Stephen Nicholas. 1988. " 'Giants of an Earlier Capitalism': The

Chartered Trading Companies as Modern Multinationals." *Business History Review* 62: 398–419.

Carroll, John M. 2005. *Edge of Empires: Chinese Elites and British Colonials in Hong Kong.* Cambridge, Mass.: Harvard University Press.

Cassis, Youssef. 1994. *City Bankers, 1890–1914.* Trans. from the French by Margaret Roques. Cambridge: Cambridge University Press.

Chalmers, Robert. 1893. *History of Currency in the British Colonies.* London: Her Majesty's Stationery Office.

Chan, Wellington K. K. 1977. *Merchants, Mandarins and Modern Enterprise in Late Ch'ing China.* Cambridge, Mass.: Harvard University Press.

———. 1996. "Personal Styles, Cultural Values and Management: The Sincere and Wing On Companies in Shanghai and Hong Kong, 1900–1941." *Business History Review* 70.2: 141–167.

Chandler, Alfred D. 1977. *The Visible Hand: The Managerial Revolution in American Business.* Cambridge, Mass.: Belknap Press.

Chang Chung-li. 1962. *The Income of the Chinese Gentry.* Seattle: University of Washington Press.

Chang Kia-ngau [Zhang Jia'ao]. 1958. *The Inflationary Spiral: The Experience in China, 1939–1950.* Cambridge, Mass.: MIT Press.

Checkland, S. G. 1953. "An English Merchant House in China after 1842." *Bulletin of the Historical Society* 27.3: 158–189.

———. 1975. *Scottish Banking: A History, 1695–1973.* Glasgow: Collins.

Chen, C. S. 1965. "Profits of British Bankers from Chinese Loans, 1895–1914." *Tsinghua Journal of Chinese Studies* 5.1: 107–120.

Ch'en, Jerome. 1980. *State Economic Policies of the Ch'ing Government, 1840–1895.* New York: Garland.

Chen, Joseph T. 1971. *The May Fourth Movement in Shanghai: The Makings of a Social Movement in Modern China.* Leiden: E. J. Brill.

Ch'en, Paul H. 1992. "The Treaty System and European Law in China: A Study of the Exercise of British Jurisdiction in Late Imperial China." In W. J. Mommsen and J. A. De Moor, eds., *European Expansion and Law: The Encounter of European and Indigenous Law in 19th- and 20th-Century Africa and Asia*, 83–100. New York: Berg.

Chen Chau-nan, Chang Pin-tsun, and Chen Shikuan. 1995. "The Sung and Ming Paper Monies: Currency Competition and Currency Bubbles." *Journal of Macroeconomics* 17.2: 273–288.

Chen Limao 陳禮茂. 2003. *Zhang Zhidong zai Zhongguo tongshang yinhang chuangban guochengzhong de yanlun shuping* 張之洞在中國通商銀行創辦過程中的言論述評 [Critical Review of Zhang Zhidong's Pronouncements during the Formation of the Imperial Bank of China]. *Anhui shixue* 5: 29–35.

Chen Shao-teh. 1932 [Rep. 1982]. *Étude sur le marché monetaire de Changhai.* New York: Garland.

Chen Zhen 陳真. 1957. *Zhongguo jindai gongye shi ziliao* 中國近代工業史資料 [Historical Materials on China's Early Modern Industry]. 4 vols. Beijing: San Lian.

Cheng Linsun. 2003. *Banking in Modern China: Entrepreneurs, Professional Managers and the Development of Chinese Banks, 1897–1937*. New York: Cambridge University Press.
Chiang Hai Ding. 1963. "A History of Straits Settlements Foreign Trade, 1870–1915." PhD dissertation, Australian National University.
Chou Shun-hsin. 1963. *The Chinese Inflation 1937–1949*. New York: Columbia University Press.
Clayton, David. 1997. *Imperialism Revisited: Political and Economic Relations between Britain and China, 1950–54*. Basingstoke, U.K.: Macmillan.
Cleveland, Harold van B., and Thomas F. Huertas. 1985. *Citibank, 1812–1970*. Cambridge, Mass.: Harvard University Press.
Clifford, Nicholas R. 1991. *Spoilt Children of Empire: Westerners in Shanghai and the Chinese Revolution of the 1920s*. Hanover, N.H.: University Press of New England.
Coble, Parks M. 1980. *The Shanghai Capitalists and the Nationalist Government, 1927–1937*. Cambridge, Mass.: Harvard University Press.
———. 1991. Book Review of *The History of the Hongkong and Shanghai Banking Corporation* (King 1987). *The International History Review* 13.1: 378–381.
Cochran, Sherman. 1980. *Big Business in China: Sino-Foreign Rivalry in the Cigarette Industry, 1890–1930*. Cambridge, Mass.: Harvard University Press.
———. 2000. *Encountering Chinese Networks: Western, Japanese, and Chinese Corporations in China, 1880–1937*. Berkeley: University of California Press.
Collins, Michael. 1988. *Money and Banking in the UK: A History*. London: Croom Helm.
Collis, Maurice. 1965. *Wayfoong: The Hongkong and Shanghai Banking Corporation*. London: Faber and Faber.
Conant, Charles Arthur. 1927. *History of Modern Banks of Issue*. New York: G. P. Putnam.
Coppieters, Emmanuel. 1955. *English Banknote Circulation: 1694–1954*. Louvain: Institute of Social and Economic Research.
Cortney, William Prideaux. 2004. "Wilson, James." In the British Academy, comp., *Oxford Dictionary of National Biography*, vol. 21, 571–573. Oxford: Oxford University Press.
Cox, Howard. 2000. *The Global Cigarette: Origins and Evolution of British American Tobacco, 1880–1945*. New York: Oxford University Press.
Cribb, Joe. 1987. *Money in the Bank: An Illustrated Introduction to the Money Collection of the Hongkong and Shanghai Banking Corporation*. London: Spink and Son.
Da Rin, Marco, and Thomas Hellman. 2002. "Banks as Catalysts for Industrialization." *Journal of Financial Intermediation* 11: 366–397.
Dai Jianbing 戴建兵. 2005. *Baiyin yu jindai Zhongguo jingji* 白银与近代中国经济 [Silver and China's Modern Economy]. Shanghai: Fudan daxue chubanshe.
Darwent, C. E. 1920. *Shanghai: A Handbook for Travellers and Residents*. Shanghai: Kelly and Walsh.
Davenport-Hines, R. P. T., and Geoffrey Jones. 1989. "British Business in Asia since 1860." In R. P. T. Davenport-Hines and Geoffrey Jones, eds., *British Business in Asia since 1860*, 1–30. Cambridge: Cambridge University Press.
Davies, Glyn. 1994. *A History of Money: From Ancient Times to the Present Day*. Cardiff: University of Wales.
Davis, Clarence B. 1982. "Financing Imperialism: British and American Bankers as Vectors of Imperial Expansion in China, 1908–1920." *Business History Review* 56.2: 236–264.

Davis, Lance E., and Douglass C. North. 1971. *Institutional Change and American Economic Growth*. London: Cambridge University Press.

Dayer, Roberta Albert. 1981. *Bankers and Diplomats in China, 1917–1925: The Anglo-American Relationships*. London: Frank Cass.

———. 1988. *Finance and Empire: Sir Charles Addis, 1861–1945*. Basingstoke, U.K.: Macmillan.

De Bary, William T. 1991. *The Trouble with Confucianism*. Cambridge, Mass.: Harvard University Press.

De Vries, Jan. 1976. *Economy of Europe in an Age of Crisis*. Cambridge: Cambridge University Press.

Deng Gang. 1999. *The Premodern Chinese Economy: Structural Equilibrium and Capitalist Sterility*. London: Routledge.

Ding Guoliang 丁國良 and Zhang Yuncai 張運才. 1993. *Xiang E Gan geming genjudi huobi shi* 湘鄂贛革命根據地貨幣史 [History of Currency in the Revolutionary Soviets of Hunan, Hubei and Jiangxi]. Beijing: Zhongguo jinrong chubanshe.

Ding Richu 丁日初. 1994. *Shanghai jindai jingji shi* 上海近代經濟史 [The Modern Economic History of Shanghai]. 2 vols. Shanghai: Shanghai renmin chubanshe.

Djang Siao-mei [Zhang Xiaomei]. 1936 [Rep. 1968]. "Banking, Currency and Credit." In Kwei Chungshu [Gui Zhongshu], ed., *The Chinese Yearbook 1935–36*, 1429–1509. Nendeln, Liechtenstein: Karus.

Documents on British Foreign Policy, 1919–1939: Far Eastern Affairs May 20, 1933–November 5, 1936. 1981. Second series, vol. 20. W. N. Medlicott and Douglas Dakin, eds. London: Her Majesty's Stationery Office.

Dong, Stella. 2001. *Shanghai: The Rise and Fall of a Decadent City*. New York: Perennial.

Dowd, Kevin, ed. 1992. *The Experience of Free Banking*. London: Routledge.

Drabble, John H. 1989. *The Emergence of the Modern Malayan Economy: The Impact of Foreign Trade in the Nineteenth Century*. Clayton, Victoria: Centre of Southeast Asian Studies.

Drake, P. J. 2004. *Currency, Credit and Commerce: Early Growth in Southeast Asia*. Aldershot, U.K.: Ashgate.

Du Xuncheng 杜恂诚. 2002. *Shanghai jinrong de zhidu, gongneng yu bianqian* 上海金融的制度、功能与变迁, 1897–1997 [The Financial System in Shanghai: Functions and Evolution, 1897–1997]. Shanghai: Shanghai renmin chubanshe.

———. 2003. *Zhongguo jinrong tongshi: Beiyang zhengfu shiqi* 中國金融通史–北洋政府時期 [A Comprehensive History of Finance in China, vol. 3: The Beiyang Government Era]. Beijing: Zhongguo jinrong chubanshe.

Dunstan, Helen. 1996. " 'Orders Go Forth in the Morning and Are Changed by Nightfall': A Monetary Policy Cycle in Qing China, November 1744–June 1745." *T'oung pao* 82: 66–136.

Eastman, Lloyd E. 1974 [Rep. 1990]. *The Abortive Revolution: China under Nationalist Rule, 1927–1937*. Cambridge, Mass.: Council on East Asian Studies, Harvard University.

Edwards, E.W. 1987. *British Diplomacy and Finance in China, 1895–1914*. Oxford: Clarendon Press.

Eldem, Edhem. 1998. *A 135-Year-Old Treasure: Glimpses from the Past in the Ottoman Bank Archives*. Istanbul: Osmanli Bankasi.

Elvin, Mark. 1967. "The Gentry Democracy in Shanghai, 1905–1914." PhD dissertation, University of Cambridge.

———. 1973. *The Pattern of the Chinese Past.* London: Eyre Methuen.

———. 1977. "Market Towns and Waterways: The County of Shanghai from 1480 to 1910." In G. William Skinner, ed., *The City in Late Imperial China,* 441–473. Stanford, Calif.: Stanford University Press.

———. 1981. "Making Progress Pay—A Basic Problem in China's Early Economic Modernization." In *Symposium on the History of the Republic of China,* vol. 3: *Northern Expedition and Period of Political Tutelage,* 254–286. Taipei, Taiwan: Compilation Committee of the Symposium on the History of the Republic of China.

———. 1999. "How Did the Cracks Open? The Origins of the Subversion of China's Late-Traditional Culture by the West." *Thesis Eleven* 57: 1–16.

———. 2001. Book Review of *The Great Divergence: Europe, China and the Making of the Modern World Economy* (Pomeranz 2000). *China Quarterly* 167: 754–758.

———. 2004. "Some Reflections on the Use of 'Styles of Scientific Thinking' to Disaggregate and Sharpen Comparisons between China and Europe from Song to Mid-Qing Times (960–1850 CE)." *History of Technology* 25: 53–103.

Endicott, Stephen L. 1973–1974. "British Financial Diplomacy in China: The Leith-Ross Mission, 1935–1937." *Pacific Affairs* 46.4: 481–501.

Eng, Robert Y. 1984. "Chinese Entrepreneurs, the Government and the Foreign Sector: The Canton and Shanghai Silk-Reeling Enterprises, 1861–1932." *Modern Asian Studies* 18.3: 353–370.

Esherick, Joseph. 1991. Book Review of *Commercialization and Agricultural Development: Central and Eastern China, 1870–1937* (Brandt 1989). *Journal of Economic History* 51.2: 501–503.

Faure, David. 1989. *The Rural Economy of Pre-Liberation China: Trade, Expansion and Peasant Livelihood in Jiangsu and Guangdong, 1870 to 1937.* Hong Kong: Oxford University Press.

———. 1994. *China and Capitalism: Business Enterprise in Modern China.* Hong Kong: Division of Humanities, Hong Kong University of Science and Technology.

———. 2006. *China and Capitalism: A History of Business Enterprise in Modern China.* Hong Kong: Hong Kong University Press.

Feuerwerker, Albert. 1958. *China's Early Industrialization: Sheng Hsuan-huai (1844–1916) and the Mandarin Enterprise.* Cambridge, Mass.: Harvard University Press.

———. 1980. "Economic Trends in the Late Ch'ing Empire, 1870–1911." In John K. Fairbank and Denis Twitchett, eds., *The Cambridge History of China,* vol. 11, 1–69. Cambridge: Cambridge University Press.

———. 1983. "Economic Trends, 1912–49." In John K. Fairbank and Denis Twitchett, eds., *The Cambridge History of China,* vol. 12, 128–207. Cambridge: Cambridge University Press.

Fewsmith, Joseph. 1985. *Party, State, and Local Elites in Republican China: Merchant Organizations and Politics in Shanghai, 1890–1930.* Honolulu: University of Hawai'i Press.

Fitzgerald, John. 1990. "Increased Disunity: The Politics and Finance of Guangdong Separatism, 1926–1936." *Modern Asian Studies* 24.4: 745–775.

Flynn, Dennis O., and Arturo Giraldez. 1994. "China and the Manila Galleons." In A. J. H. Latham and H. Kawakatsu, eds., *Japanese Industrialization and the Asian Economy*, 71–90. London: Routledge.

Fogel, Joshua A. 2000. " 'Shanghai-Japan': The Japanese Residents' Association in Shanghai." *Journal of Asian Studies* 59.4: 927–950.

Foreign Relations of the United States: Diplomatic Papers. Vol. 3: *The Far East*. 1935 [Rep. 1950]. Washington, D.C.: U.S. Government Printing Office.

The Foreign Trade of China 1925: Reports and Abstracts of Statistics. 1926. Chinese Maritime Customs, comp. Shanghai: Inspector General of Customs.

Fox, Josephine J. 1994. "Access to Work in Republican China: Technology, Patronage and Industrial Conflict." PhD dissertation, Australian National University.

Frank, Andre Gunder. 1998. *ReOrient: Global Economy in the Asian Age*. Berkeley: University of California Press.

Frazier, Martin W. 1994. "Mobilizing a Movement: Cotton Mill Foremen in the Shanghai Strikes of 1925." *Republican China* 20.1: 1–45.

Freeth, Stephen. 1991. "Destroying Archives: A Case Study of the Records of Standard Chartered Bank." *Journal of the Society of Archivists* 12.2: 85–94.

Friedman, Irving S. 1940. *British Relations with China: 1931–39*. New York: Institute of Pacific Relations.

Friedman, Milton. 1992. "Franklin D. Roosevelt, Silver, and China." *Journal of Political Economy* 100.1: 62–83.

Friedman, Milton, and Anna Jacobson Schwartz. 1963. *A Monetary History of the United States, 1867–1960*. Princeton, N.J.: Princeton University Press.

Fung, Edmund S. K. 1991. *The Diplomacy of Imperial Retreat: Britain's South China Policy, 1924–1931*. Hong Kong: Oxford University Press.

Gallagher, John, and Ronald Robinson. 1953. "The Imperialism of Free Trade." *The Economic History Review*, New Series 6.1: 1–15.

Gao Yang 高陽. 1981. *Chen Guangfu waizhuan* 陳光甫外傳 [Anecdotal Notes on Chen Guangfu]. Taipei: Nanjing chuban gongsi.

Gardella, Robert. 1992. "Squaring Accounts: Commercial Bookkeeping Methods and Capitalist Rationalism in Late Qing and Republican China." *The Journal of Asian Studies* 51.2: 317–339.

Gerschenkron, Alexander. 1966. *Economic Backwardness in Historical Perspective: A Book of Essays*. Cambridge, Mass.: Harvard University Press.

Gerth, Karl. 2003. *China Made: Consumer Culture and the Creation of the Nation*. Cambridge, Mass.: Harvard University Press.

Gillin, Donald G. 1967. *Warlord: Yen Hsi-shan in Shansi Province, 1911–1949*. Princeton, N.J.: Princeton University Press.

Goetzmann, William N., and Elisabeth Köll. 2004. "The History of Corporate Ownership in China: State Patronage, Company Legislation, and the Issue of Control." Yale International Centre for Finance Working Paper no. 4-29.

Goldstone, Jack A. 1991. *Revolution and Rebellion in the Early Modern World*. Berkeley: University of California Press.

———. 1996. "Gender, Work and Culture: Why the Industrial Revolution Came Early to England But Late to China." *Sociological Perspectives* 39.1: 1–21.

———. 2002. "Efflorescences and Economic Growth in World History: Rethinking 'The Rise of the West' and the Industrial Revolution." *Journal of World History* 13.2: 323–389.

Gongbuju dongshihui huiyilu 公部局董事會會議錄 [The Minutes of the Shanghai Municipal Council]. 2001. Shanghai Municipal Archive, comp. Shanghai: Shanghai guji chubanshe.

Gonjō Yasuo. 1993. *Banque coloniale ou banque d'affaires: La Banque de l'Indochine sous la IIIe République*. Paris: Comité pour l'histoire économique et financière de la France.

Goodman, Bryna. 1995. *Native Place, City, and Nation: Regional Networks and Identities in Shanghai, 1853–1937*. Berkeley: University of California Press.

———. 2004. "Semi-Colonialism, Transnational Networks and News Flows in Early Republican Shanghai." *The China Review* 4.1: 55–88.

Goto-Shibata, Harumi. 1995. *Japan and Britain in Shanghai, 1925–31*. New York: St. Martin's Press.

Green, E. H. H. 1988. "Rentiers versus Producers? The Political Economy of the Bimetallic Controversy c. 1880–1898." *The English Historical Review* 103.408: 588–612.

Green, Edwin, and Sara Kinsey. 1999. *The Paradise Bank: The Mercantile Bank of India, 1893–1984*. Aldershot, U.K.: Ashgate.

Greenberg, Michael. 1951. *British Trade and the Opening of China, 1800–42*. Cambridge: Cambridge University Press.

Greif, Avner. 2005. "Institutions and the Path to the Modern Economy: Lessons from Medieval Trade." In Claude Ménard and Mary M. Shirley, eds., *Handbook of New Institutional Economics*, 727–786. New York: Springer.

Grossman, Richard S. 2001. "Charters, Corporations and Codes: Entry Restrictions in Modern Banking Law." *Financial History Review* 8.2: 107–121.

Guo Xiaoxian 郭孝先. 1935 [Rep. 2005]. *Shanghai de yinhang* 上海的銀行 [Banks in the City of Shanghai]. Beijing: Quanguo tushuguan wenxian suowei fuzhi zhongxin.

Hall, Ray Ovid. 1921. *Chinese National Banks: From Their Founding to the Moratorium*. Berlin: S.N.

Hamashita Takeshi 濱下武志. 1980. *Chūgoku tsūshō ginkō no setsuritsu to Honkon Shanhai ginkō* 中国通商銀行の設立と香港上海銀行 [The Establishment of the Imperial Bank of China and the Hongkong and Shanghai Bank]. *Hitotsubashi ronsō* 84.4: 448–464.

———. 1983. "History of the Japanese Silver Yen and the Hongkong and Shanghai Banking Corporation, 1871–1913." In Frank H. H. King, ed., *Eastern Banking: Essays in the History of the Hongkong and Shanghai Banking Corporation*, 321–349. London: Athlone Press.

———. 1984. "Foreign Trade Finance in China, 1810–1850." Trans. from the Japanese by Takechi Manabu. In Linda Grove and Christian Daniels, eds., *State and Society in China*, 387–435. Tokyo: Tokyo University Press.

———. 1989. *Chūgoku kindai keizaishi kenkyū—Shinmatsu kaikan saisei to kaikō shijō ken* 中国近代経済史研究—清末海関財政と開港市場圏 [China's Early Modern Economic History: The Late-Qing Maritime Customs and the Opening of the Treaty-Ports]. Tokyo: Tokyo University.

———. 1994. "Overseas Chinese Remittance and Asian Banking History." In Olive Checkland, Nishimura Shizuya, and Tamaki Norio, eds., *Pacific Banking, 1859–1959: East Meets West*, 52–60. Basingstoke, U.K.: St. Martin's Press.

Hanna, Hugh H., Charles A. Conant, and Jeremiah W. Jenks. 1904. *Report on the Introduction of the Gold-Exchange Standard into China, the Philippine Islands, Panama, and Other Silver-Using Countries*. Washington, D.C.: U.S. Government Printing Office.

Hao Yen-p'ing. 1970. *The Comprador in Nineteenth Century China: A Bridge between East and West*. Cambridge, Mass.: Harvard University Press.

Harvey, Charles, and Peter Taylor. 1987. "Mineral Wealth and Economic Development: Foreign Direct Investment in Spain, 1851–1913." *Economic History Review* 40.2: 185–207.

Heckscher, Eli F. 1954. *An Economic History of Sweden*. Trans. from the Swedish by G. Ohlin. Cambridge, Mass.: Harvard University Press.

Helleiner, Eric. 2003. *The Making of National Money: Territorial Currencies in Historical Perspective*. Ithaca, N.Y.: Cornell University Press.

Henriot, Christian. 2001. *Prostitution and Sexuality in Shanghai: A Social History 1849–1949*. Trans. from the French by Noel Castelino. Cambridge: Cambridge University Press.

Hickson, C. R., and J. D. Turner. 2004. "Free Banking and the Stability of Early Joint-Stock Banking." *Cambridge Journal of Economics* 28: 903–919.

Hirase Minokichi 平瀬巳之吉. 1942. *Kindai shina keizaishi* 近代支那経済史 [Economic History of Modern China]. Tokyo: Chūō Kōronsha.

Ho, Virgil Kit-yiu. 1991. "The Limits of Hatred: Popular Attitudes towards the West in Republican Canton." *East Asian History* 2: 87–104.

Ho Hon-wai [He Hanwei] 何漢威. 1993. "Cong yinqian huang dao tongyuan fanlan—Qingmo xin huobi de faxing ji qi yingxiang" 從銀錢荒到銅元汎濫—清末新貨幣的發行及其影響 [From the Devaluing of Silver and the Scarcity of Money to the Over-supply of Copper Coinage: The Issuing of New Currency in the Late Ch'ing and Its Effects]. *Zhongyang yanjiuyuan lishi yuyan yanjiusuo jikan* [Bulletin of the Institute of History and Philology, Academia Sinica] 62.3: 389–494.

Hobson, John M. 2004. *The Eastern Origins of Western Civilisation*. New York: Cambridge University Press.

Hong Jiaguan 洪葭管. 1989. *Jindai Shanghai jinrong shichang* 近代上海金融市场 [Financial Markets in Modern Shanghai]. Shanghai: Shanghai renmin chubanshe.

———. 2003. *Shanghai jinrong zhi* 上海金融志 [Handbook for Shanghai Finance]. Shanghai: Shanghai shehui kexueyuan chubanshe.

———. 2004. *Ershi shiji de Shanghai jinrong* 20世纪的上海金融 [Shanghai Finance in the Twentieth Century]. Shanghai: Shanghai renmin chubanshe.

Hong Kong: Copy of Correspondence between the Secretary of State for the Colonies and the Governor of Hong Kong upon the Subject of the Currency of the Colony. 1863. London: Her Majesty's Stationery Office.

Horesh, Niv. 2006. "Printed in London, Disbursed on the Bund: The Hongkong Bank and Its Early Note Issue in Shanghai, 1865–1911." *Late Imperial China* 27.1: 109–140.

———. 2007. "The Bund and Beyond: Re-thinking the Sino-Foreign Financial Grid in Pre-war Shanghai." *China Review* 7.1: 1–26.

———. 2008a. "Between Legal and Illegal Tender: The Chartered Bank's Note Issue in China." *Modern China* 34.2: 276–298.

———. 2008b. " 'Many a Long Day': HSBC and Its China Note Issue in the Republican Era, 1912–1937." *Enterprise & Society* 9.1: 6–43.

Hou Chi-ming. 1965. *Foreign Investment and Economic Development in China 1840–1937*. Cambridge, Mass.: Harvard University Press.

Howe, A. C. 1990. "Bimetallism, c. 1880–1898: A Controversy Reopened?" *The English Historical Review* 105.415: 377–391.

Hsiao Liang-lin. 1974. *China's Foreign Trade Statistics, 1864–1949*. Cambridge, Mass.: Harvard University Press.

Hsu Yih-tzong [Xu Yizong] 許義宗. 1997. *Qing dai zhibi tushuo* 清代紙幣圖說 [Banknotes of the Ching Dynasty, 1853–1911]. Taipei: Hsu Yih-tzong.

———. 1998. *Zhongguo Huashang zhibi tushuo* 中國華商紙幣圖說 [Banknotes of the Commercial Banks of China, 1898–1938]. Taipei: Hsu Yih-tzong.

Huang, Philip C. 1990. *The Peasant Family and Rural Development in the Yangzi Delta, 1350–1988*. Stanford, Calif.: Stanford University Press.

———. 1991. "The Paradigmatic Crisis in Chinese Studies: Paradoxes in Social and Economic History." *Modern China* 17.3: 299–341.

Huang, Ray. 1974. *Taxation and Governmental Finance in Sixteenth-Century Ming China*. Cambridge: Cambridge University Press.

Huang Hanmin 黃漢民 and Lu Xinglong 陸興龍. 2002. *Jindai Shanghai gongye qiye fazhan shi lun* 近代上海工業企業發展史論 [The History of Industrial Development in Shanghai]. Shanghai: Caijing daxue chubanshe.

Huang Hengjun 黃亨俊. 2001. *Qingdai guan yinqianhao faxing shi* 清代官銀錢號發行史 [The History of Issuance of Official Currency in the Ching Dynasty]. Taipei: Guoli lishi bowuguan.

Huang Jianhui 黃鑒暉. 1994. *Zhongguo yinhang yeshi* 中國銀行業史 [The History of Banking in China]. Taiyuan: Shanxi jingji chubanshe.

Huang Yihai and Wang Yunting. 2004. *Chinese Specimens Printed by the American Bank Note Company*. 3 vols. Hong Kong: Zhongguo tong chubanshe.

Hurley, R. C. 1903. *The Tourists' Guide to Canton, the West River and Macao*. Hong Kong: Hongkong Printing Press.

Huxley, Aldous. 1926 [1991]. *Jesting Pilate: Travels through India, Burma, Malaya, Japan, China, and America*. New York: Paragon House.

Ingram, James Carlton. 1971. *Economic Change in Thailand since 1850*. 2nd ed. Stanford, Calif.: Stanford University Press.

Isaacs, Harold Robert. 1961. *The Tragedy of the Chinese Revolution*. Stanford, Calif.: Stanford University Press.

Isett, Christopher M. 2007. *State, Peasant, and Merchant in Qing Manchuria, 1644–1862*. Stanford, Calif.: Stanford University Press.

Ishii Kanji. 2002. "British-Japanese Rivalry in Trading and Banking." In Janet E. Hunter and

Sugiyama Shinya, eds., *The History of Anglo-Japanese Relations, 1600–2000*, vol. 4: *Economic and Business Relations*, 110–132. Basingstoke, U.K.: Macmillan.

Jain, Lakshmi Chandra. 1929. *Indigenous Banking in India*. London: Macmillan.

Jao, Y. C., and Frank H. H. King. 1990. *Money in Hong Kong: Historical Perspective and Contemporary Analysis*. Hong Kong: University of Hong Kong, Centre of Asian Studies.

Jernigan, Thomas R. 1904. *China's Business Methods and Policy*. Shanghai: Kelly and Walsh.

Ji Zhaojin. 2003. *A History of Modern Shanghai Banking: The Rise and Decline of China's Finance Capitalism*. Armonk, N.Y.: M. E. Sharpe.

Jiang Hongye 姜宏業. 1991. *Zhongguo difang yinhang shi* 中國地方銀行史 [History of Chinese Local Banks]. Changsha: Hunan chubanshe.

Jindai Shanghai chengshi yanjiu 近代上海城市研究 [An Urban Study of Modern Shanghai]. 1990. Zhang Zhongli 張仲禮, comp. Shanghai: Shanghai renmin chubanshe.

Jindai Shanghai diqu fangzhi jingji shiliao xuanji 近代上海地區方誌經濟史料選輯 [Select Historic Materials from Gazetteers on the Modern Shanghai-Region Economy]. 1984. Huang Wei 黃葦 and Xia Lingen 夏林根, comps. Shanghai: Shanghai renmin chubanshe.

Johnson, Linda Cook. 1995. *Shanghai: From Market Town to Treaty Port, 1074–1858*. Stanford, Calif.: Stanford University Press.

Johnstone, William Crane. 1937 [Rep. 1973]. *The Shanghai Problem*. Westport, Conn.: Hyperion Press.

Jones, Charles. 1977. "Commercial Banks and Mortgage Companies." In D. C. M. Platt, ed., *Business Imperialism, 1840–1930: An Inquiry Based on British Experience in Latin America*. Oxford: Clarendon Press.

Jones, Geoffrey. 1990. "Competitive Advantages in British Multinational Banking since 1890." In Geoffrey Jones, ed., *Banks as Multinationals*, 30–61. London: Routledge.

———. 1993. *British Multinational Banking, 1830–1990*. Oxford: Clarendon Press.

———. 1994. "British Multinational Banking in Asia before 1960: Lending Strategies and Human Resource Management." In Olive Checkland, Nishimura Shizuya, and Tamaki Norio, eds., *Pacific Banking, 1859–1959: East Meets West*, 151–168. Basingstoke, U.K.: St. Martin's Press.

Jones, Susan Mann. 1972. "Finance in Ningpo: The 'Ch'ien Chuang', 1750–1880." In W. E. Willmott, ed., *Economic Organization in Chinese Society*, 47–77. Stanford, Calif.: Stanford University Press.

Jordan, Donald A. 1991. *Chinese Boycotts versus Japanese Bombs: The Failure of China's "Revolutionary Diplomacy," 1931–32*. Ann Arbor: University of Michigan Press.

Joslin, David Maelgwyn. 1963. *A Century of Banking in Latin America*. London: Oxford University Press.

Kann, Eduard. 1927. *The Currencies of China*. Shanghai: Kelly and Walsh.

Kapp, Robert A. 1973. *Szechwan and the Chinese Republic: Provincial Militarism and Central Power, 1911–1938*. New Haven, Conn.: Yale University Press.

Katō Shigeru 加藤繁. 1944 [Rep. 1970]. *Tang Song shidai jinyin zhi yanjiu* 唐宋時代金銀之研究 [On Gold and Silver during the Tang and Song Eras]. 2 vols. Hong Kong: Longmen shudian.

———. 1959. *Zhongguo jingji shi kaozheng* 中國經濟史考證 [A Textual Survey of Chinese Economic History]. 2 vols. Trans. from Japanese into Chinese by Wu Jie 吳傑. Beijing: Shangwu yinshuguan.

Kawamura Tomotaka 川村朋貴. 2005. "Higashi Indo kaisha kaisan izen no isutan banku mondai, 1847–1857 nen" 東インド会社解散以前のイースタンバンク問題、1847–1857 年 [The Problematic of Eastern Exchange Banking prior to the Dissolution of the East India Co., 1847–1857]. *Shakai keizai shigaku* 71.2: 25–47.

Keeton, George Williams. 1928. *The Development of Extraterritoriality in China.* 2 vols. London: Longmans.

Kikuchi Takaharu 菊池貴晴. 1966. *Chūgoku minzoku undō no kihon gozō: tai boikotto no kenkyū* 中国民族運動の基本構造ー対ボイコットの研究 [The Historical Background of the Chinese National Movement: A Study of Anti-Foreign Boycotts in Modern China]. Tokyo: Daian.

King, Frank H. H. 1965. *Money and Monetary Policy in China, 1845–1895.* Cambridge, Mass.: Harvard University Press.

———. 1979. *Survey Our Empire! Robert Montgomery Martin (1801?–1868): A Bio-Bibliography.* Hong Kong: University of Hong Kong Press.

———. 1983. "Defending the Chinese Currency: The Role of the Hongkong and Shanghai Banking Corporation, 1938–1941." In Frank H. H. King, ed., *Eastern Banking: Essays in the History of the Hongkong and Shanghai Banking Corporation*, 279–320. London: Athlone Press.

———. 1987. *The History of the Hongkong and Shanghai Banking Corporation.* 4 vols. New York: Cambridge University Press.

———. 1990. "The Extraordinary Survival of Hong Kong's Private Note Issue: From Profit Making to Public Service." In Y. C. Jao and Frank H. H. King, *Money in Hong Kong: Historical Perspective and Contemporary Analysis*, 1–50. Hong Kong: University of Hong Kong, Centre of Asian Studies.

———. 2004. "Hillier, Edward Guy." In the British Academy, comp., *Oxford Dictionary of National Biography*, vol. 27, 224–225. Oxford: Oxford University Press.

King, W. T. C. 1936. *History of the London Discount Market.* London: Routledge.

Kirby, William C. 1995. "China Unincorporated: Company Law and Business Enterprise in Twentieth-Century China." *Journal of Asian Studies* 54.1: 43–63.

———. 2000. "The Internationalization of China: Foreign Relations at Home and Abroad in the Republican Era." In Frederic Wakeman Jr. and Richard L. Edmonds, eds., *Reappraising Republican China*, 179–204. New York: Oxford University Press.

Kiser, Edgar, and Tong Xiaoxi. 1992. "Determinants of the Amount and Type of Corruption in State Fiscal Bureaucracies: An Analysis of Late Imperial China." *Comparative Political Studies* 25.3: 300–331.

Koehn, Nancy F. 1994. *The Power of Commerce: Economy and Governance in the First British Empire.* Ithaca, N.Y.: Cornell University Press.

Kolsky, Maurice, and Maurice Muszynski. 1996. *Les billets de la Banque de l'Indochine.* Monaco: V. Gadoury.

Kotenev, Anatol M. 1925 [Rep. 1968]. *Shanghai: Its Mixed Court and Council.* Taipei: Ch'eng-Wen.

———. 1927. *Shanghai: Its Municipality and the Chinese*. Shanghai: North-China Daily News and Herald.

Ku Hung-ting. 1984. "Urban Mass Movement in Action: The Shakee Incident and the Canton-Hongkong Strike." In Academia Sinica, comp., *Proceedings of the Conference on the Early History of the Republic of China, 1912–1927*, 849–872. Taipei: Academia Sinica.

Kuroda, Akinobu. 2005. "The Collapse of the Chinese Imperial Monetary System." In Sugihara Kaoru ed., *Japan, China and the Growth of the Asian International Economy, 1850–1949*, 103–126. Oxford: Oxford University Press.

Kwan Man Bun. 2001. *The Salt Merchants of Tianjin: State-Making and Civil Society in Late Imperial China*. Honolulu: University of Hawai'i Press.

Lai, Cheng-Chung, and Joshua Jr-Shiang Gau. 2003. "The Chinese Silver Standard Economy and the 1929 Great Depression." *Australian Economic History Review* 43.2: 155–168.

Landes, David S. 2003. *Unbound Prometheus: Technological Change and Industrial Development in Western Europe from 1750 to the Present*. 2nd ed. New York: Cambridge University Press.

Lao Shanghai ditu 老上海地圖 [Album of Shanghai during the Past 150 Years]. 2001. Shanghai Municipal Library, comp. Shanghai: Shanghai huabao chubanshe.

Le Fevour, Edward. 1968. *Western Enterprise in Late Ch'ing China: A Selective Survey of Jardine, Matheson and Company's Operations, 1842–1895*. Cambridge, Mass.: Harvard University Press.

Lee, Frederic Edward. 1926 [Rep. 1982]. *Currency, Banking, and Finance in China*. New York: Garland.

Lee En-han. 1981. "China's Restoration of the British Hankow and Kiukiang Concessions in 1927: A Study of the Chinese Nationalist Party's Revolutionary Diplomacy during the Northern Expedition Period." In Academia Sinica, comp., *Proceedings of the International Conference on Sinology*, vol. 5, 1431–1464. Taipei: Academia Sinica.

Leith-Ross, Frederick, Sir. 1968. *Money Talks: Fifty Years of International Finance*. London: Hutchison.

Li, Lillian M. 2007. *Fighting Famine in North China: State, Market, and Environmental Decline, 1690s–1990s*. Stanford, Calif.: Stanford University Press.

Li Bozhong. 1998. *Agricultural Development in Jiangnan, 1620–1850*. New York: St. Martin's Press.

Li Hong 李宏. 1988. *Xianggang da shi ji* 香港大事記 [A Chronicle of Hong Kong History from 214 BCE to 1987]. Beijing: Renmin ribao chubanshe.

Li Jianmin 李建民. 1986. *Wusa can'an hou de fanYing yundong* 五卅慘案後的反英運動 [The Anti-British Movement Following the May Thirtieth Incident]. Taipei: Academia Sinica.

Li Taichu [Lee Taichu] 李泰初. 1936. *Xianggang zhibi yu Guangzhou wujia guanxi zhi chubu yanjiu* 香港紙幣與廣州物價關係之初步研究 [The Hong Kong Dollar: A Statistical Study of Its Relation to Wholesale Prices in Canton]. Guangzhou: Guangdong shengli rangqin daxue shangxue yuan.

Li Xizhu 李細珠. 2003. *Zhang Zhidong yu Qingmo xinzheng yanjiu* 張之洞與清末新政研究 [On Zhang Zhidong and the Late-Qing Reforms]. Shanghai: Shanghai shudian.

Lieu, D. K. [a.k.a. Liu Ta-chun; see below] 1929. *Foreign Investments in China.* Nanjing: Chinese Government Bureau of Statistics.

Lin, Alfred H. Y. 2002. "Building and Funding a Warlord Regime: The Experience of Chen Jitang in Guangdong." *Modern China* 28.2: 177–212.

Lin Man-houng. 1991. "Two Social Theories Revealed: Statecraft Controversies over China's Monetary Crisis, 1808–1854." *Late Imperial China* 12.2: 1–35.

———. 2001. "Overseas Chinese Merchants and Multiple Nationality: A Means of Reducing Commercial Risk, 1895–1935." *Modern Asian Studies* 35.4: 985–1009.

Lin Wei-Ying [W. Y. Lin]. 1936. *The New Monetary System of China: A Personal Interpretation.* Shanghai: Kelly and Walsh.

Little, Daniel. 1992. Book Review of *Commercialization and Agricultural Development: Central and Eastern China, 1870–1937* (Brandt 1989). *Economic Development and Cultural Change* 40.2: 425–432.

Liu Ta-Chun. 1936. *The Growth and Industrialization of Shanghai.* Shanghai: China Institute of Pacific Relations.

Lloyd George, David. 1927. Foreword. In Arthur Ransome, *The Chinese Puzzle*, 9–11. London: George Allen and Unwin.

Lu Hanchao. 1999. *Beyond the Neon Lights: Everyday Shanghai in the Early Twentieth Century.* Berkeley: University of California Press.

Lyons, Thomas P. 2003. *China Maritime Customs and China's Trade Statistics 1859–1948.* Trumansburg, N.Y.: Willow Creek.

Ma Chuande 馬傳德, Xu Yuan 徐淵, and Hu Youwen 胡幼文. 2000. *Shanghai-tan huobi* 上海灘貨幣 [The Currency of Shanghai's Bund]. Shanghai: Shanghai jiaoyu chubanshe.

Ma Debin. 2004. "Growth, Institutions and Knowledge: A Review and Reflection on the Historiography of Eighteenth–Twentieth Century China." *Australian Economic History Review* 44.3: 259–277.

———. 2005. "Modern Economic Growth in the Lower Yangzi in 1911–1937: A Quantitative, Historical and Institutional Analysis." Unpublished Discussion Paper. Tokyo: Foundation for Advanced Studies on International Development.

Mackenzie, A. D. 1953. *The Bank of England Note Issue: A History of Its Printing.* Cambridge: Cambridge University Press.

Mackenzie, Compton. 1954. *Realms of Silver: One Hundred Years of Banking in the East.* London: Routledge and Kegan Paul.

Mao Chih-Li [Mao Zhili] 毛知礪. 1996. *Zhang Jia'ao yu Zhongguo yinhang de jingying yu fazhan* 張嘉璈與中國銀行的經營與發展 [Chang Kia-ngau and the Management and Development of the Bank of China, 1912–1935]. Taipei: Guoshiguan.

Mao King On. 1977. *History of Chinese Paper Currency.* 2 vols. Kowloon, Hong Kong: K. O. Mao.

Marcus, Harold G. 2002. *A History of Ethiopia.* Berkeley: University of California Press.

Martin, Brian. 1996. *The Shanghai Green Gang: Politics and Organized Crime, 1919–1937.* Berkeley: University of California Press.

Marx, Karl. 1867 [Rep. 1990]. *Capital: A Critique of Political Economy.* 3 vols. Trans. from the German by Ben Fowkes. London: Penguin Classics.

Marybon, Charles B. 1929. *Histoire de la concession française de changhai*. Paris: Plon.

McCord, Edward A. 1993. *The Power of the Gun: The Emergence of Modern Chinese Warlordism*. Berkeley: University of California Press.

McElderry, Andrea Lee. 1976. *Shanghai Old-style Banks (Ch'ien-Chuang), 1800–1925: A Traditional Institution in a Changing Society*. Ann Arbor: Center for Chinese Studies, University of Michigan.

———. 1991. Book Review of *The History of the Hongkong and Shanghai Banking Corporation* (King 1987). *Journal of Asian Studies* 50.4: 914–915.

———. 2001. *Shanghai Securities Exchanges: Past and Present*. Occasional Paper Series in Business History 4. Queensland: University of Queensland, Asian Business History Centre.

McGuire, John. 2004. "The Rise and Fall of the Oriental Bank in the Nineteenth Century: A Product of the Transformation that Occurred in the World Economy or the Result of Its Own Mismanagement." In *Proceedings of the Fifteenth Biennial Conference of the Asian Studies Association of Australia*, 1–20. Canberra: Asian Studies Association of Australia.

McLean, David. 1976. "Finance and 'Informal Empire' before the First World War." *The Economic History Review* 29.2: 291–305.

Medlicott, W. N. 1981. Preface. In W. N. Medlicott and Douglas Dakin, eds., *Documents on British Foreign Policy, 1919–1939*, Second Series, vol. 20, v–xvi. London: Her Majesty's Stationery Office.

Meiguo Huaqi yinhang zai Hua shiliao 美国花旗银行在华史料 [Historical Materials on Citibank in China]. 1990. The People's Bank of China, comp. Beijing: Zhongguo jinrong chubanshe.

Meissner, Daniel J. 2005. "The Business of Survival: Competition and Cooperation in the Shanghai Flour Milling Industry." *Enterprise and Society* 6.3: 364–394.

Meyer, Maisie J. 2003. *From the Rivers of Babylon to the Whangpoo: A Century of Sepharadi Jewish Life in Shanghai*. Lanham, Md.: University Press of America.

Michie, Ranald C. 1999. *The London Stock Exchange: A History*. New York: Oxford University Press.

Mickey, Georgia A. 2004. "Politics of Reform: The Bank of China and Its Shareholders, 1904–1919." PhD dissertation, Columbia University.

Miller, G. E. 1937. *Shanghai: The Paradise of Adventurers*. New York: Orsay.

Miners, Norman. 1987. *Hong Kong under Imperial Rule, 1912–1941*. Hong Kong: Oxford University Press.

Mittler, Barbara. 2004. *A Newspaper for China: Power, Identity, and Change in Shanghai's New Media, 1872–1912*. Cambridge, Mass.: Harvard University Press.

Miyazaki Ichisada 宮崎市定. 1977. *Chūgoku shi* 中国史 [History of China]. 2 vols. Tokyo: Iwanami shoten.

Mokyr, Joel. 1976. *Industrialization in the Low Countries, 1795–1850*. New Haven, Conn.: Yale University Press.

Morse, Hosea Ballu. 1921 [Rep. 1967]. *The Trade and Administration of China*. New York: Russell and Russell.

Motono Eiichi. 2000. *Conflict and Cooperation in Sino-British Business, 1860–1911: The Impact of the Pro-British Commercial Network in Shanghai*. Basingstoke, U.K.: Macmillan.

Moulder, Frances V. 1977. *Japan, China and the Modern World Economy*. Cambridge: Cambridge University Press.

Muirhead, Stuart. 1996. *Crisis Banking in the East: The History of the Chartered Mercantile Bank of India, London and China, 1853–93*. London: Scolar Press.

Müller-Jabusch, Maximilian. 1940. *Fünfzig Jahre Deutsch-Asiatische Bank, 1890–1939*. Berlin: Die Bank.

Murphey, Rhoads. 1953. *Shanghai: Key to Modern China*. Cambridge, Mass.: Harvard University Press.

———. 1974. "The Treaty-Ports and China's Modernization." In William G. Skinner and Mark Elvin, eds., *The Chinese City between Two Worlds*, 17–71. Stanford, Calif.: Stanford University Press.

Myers, Ramon H. 1970. *The Chinese Peasant Economy: Agricultural Development in Hopei and Shantung, 1890–1949*. Cambridge, Mass.: Harvard University Press.

———. 1991. "How Did the Modern Chinese Economy Develop? A Review Article." *Journal of Asian Studies* 50.3: 604–628.

Negishi Tadashi 根岸佶. 1948. *Baiben seido no kenkyū* 買辦制度の研究 [A Study of the Comprador System]. Tokyo: Nihon tosho kabushiki kaisha.

Nelson, Evan W. 1983. "The Hongkong and Shanghai Banking Corporation Factor in the Progress toward a Straits Settlements Government Note Issue, 1881–1889." In Frank H. H. King, ed., *Eastern Banking: Essays in the History of the Hongkong and Shanghai Banking Corporation*, 155–179. London: Athlone Press.

———. 1984. "The Imperial Administration of Currency and British Banking in the Straits Settlements, 1867–1908." PhD dissertation, Duke University.

Nishijima Sadao. 1984. "The Formation of the Early Chinese Cotton Industry." Trans. from the Japanese by Linda Grove. In Linda Grove and Christian Daniels, eds., *State and Society in China: Japanese Perspectives on Ming-Qing Social and Economic History*, 17–77. Tokyo: Tokyo University Press.

Nishimura Shizuya. 1994. "The Flow of Funds within the Hongkong and Shanghai Banking Corporation in 1913." In Olive Checkland, Nishimura Shizuya, and Tamaki Norio, eds., *Pacific Banking: 1859–1959: East Meets West*, 24–51. Basingstoke, U.K.: St. Martin's Press.

———. 1997. "British Banks in Shanghai." In Nishimura Shizuya and Yasutomi Ayumu, *International Banking in the China Market before the Second World War*, 1–19. London: London School of Economics and Political Science.

———. 西村閑也 2003. "Eikei kokusai ginkō to Ajia 1890–1913 nen (1)" 英系国際銀行とアジア, 1890–1913 年 (1) [British International Banks and Asia between 1890–1913, Part 1]. *Keiei shirin* 40.2: 1–17.

———. 2004. "Eikei kokusai ginkō to Ajia 1890–1913 nen (2)" 英系国際銀行とアジア, 1890–1913 年 (2) [British International Banks and Asia between 1890–1913, Part 2]. *Keiei shirin* 40.4: 1–29.

———. 2005. "The Foreign and Native Banks in China: Chop Loans in Shanghai and Hankow before 1914." *Modern Asian Studies* 39.1: 109–132.

North, Douglass C., and Robert Thomas. 1973. *The Rise of the Western World: A New Economic History*. Cambridge: Cambridge University Press.

Notar, Beth E. 2002. "Viewing Currency Chaos: Paper Money for Advertising, Ideology, and Resistance in Republican China." In Terry Bodenhorn, ed., *Defining Modernity: Guomindang Rhetorics of a New China, 1920–1970*, 123–149. Ann Arbor: Center for Chinese Studies, University of Michigan.

O'Brien, Patrick K. 1988. "The Costs and Benefits of British Imperialism 1846–1914." *Past and Present* 120: 163–200.

O'Brien, Patrick K., and Geoffrey Allen Pigman. 1992. "Free Trade, British Hegemony and the International Economic Order in the Nineteenth Century." *Review of International Studies* 18: 89–113.

Orbell, John, and Alison Turton. 2001. *British Banking: A Guide to Historical Records*. Aldershot, U.K.: Ashgate.

Orchard, Dorothy J. 1930. "China's Use of the Boycott as a Political Weapon." *The Annals of the American Academy of Political and Social Science—China* 152: 252–261.

Osterhammel, Jürgen. 1984. "Imperialism in Transition: British Business and the Chinese Authorities, 1931–1937." *China Quarterly* 98: 260–286.

———. 1989. "British Business in China, 1860s–1950s." In R. P. T. Davenport-Hines and Geoffrey Jones, eds., *British Business in Asia since 1860*, 189–216. Cambridge: Cambridge University Press.

———. 1997. *Shanghai, 30. Mai 1925: Die chinesische revolution*. Munich: Deutscher Taschenbuch Verlag.

———. 1999. "Britain and China, 1842–1914." In Andrew Porter, ed., *The Oxford History of the British Empire*, vol. 3, 146–169. Oxford: Oxford University Press.

Paauw, Douglas S. 1950. "Chinese Public Finance during the Nanking Government Period." PhD dissertation, Harvard University.

Pan Liangui 潘連貴. 2004. *Shanghai huobi shi* 上海貨幣史 [The History of Shanghai's Currency]. Shanghai: Shanghai renmin chubanshe.

Pelcovits, Nathan A. 1948. *Old China Hands and the Foreign Office*. New York: King's Crown Press.

Peng Xinwei 彭信威. 1958. *Zhongguo huobi shi* 中國貨幣史 [The History of Chinese Currency]. Shanghai: Shanghai renmin chubanshe.

Pennell, W. V. 1961. *History of the Hong Kong General Chamber of Commerce, 1861–1961*. Hong Kong: Cathay Press.

Perkins, Dwight H. 1969. *Agricultural Development in China, 1368–1968*. Edinburgh: Edinburgh University Press.

Perry, Elizabeth J. 1993. *Shanghai on Strike: The Politics of Chinese Labour*. Stanford, Calif.: Stanford University Press.

Philips, C. H. 1961. *The East India Company, 1784–1834*. London: Routledge.

Pick, Albert. 1990. *Standard Catalog of World Paper Money*. 6th ed. 2 vols. Iola, Wis.: Krause Publications.

Pinnick, A. W. 1930. *China and Silver: An Investigation of the Monetary Principles Governing China's Trade and Prosperity*. Shanghai: Kelly and Walsh.

Platt, D. C. M. 1968. *Finance, Trade and Politics in British Foreign Policy, 1815–1914*. Oxford: Clarendon Press.

Polo, Marco. [Rep. 1903]. *The Book of Ser Marco Polo*. Trans. from the Venetian by Henry Yule. London: J. Murray.

———. [Rep. 1987]. *The Travels of Marco Polo*. Trans. from the Venetian by R. E. Latham. Harmondsworth, U.K.: Penguin.

Pomeranz, Kenneth. 1993. *The Making of a Hinterland: State, Society, and Economy in Inland North China, 1853–1937*. Berkeley: University of California Press.

———. 2000. *The Great Divergence: Europe, China and the Making of the Modern World Economy*. Princeton, N.J.: Princeton University Press.

Pugach, Noel H. 1997. *Same Bed, Different Dreams: A History of the Chinese American Bank of Commerce, 1919–1937*. Hong Kong: Centre of Asian Studies, Hong Kong University.

Pye, Lucian W. 1971. *Warlord Politics: Conflict and Coalition in the Modernization of Republican China*. New York: Praeger.

Qi Xia 漆俠. 1987. *Song dai jingji shi* 宋代經濟史 [Economic History of the Song Dynasty]. 2 vols. Shanghai: Shanghai renmin chubanshe.

Qian Yizhang 錢益璋. 1987. *Shaji tongshi* 沙基痛史 [The Tragic Events in Shaji]. Taipei: Wenhai chubanshe.

Quan Hansheng 全漢昇. 1972. *Zhongguo jingjishi luncong* 中國經濟史論叢 [Essays on China's Economic History]. 2 vols. Hong Kong: Chinese University of Hong Kong.

Randall, Laura. 1977. *A Comparative Economic History of Latin America: 1500–1914*, vol. 2: *Argentina*. Ann Arbor: University Microfilms International.

Ransome, Arthur. 1927. *The Chinese Puzzle*. London: George Allen and Unwin.

Rawski, Thomas G. 1989. *Economic Growth in Prewar China*. Berkeley: University of California Press.

———. 1993. "Milton Friedman, Silver, and China." *Journal of Political Economy* 101.4: 755–758.

Remer, C. F. 1933 [Rep. 1968]. *Foreign Investments in China*. New York: H. Fertig.

———. 1933. *A Study of Chinese Boycotts: With Special Reference to Their Economic Effectiveness*. Baltimore, Md.: Johns Hopkins University Press.

Richardson, Philip. 1999. *Economic Change in China, c. 1800–1950*. Cambridge: Cambridge University Press.

Rigby, Richard W. 1980. *The May 30 Movement: Events and Themes*. Canberra: Australian National University.

Rippy, J. Fred. 1959. *British Investments in Latin America, 1822–1949: A Case Study in the Operations of Private Enterprise in Retarded Regions*. Minneapolis: Minnesota University Press.

Ristaino, Marcia R. 2001. *Port of Last Resort: The Diaspora Communities of Shanghai*. Stanford, Calif.: Stanford University Press.

Rosenberg, Nathan, and L. E. Birdzell Jr. 1985. *How the West Grew Rich: The Economic Transformation of the Industrial World*. New York: Basic Books.

Rothwell, V. H. 1975. "The Mission of Sir Frederick Leith-Ross to the Far East, 1935–1936." *Historical Journal* 18.1: 147–169.

Roux, Alain. 1993. *Le Shanghai ouvrier des années trente: Coolies, gangsters et syndicalistes.* Paris: L'Harmattan.

Rowe, William T. 1984. *Hankow: Commerce and Society in a Chinese City, 1796–1889.* Stanford, Calif.: Stanford University Press.

Salter, Arthur. 1934. *China and Silver.* New York: Economic Forum.

Sanminzhuyi qianzike 三民主義千字課 [The Three Principles of the People: A Reader]. 1928. Xiaozhuang Society for Popular School Education, comp. Nanjing: Xin shidai jiaoyu she.

Schenk, Catherine R. 2000. "Another Asian Financial Crisis: Monetary Links between Hong Kong and China 1945–50." *Modern Asian Studies* 34.3: 739–764.

Schifferli, Christoph. 1986. "Le système monétaire au sichuan vers la fin du Xe siècle." *T'oung Pao* 72: 269–290.

Schuler, Kurt. 1992. "The World History of Free Banking: An Overview." In Kevin Dowd, ed., *The Experience of Free Banking,* 7–47. London: Routledge.

Schurtz, William L. 1959. *The Manila Galleon.* New York: E. P. Dutton.

Schwarcz, Vera. 1986. *The Chinese Enlightenment: Intellectuals and the Legacy of the May Fourth Movement of 1919.* Berkeley: University of California Press.

Scott, William R. 1912. *The Constitution and Finance of English, Scottish and Irish Joint-Stock Companies to 1720.* 3 vols. Cambridge: Cambridge University Press.

Selgin, George A. 1988. *The Theory of Free Banking: Money Supply under Competitive Note Issue.* Totowa, N.J.: Rowman and Littlefield.

———. 1992. "Free Banking in Foochow." In Kevin Dowd, ed., *The Experience of Free Banking,* 103–122. London: Routledge.

Semmel, Bernard. 1970. *The Rise of Free Trade Imperialism: Classical Political Economy, the Empire of Free Trade and Imperialism.* Cambridge: Cambridge University Press.

Senryōchi tsūka kōsaku 占領地通貨工作 [Materials on Monetary Measures in Japanese Occupied Areas]. 1983. Tatai Yoshio 多田井喜生, comp. Tokyo: Misuzu Shobō.

Sergeant, Harriet. 1990. *Shanghai: Collision Point of Cultures, 1918–1939.* New York: Crown.

Sha Weikai 沙為楷. 1927. *Zhongguo maiban zhi* 中國買辦制 [The Compradoric System in China]. Shanghai: Shangwu yinshuguan.

Shai, Aron. 1996. *The Fate of British and French Firms in China, 1949–54: Imperialism Imprisoned.* Basingstoke, U.K.: Macmillan.

Shanghai minzu jiqi gongye 上海民族机器工业 [The Privately Owned Machinery Industry in Shanghai]. 1979. Shanghai Bureau of Industrial and Commercial Administration, comp. Beijing: Zhonghua shuju.

Shanghai minzu xiangjiao gongye 上海民族橡胶工业 [The Privately Owned Rubber Industry in Shanghai]. 1979. Shanghai Bureau of Industrial and Commercial Administration, comp. Beijing: Zhonghua shuju.

Shanghai qianzhuang shiliao 上海錢莊史料 [Historical Records on Shanghai's Moneyshops]. 1960. The People's Bank of China, comp. Shanghai: Shanghai renmin chubanshe.

Sheehan, Brett. 2003. *Trust in Troubled Times: Money, Banks and State-Society Relations in Republican Tianjin.* Cambridge, Mass.: Harvard University Press.

———. 2004. "The History of Chinese Money and Banking: A Mini Explosion." *Chinese Business History* 14.1: 1–2, 10.

———. 2005. "Myth and Reality in Chinese Financial Cliques in 1936." *Enterprise and Society* 6.3: 452–491.

Shen Lyn Yu. 1941 [Rep. 1980]. *China's Currency Reform: A Historical Survey*. New York: Garland.

Sheng Gang da bagong ziliao 省港大罷工資料 [Materials on the Great Strike in Guangdong Province and Hong Kong]. 1980. Guangdong Institute of Philosophy and Social Sciences, comp. Guangzhou: Guangdong renmin chubanshe.

Sheridan, James E. 1966. *Chinese Warlord: The Career of Feng Yu-hsiang*. Stanford, Calif.: Stanford University Press.

———. 1975. *China in Disintegration: The Republican Era in Chinese History, 1912–1949*. New York: Free Press.

Shiba Yoshinobu. 1968. *Sōdai shōgyōshi kenkyū* 宋代商業史研究 [The Mercantile History of the Song Dynasty]. Tokyo: Kazama shobō.

Shiroyama Tomoko. 2008. *China during the Great Depression: Market, State, and the World Economy, 1929–1937*. Cambridge, Mass.: Harvard University Press.

Shiue, Carol H. 2002. "Transport Costs and the Geography of Arbitrage in Eighteenth-Century China." *The American Economic Review* 92.5: 1406–1419.

Shiue, Carol H., and Wolfgang Keller. 2004. "Markets in China and Europe on the Eve of the Industrial Revolution." National Bureau of Economic Research Working Paper 10778.

Sinn, Elizabeth. 1994. *Growing with Hong Kong: The Bank of East Asia, 1919–1994*. Hong Kong: The Bank of East Asia.

Skinner, G. William. 1993. *Marketing and Social Structure in Rural China*. Ann Arbor, Mich.: Association for Asian Studies.

Smith, S. A. 2000. *A Road Is Made: Communism in Shanghai, 1920–1927*. Honolulu: University of Hawai'i Press.

Spalding, William Frederick. 1924. *Eastern Exchange, Currency and Finance*. London: Pitman.

Strauss, Julia C. 1998. *Strong Institutions in Weak Polities: State Building in Republican China, 1927–1940*. Oxford: Clarendon Press.

Sugihara, Kaoru. 1996. "Patterns of Asia's Integration into the World Economy, 1880–1913." In C. Knick Harley, ed., *The Integration of the World Economy, 1850–1914*, vol. 2, 700–719. Cheltenham, U.K.: Edward Elgar.

Sun Yixian [Sun Yat-sen]. 1989. *Guofu quanji* 國父全集 [Collected Works of the Father of the Nation]. 12 vols. Taipei: Jindai Zhongguo chubanshe.

Takahashi Kōsuke 高橋孝助 and Furumaya Tadao 古厩忠夫. 1995. *Shanhai shi: Kyodai toshi no keisei to hitobito no itonami* 上海史: 巨大都市の形成と人々の営み [The History of Shanghai: The Formation of a Metropolis and Its Everyday Life]. Tokyo: Tōhō shoten.

Tamagna, Frank. 1942. *Banking and Finance in China*. New York: Institute of Pacific Relations.

Tang Chuansi 唐傳泗 and Huang Hanmin 黃漢民. 1980. "1890–1936 Nian waiguo zai Hua yinhang zhibi faxingliang de chongxin guji" 1890–1936 年外國在華銀行紙幣發行量的重新估計 [A Revised Estimate of Foreign Bank Note Circulation Volume in China between 1890–1936]. *Shanghai shehui kexueyuan: Jingji xueshu ziliao* 8: 45–50.

———. 1985. "Shilun 1927 nian yiqian de Zhongguo yinhangye" 試論 1927 年以前的中國銀行業 [A Tentative Exposition of Banking in China before 1927]. *Zhongguo jindai jingjishi yanjiu ziliao* 4: 57–89.

Tang Zhenchang 唐振常. 1989. *Shanghai shi* 上海史 [History of Shanghai]. Shanghai: Shanghai renmin chubanshe.

Taylor, James. 2006. *Creating Capitalism: Joint-Stock Enterprise in British Politics and Culture, 1800–1870*. Rochester, N.Y.: Royal Historical Society/Boydell Press.

Thomas, W. A. 1989. Book Review of *The History of the Hongkong and Shanghai Banking Corporation* (King 1987). *China Quarterly* 118: 376.

———. 2001. *Western Capitalism in China: A History of the Shanghai Stock Exchange*. Aldershot, U.K.: Ashgate.

Tom, C. F. Joseph. 1964. *The Entrepôt Trade and the Monetary Standards of Hongkong, 1842–1941*. Hong Kong: K. Weiss.

Tortella Casares, Gabriel. 2000. *The Development of Modern Spain: An Economic History of the Nineteenth and Twentieth Centuries*. Trans. from the Spanish by Valerie J. Herr. Cambridge, Mass.: Harvard University Press.

Triffin, Robert. 1985. "The Myths and Realities of the So-Called Gold Standard." In Barry Eichengreen, ed., *The Gold Standard in History and Theory*, 121–140. New York: Methuen.

Trotter, Ann. 1975. *Britain and East Asia, 1933–1937*. London: Cambridge University Press.

Tsang, Steve Yui-Sang. 2004. *A Modern History of Hong Kong*. London: I. B. Tauris.

Tsin, Michael. 1999. *Nation, Governance and Modernity in China: Canton, 1900–1927*. Stanford, Calif.: Stanford University Press.

Tullock, Gordon. 1958. "Paper Money—a Cycle in Cathay." *Economic History Review* 9.3 (second series): 393–407.

Twitchett, Denis C. 1970. *Financial Administration under the T'ang Dynasty*. 2nd ed. Cambridge: Cambridge University Press.

Tyson, Geoffrey. 1963. *100 Years of Banking in Asia and Africa*. London: National and Grindlays Bank.

Van de Ven, Hans J. 1996. "Public Finance and the Rise of Warlordism." *Modern Asian Studies* 30.4: 831–835.

———. 2003. *War and Nationalism in China, 1925–1945*. London: RoutledgeCurzon.

Van der Eng, Pierre. 1998. "Exploring Exploitation: The Netherlands and Colonial Indonesia, 1870–1940." *Revista de Historia Económica* 16.1: 291–321.

———. 1999. "The Silver Standard and Asia's Integration into the World Economy, 1850–1914." *Journal of Asian and Pacific Studies* 18: 59–85.

———. 2004. "Economic History of Asia: Comparative Perspectives." *Australian Economic History Review* 44.3: 215–220.

Van Dyke, Paul. 2005. *The Canton Trade: Life and Enterprise on the China Coast, 1700–1845*. Hong Kong: Hong Kong University Press.

Verdier, Daniel. 2003. "Explaining Cross-National Variations in Universal Banking in Nineteenth-Century Europe, North America, and Australia." In Douglas J. Forsyth and Daniel Verdier, eds., *The Origins of National Financial Systems: Alexander Gerschenkron Reconsidered*, 23–42. New York: Routledge.

Vissering, G. 1914. *On Chinese Currency: Preliminary Remarks on the Monetary and Banking Reform in China.* 2 vols. Amsterdam: De Bussy.

Von Glahn, Richard. 1996. *Fountain of Fortune: Money and Monetary Policy in China 1000–1700*. Berkeley: University of California Press.

———. 2007. "Foreign Silver Coins in the Market Culture of Nineteenth Century China." *International Journal of Asian Studies* 4.1: 51–78.

Von Hayek, Friedrich August. 1976. *Denationalisation of Money: An Analysis of the Theory and Practice of Concurrent Currencies*. London: Institute of Economic Affairs.

Vort-Ronald, Michael P. 1982. *Banks of Issue in Australia*. Whyalla Norrie, Australia: Vort-Ronald.

Vries, Peer. 2003. "Via Peking Back to Manchester: Britain, the Industrial Revolution, and China." *Studies in Overseas History* 4: 1–109.

Wagel, Srinivas R. 1914 [Rep. 1980]. *Finance in China*. New York: Garland.

———. 1915. *Chinese Currency and Banking*. Shanghai: North China Daily News and Herald.

Wakeman, Frederic, Jr. 1996. *Policing Shanghai, 1927–1937*. Berkeley: University of California Press.

Waldron, Arthur. 1995. *From War to Nationalism: China's Turning Point, 1924–1925*. Cambridge: Cambridge University Press.

Wang Guanghua. 2001. *In Search of Justice: The 1905–1906 Anti-American Boycott*. Cambridge, Mass.: Harvard University Press.

Wang Hongbin 王宏斌. 2001. *Jindai Zhongguo jiazhi chidu yu yapian wenti* 近代中國價值尺度與鴉片問題 [Pricing and Opium in Early Modern China]. Beijing: Dongfang chubanshe.

Wang Jingyu 汪敬虞. 1963. "Shijiu shiji waiguo zai Hua yinhang shili de kuozhang ji qi dui Zhongguo tongshang kou'an jinrong shichang de kongzhi" 十九世紀外國在華銀行實力的擴張及其對中國通商口岸金融市場的控制 [Foreign Banks' Expansion in Nineteenth-Century China and Their Domination of Treaty-Port Finance]. *Lishi yanjiu* 5: 51–74.

———. 1965. "Shijiu shiji waiguo qinHua qiyezhong de Huashang fugu huodong" 十九世紀外國侵華企業中的華商附股活動 [Ethnic Chinese Shareholders of Foreign Companies Operating in Nineteenth-Century China]. *Lishi yanjiu* 4: 39–74.

———. 1983a. "Cong Liru yinhang de lishi kan shijiu shiji waiguo yinhang qinlüe Zhongguo de tedian he jincheng" 從麗如銀行的歷史看十九世紀外國銀行侵略中國的特點和進程 [The History of the Oriental Bank Corporation: A Case Study of Foreign Bank Inroads into China in the Nineteenth Century]. *Zhongguo shehui kexueyuan: Jingji yanjiusuo jikan* 4: 218–277.

———. 1983b. "Huifeng yinhang de chengli ji qi zai Zhongguo de chuqi huodong" 匯丰銀行的成立及其在中國的初期活動 [The Establishment of HSBC and Its Early China Operation]. *Zhongguo shehui kexueyuan: Jingji yanjiusuo jikan* 5: 267–297.

Wang Yeh-chien. 1973. *Land Taxation in Imperial China: 1750–1911*. Cambridge, Mass.: Harvard University Press.

Wasserstrom, Jeffrey N. 1991. *Student Protests in Twentieth-Century China: The View from Shanghai*. Stanford, Calif.: Stanford University Press.

Weber, Max. 1922 [Rep. 1951]. *The Religion of China: Confucianism and Taoism*. Trans. from the German by Hans H. Gert. New York: Macmillan.

Wei, Betty Peh-T'i. 1987. *Shanghai: Crucible of Modern China*. Hong Kong: Oxford University Press.

Wei Jianyou 魏建猷. 1955. *Zhongguo jindai huobi shi* 中國近代貨幣史 [The History of Currency in Modern China]. Shanghai: Qunlian chubanshe.

Wei Wen Pin. 1914. *The Currency Problem in China*. New York: Columbia University.

White, Lawrence H. 1984. *Free Banking in Britain: Theory, Experience, and Debate, 1800–1845*. Cambridge: Cambridge University Press.

———. 1993. *Free Banking*. 3 vols. Aldershot, U.K.: Edward Elgar.

Wilkins, Mira. 1986. "The Impacts of American Multinational Enterprise on American-Chinese Economic Relations, 1786–1949." In Ernest R. May and John K. Fairbank, eds., *America's China Trade in Historical Perspective: The Chinese and American Performance*, 259–292. Cambridge, Mass.: Harvard University Press.

Wittfogel, Karl August. 1957. *Oriental Despotism: A Comparative Study of Total Power*. New Haven, Conn.: Yale University Press.

Wong, R. Bin. 1997. *China Transformed: Historical Change and the Limits of European Experience*. Ithaca, N.Y.: Cornell University Press.

Wong, Sin Kiong. 2002. *China's Anti-American Boycott Movement in 1905: A Study in Urban Protest*. New York: Peter Lang.

Wood, Frances. 1998. *No Dogs and Not Many Chinese: Treaty-Port Life in China, 1843–1943*. London: John Murray.

Woodhead, H. G. W. 1929 [Rep. 1980]. *Extraterritoriality in China: The Case against Abolition*. New York: Garland.

Wou, Odoric Y. K. 1989. "The Chinese Communist Party and the Labor Movement: The May 30th Movement in Henan." *Chinese Studies in History* 23.1: 70–104.

Wright, Tim. 1984. *Coal Mining in China's Economy and Society, 1895–1937*. Cambridge: Cambridge University Press.

———. 1986. "Imperialism and the Chinese Economy: A Methodological Critique of the Debate." *Bulletin of Concerned Asian Scholars* 18.1: 36–45.

———. 1991. "Shanghai Imperialists versus Rickshaw Racketeers: The Defeat of the 1934 Rickshaw Reforms." *Modern China* 17.1: 76–111.

———. 2000. "Distant Thunder: The Regional Economies of Southwest China and the Impact of the Great Depression." *Modern Asian Studies* 34.3: 697–738.

Wu Ping 吳平. 1994. *Huanan geming genjudi huobi shi* 華南革命根據地貨幣史 [History of Currency in the Revolutionary Soviets of South China]. Beijing: Zhongguo jinrong chubanshe.

Wusa yundong shiliao 五卅運動史料 [Historical Records of the May Thirtieth Movement]. 1981. Shanghai Academy of Social Sciences, comp. Shanghai: Shanghai renmin chubanshe.

Xia Dongyuan 夏東元. 1981. *Zheng Guanying zhuan* 鄭觀應傳 [Zheng Guanying: A Biography]. Shanghai: Huadong shifan daxue chubanshe.

Xian Ke 獻可. 1958. *Jin bainianlai diguo zhuyi zai Hua yinhang faxing zhibi gaikuang* 近百年來帝國主義在華銀行發行紙幣概況 [A Survey of Banknote Issuance by Imperialist Banks in China in the Last Century]. Shanghai: Shanghai renmin chubanshe.

Xu Jiqing 徐寄廎. 1932 [Rep. 1970]. *Shanghai jinrong shi* 上海金融史 [A History of Shanghai Finance]. Taipei: Xuehai chubanshe.

Xu Xiaoqun. 2001. *Chinese Professionals and the Republican State: The Rise of Professional Associations in Shanghai, 1912–1937*. Cambridge: Cambridge University Press.

Yamane Yukio. 1984. "Reforms in the Service Levy System in the Fifteenth and Sixteenth Centuries." Trans. from the Japanese by Helen Dunstan. In Linda Grove and Christian Daniels, eds., *State and Society in China: Japanese Perspectives on Ming-Qing Social and Economic History*, 279–310. Tokyo: Tokyo University Press.

Yang Duanliu 楊端六. 1962. *Qingdai huobi jinrong shigao* 清代貨幣金融史稿 [Historic Overview of Currency and Finance during the Qing Dynasty]. Beijing: Xinhua shudian.

Yang Lien-sheng. 1952. *Money and Credit in China: A Short History*. Cambridge, Mass.: Harvard University Press.

Yang Yinpu 楊蔭溥. 1930 [Rep. 1972]. "Shanghai jinrong zuzhi gaiyao" 上海金融組織概要 [Overview of Shanghai's Financial Structure]. In Yang Yunpu, ed., *Zhongguo zhi yinhang shiliao sanzhong* 中國之銀行史料三種 [Three Historic Treatises on China's Banks], vol. 2. Taipei: Xuehai chubanshe.

Yasutomi Ayumu 安富步. 2003. "Honkon Shanhai ginkō no shikin kōzō, 1913–1941 nen" 香港上海銀行の資金構造、1913–1941 年 [The Capital Structure of the Hongkong and Shanghai Banking Corporation, 1913–1941]. *Ajia keizai* 44.10: 27–53.

Ye Shichang 葉世昌. 1963. *Yapian zhanzheng qianhou woguo de huobi xueshuo* 鴉片戰爭前后我國的貨幣學説 [China's Monetary Discourse before and after the Opium War]. Shanghai: Shanghai renmin chubanshe.

———. 2002. *Zhongguo jinrong tongshi diyijuan: Xian Qin zhi Qing yapian zhanzheng shiqi* 中國金融通史一先秦至清鴉片戰爭時期 [A Comprehensive History of Finance in China, vol. 1: From the Pre-Qin Era to the Opium War]. Beijing: Zhongguo jinrong chubanshe.

Yeh, Catherine Vance. 2002. "Representing the City: Shanghai and Its Maps." In David Faure and Tao Tao Liu, eds., *Town and Country in China: Identity and Perception*, 166–202. New York: Palgrave.

Yeh Wen-Hsin. 1995. "Corporate Space, Communal Time: Everyday Life in Shanghai's Bank of China." *American Historical Review* 100.1: 97–122.

Yokouchi Masao 横内正雄. 1990. "Makantairu ginkō, 1893–1918 nen" マーカンタイル銀行、1893–1918 年 [The Mercantile Bank of India, 1893–1918]. *Niigata Daigaku shōgaku ronshū* 22.3: 55–108.

———. 1996. "Dai'ichiji taisen mae ni okeru Tōyō kawase ginkō no soshiki teki kōdō" 第一次大戦前における東洋為替銀行の組織的行動 [The Cartelistic Policies of the Eastern Exchange Banks before World War I]. In Gonjō Yasuo 権上康男, Hirota Akira 廣田明, and Ōmori Hiroyoshi 大森弘喜, eds., *Nijū Seiki shi'hon shugi no seisei: Jiyū to soshikika* 20 世紀資本主義の生成: 自由と組織化 [The Formation of Capitalism in the Twentieth Century: Freedom and Structure], 151–185. Tokyo: Tokyo University Press.

Young, Arthur N. 1971. *China's Nation-Building Effort, 1927–1937: The Financial and Economic Record*. Stanford, Calif.: Hoover Institution Press.

Yunnan jindai huobishi ziliao huibian 雲南近代貨幣史資料彙編 [A Collection of Historic Records on Currency in Early-Modern Yunnan Province]. 1984. The People's Bank of China, comp. Yunnan: Zhongguo renmin yinhang.

Zelin, Madeleine. 1988. "Capital Accumulation and Investment Strategies in Early Modern China: The Case of the Furong Salt Yard." *Late Imperial China* 9.1: 79–122.

———. 1998. "Critique of Scholarship on Chinese Business in the People's Republic of China and Taiwan." *Chinese Studies in History* 31.3–4: 95–105.

Zeng Xianming 曾憲明. 2002. "Shanhai shōgyō chochiku ginkō ni miru chūgoku ginkōgyō no keisei katei" 上海商業儲蓄銀行にみる中国銀行業の形成過程 1920–1931 年 [The Establishment of Modern Banking in China: An Analysis of the Loan Business of the Shanghai Commercial and Savings Bank, 1920–1931]. *Shakai keizai shigaku* 67.5: 71–88.

Zhang Guohui 張國煇. 1963. "Shijiu shiji houbanqi Zhongguo qianzhuang de maibanhua" 十九世紀后半期中國錢莊的買辦化 [The Compradorization of China's Moneyshops in the Latter Half of the Nineteenth Century]. *Lishi yanjiu* 6: 85–98.

———. 1989. *Wan Qing qianzhuang he piaohao yanjiu* 晚清錢莊和票號研究 [A Study of Moneyshops and Remittance Houses in the Late-Qing Period]. Beijing: Xinhua shuju.

———. 2002. *Zhongguo jinrong tongshi: Qing yapian zhanzheng shiqi zhi qingmo shiqi* 中國金融通史一清鴉片戰爭時期至清末時期 [A Comprehensive History of Finance in China, vol. 2: From the Opium War to the Late-Qing Period]. Beijing: Zhongguo jinrong chubanshe.

Zhang Naiqi 章乃器. 1936. *Zhongguo huobi jinrong wenti* 中國貨幣金融問題 [The Monetary and Financial Problems of China]. Shanghai: Shenghuo shudian.

Zhang Ning 張寧. 2002. Qingdai houqi de waibi liutong 清代後期的外幣流通 [Foreign Currency Circulation during the Late-Qing Period]. *Wuhan daxue xuebao: Renwen kexueban* 3: 307–312.

Zhang Zhizhong 張志中. 1997. *Zhongguo jindai zhibi, piaoquan tujian* 中國近代紙幣、票券圖鑒 [An Illustrated Handbook of Banknotes and Scrip in Modern China]. Beijing: Zhishi chubanshe.

Zheng Guanying 鄭觀應. 1921 [Rep. 1969]. *Shengshi weiyan houbian* 盛世危言後編 [Threats to the Prosperity of the Age: Postscript]. Taipei: Taiwan datong shuju.

———. 1982. *Zheng Guanying ji* 鄭觀應集 [The Collected Works of Zheng Guanying]. 2 vols. Shanghai: Shanghai renmin chubanshe.

Zheng Jiadu 鄭家度. 1981. *Guangxi jin bainian huobi shi* 廣西近百年貨幣史 [A Centennial History of Guangxi Currency]. Nanning: Guangxi renmin chubanshe.

Zhong Xiangcai 鈡祥才. 1995. *Fabi zhengce qianhou Zhongguo de huobi lilun* 法幣政策前後中國的貨幣理論 [Monetary Polemics Surrounding the Fabi Reform]. Shanghai: Shanghai shehui kexueyuan chubanshe.

Zhongguo di yi jia yinhang—Zhongguo tongshang yinhang de chuchuang shiqi 中國第一家銀行 [China's First Bank—The Inception of the Imperial Bank of China, 1897–1911]. 1982. Institute of Modern History—Chinese Academy of Social Sciences, comps. Beijing: Zhongguo shehui kexue chubanshe.

Zhongguo jindai zhibi shi 中國近代紙幣史 [The History of Banknotes in Modern China]. 2001. Monetary Society of Jiangsu, comp. Beijing: Zhongguo jinrong chubanshe.

Zhongguo yinhang hangshi 中國銀行行史 [The History of the Bank of China]. 1995. Editorial Committee for the History of the Bank of China, comp. Beijing: Zhongguo jinrong chubanshe.

Zhongguo zhibi biaozhun tulu 中國紙幣標準圖錄 [The Standard Catalogue of Paper Money in China]. 1994. Beijing shi qianbi xuehui 北京市錢幣學會 [Beijing Numismatic Society], comp. Beijing: Beijing chubanshe.

Zhongguo ziben zhuyi gongshangye de shehui zhuyi gaizao—Shanghai juan 中國資本主義工商業的社會主義改造：上海卷 [The Re-socialization of China's Capitalism: Shanghai]. 1993. Archive Committee of the CCP in Shanghai, comp. Beijing: Zhonggong dangshi.

Zhonghua minguo huobishi ziliao 中華民國貨幣史資料 [Materials on the Monetary History of Republican China]. 2 vols. 1989. The People's Bank of China, comp. Shanghai: Shanghai renmin chubanshe.

Zhu Zhiqian 朱志騫. 1972. *Zhang Jian de shiye zhuzhang* 張謇的實業主張 [Zhang Jian's Propositions on Industry]. Taipei: Guoli Taiwan daxue.

Ziben zhuyi guojia zai jiu Zhongguo faxing he liutong de huobi 資本主義國家在舊中國發行和流通的貨幣 [Issuance and Circulation of Currency by Capitalist Powers in Old China]. 1992. The People's Bank of China, comp. Beijing: Wenwu chubanshe.

Index

Note: Page numbers followed by *f* and *t* indicate figures and tables.